D1604006

3 8700 10868 7053

The Black Shore

Sketch of Joseph O'Neill. This sketch appeared as the frontispiece to the 1915 Talbot Press publication of O'Neill's *The Kingdom Maker*. It was done by his wife, Mary Devenport O'Neill.

The Black Shore

by Joseph O'Neill (Michael Malía)

Edited, Annotated, and with an Introduction
by M. Kelly Lynch

Lewisburg
Bucknell University Press
London: Associated University Presses

Associated University Presses
440 Forsgate Drive
Cranbury, NJ 08512

Associated University Presses
16 Barter Street
London WC1A 2AH, England

Associated University Presses
P.O. Box 338, Port Credit
Mississauga, Ontario
Canada L5G 4L8

The paper used in this publication meets the requirements of the American National Standard for Permanence of Paper for Printed Library Materials Z39.48–1984.

Library of Congress Cataloging-in-Publication Data

O'Neill, Joseph.
  The black shore / by Joseph O'Neill (Michael Malía);
  edited, annotated, with an introduction by M. Kelly Lynch.
    p. cm.
  Includes bibliographical references.
  ISBN 0-8387-5431-7 (alk. paper)
  I. Title.   II. Lynch, M. Kelly, 1942–

  PR6029.N43 B57   2000
  823'.912 21—dc21   99-045135

Contents

Introduction to *The Black Shore*

M. KELLY LYNCH

I

THE BLACK SHORE BY MICHAEL MALÍA, PRINTED HERE FOR THE FIRST time, has a somewhat mysterious history. Completed in 1948, it is actually the final major work of Irish historical and counter-utopian novelist Joseph O'Neill. When it was completed, O'Neill, departing from his usual custom, sent it neither to his London publisher, Victor Gollancz, nor to *The Dublin Magazine*, which had regularly published O'Neill's poetry and serialized fiction. Instead, in late August, 1948, he sent the typescript to Padraic Colum, who was living in New York at the time, and asked him to find an American publisher for the new book.

Colum was mystified as to why O'Neill had chosen him as a literary agent. Although their lives had overlapped briefly in Dublin literary circles at the turn of the century, Colum and O'Neill had rarely seen each other and corresponded only sporadically for the nearly fifty years since Colum's permanent emigration to the United States in 1914. Then, suddenly, *The Black Shore* arrived on Colum's doorstep on Central Park West with the admonition that "neither the subject matter nor the author [be] associated with Joseph O'Neill, the writer of historical romances."[1]

Colum made little effort to find a publisher for *The Black Shore* and abandoned the project at O'Neill's death in 1953. There, on a bookshelf in Colum's living room, the pages of the yellowed typescript gathered dust until the winter of 1966, when graduate research in Anglo-Irish literature brought me to the same doorstep. Colum's and my acquaintance ripened quickly. I visited him frequently in Manhattan and on Cape Cod, Massachusetts, where he had a summer home. In the autumn of 1967, Colum simply gave me the typescript, hoping I would have better luck with it than he had.

Colum died in 1972 while I was teaching in Ireland. Although thoughts of finding a publisher for *The Black Shore* occasionally crossed my mind, I was otherwise engaged. Not until 1983, when I wrote a literary life of Joseph O'Neill for *The Journal of Irish Literature*, did I realize how important the unpublished novel was to a complete understanding of O'Neill's works. It is a final work which not only would change the way in which his published novels have been read, but, to a large extent, would give them a credibility and integrity they had never enjoyed singly. *The Black Shore* significantly changes O'Neill's importance—from a writer of somewhat donnish historical romances and science fiction to one who used these works to voice his grave concerns about the country and the world in which he lived.

II

The Black Shore differs from O'Neill's other works in two major ways: it is set in his contemporary Ireland, and it is written under a pseudonym. Had O'Neill written the novel earlier in his career, his wish to remain anonymous would have been understandable. The novel is a bitter castigation of Ireland, Irish culture, and the Irish Catholic Church. Still, *The Black Shore* is no more critical of Ireland than works by many of O'Neill's contemporaries—Liam O'Flaherty or Frank O'Connor, for example. Rejection by an Irish publisher would not have been an issue, since O'Neill had published throughout his career with Jonathan Cape and Victor Gollancz of London. Only one great difference between Joseph O'Neill and his literary contemporaries accounts for his wish not to have his name associated with the novel: O'Neill was not only a writer, but from 1922 until his retirement in 1945, the highly respected and skilled Permanent Secretary of Education, a civil servant and high-ranking official of the Irish Free State.

O'Neill's civil service career, not his writing, was his livelihood and the only means of support for himself and his wife Mary. Although he accepted this position grudgingly, complaining that he was buried under "obs[ervations] and files,"[2] he played his role well and was, by and large, a successful bureaucrat. By 1948, however, O'Neill already had been retired from his post for three years. He was seventy years of age and planning to live the remainder of his days in Nice. Why, then, should he have cared or worried that a novel written under his name should find criticism among his fellow civil servants or cloud his reputation?

Had his reputation as a civil servant been sterling, one could surmise that he might have wanted to keep the image intact. However, he did not, in fact, have much of a professional reputation to protect. For twenty-three years, O'Neill had remained an enigma to his colleagues: he was suspiciously "arty," owned a home at 2 Kenilworth Square at the heart of the "Rathgar Group," and hosted a Thursday "Evening at Home" attended by a crowd of literary types and moral renegades, including W. B. Yeats, Austin Clark, and George Russell. His wife, Mary Devenport O'Neill, was a published poet and an artist well known for conversation disdaining the provinciality of Dublin life and very likely to engage in talk about Peguy and Proust and life on the Left Bank. The members of the Board of Education did not trust either of the O'Neills, nor, except for patriot and member of the Dail, Michael Collins, did they number among the O'Neills' guests or friends. It seems unlikely, therefore, that O'Neill would have been concerned about his novel's potential for offending his colleagues.

In addition, publishing *The Black Shore* under his own name might have helped dispel O'Neill's equally questionable reputation among his literary friends. To the members of the "Evening at Home," O'Neill was primarily a civil servant, a writer by avocation whose works, though charming, were throwbacks, often compared to those of Bulwer-Lytton or H. G. Wells, or works of his contemporaries Sigrid Undset and Helen Waddell.

Joseph O'Neill's house at #2 Kenilworth Square.

Indeed, throughout his literary life, O'Neill complained that he was misunderstood and misread. Presumably, he meant that his exotic historical and imaginative settings had been taken too literally and read entirely at face value. In this case, publication of *The Black Shore* under his own name might have shown that his previous books, in spite of their settings, could easily be read as metaphors for his contemporary Ireland; and that he was, obliquely, writing in the mainstream with O'Flaherty and O'Connor. Published under his name, *The Black Shore* might have rescued his somewhat skewed literary reputation.

In boldly claiming *The Black Shore*, O'Neill would also have had a chance to choose for posterity which of the two lives he led would be remembered. That he did not make this choice is entirely characteristic. For O'Neill, for varied and complicated reasons, the act of choosing a single identity was fraught with neurotic complexity. Reading his works, reading his life, it seems that O'Neill was torn by the same duality that caused him such discomfort as a civil servant among writers and as a writer among civil servants. It may well be that his life's work was consciously focused on exploring the difficulty of the double identity which this final novel possibly resolves. At least he splits the dual nature of the protagonist in *The Black Shore* into separate characters and observes them as the objective narrator, "Michael Malía," the "other" Joseph O'Neill. All his other exploratory novels, in contrast, had been written in the first person.

O'Neill's voyage within to discover his "real" self caused some rather bizarre behavior. O'Neill was obsessed with throwing up smoke screens about his life and creating a variety of personal mythologies. His habit of taking on an identity (in his books and in his life), living it, and then abandoning it, was a lifelong pattern.

One can speculate endlessly about the reasons for this behavior. Odd as this may sound, the most likely is that, as the only child of Martin O'Neill, a member of the Royal Irish Constabulary, he grew up under the suspicion with which all policemen and their families traditionally have been regarded by the Irish.[3] He often falsified his date and place of birth, claiming that he had been born in 1884 on the Aran Islands and had lived there throughout his youth, when, in fact, he had been born in 1878, a native of Tuam, County Galway, who spent three years on Aran when his father was stationed there. Nor did he ever admit—it might have been the single most important admission he could have made—that he had been a matriculant at Maynooth, the Jesuit seminary outside Dublin, but had abruptly left his pursuit of the priesthood after only two months.

After his precipitous departure from Maynooth, O'Neill began to forge a second identity as a Celtic scholar and philologist. Because of his brilliant record at Queen's College Galway, and his fluency in both English and Irish, O'Neill, in his twenties, found himself the protégé of Celtic philologist, Kuno Meyer. He was the recipient of scholarships to the School of Irish Learning, the University of Freiburg, and Victoria College Manchester; he was a scholar of even greater promise than his friends and fellow students Osborne Bergin and Richard I. Best, who later achieved fame as Ireland's two leading Celtic philologists. Before O'Neill's decision to abandon Celtic scholarship, however, he had spent ten years studying Gaelic culture. An obvious reason for this abrupt move from a position that would have assured him a university professorship to the Department of Education was probably related, at least in part, to financial pressure. Prestigious penury did not appeal to O'Neill in 1907, as he was contemplating marriage to Mary Devenport. When Joseph Starkie (Walter Starkie's father), the Resident Commissioner of Education, offered O'Neill a job in the system, he accepted it, and along with it, a comfortable salary and the mark among his scholar friends, particularly Osborne Bergin, of one who had "sold out."

O'Neill's motives were not entirely superficial, however. Intellectual integrity also contributed to his decision to leave a life of scholarship. Philological studies, ironically, had convinced O'Neill that the Irish language, rooted in peasant culture, was incapable of the expressive power of the modern European tongues. Simultaneously, and in apparent contradiction of this feeling, O'Neill found that his first duty as Permanent Secretary was to implement compulsory Irish in the school curriculum, toward which end he wrote a series of impassioned articles for *The Irish Statesman* about the glories of the Irish language and culture in a positive and wholly uncharacteristic orgy of nationalist sentiment.

These articles may point to yet another reason for O'Neill's abandonment of scholarship and academic research. Cool and unimpassioned study seems to have been in direct variance with another of O'Neill's fantasies. The mythic Celt he created for *The Irish Statesman* articles was an unlikely "giant astride the world at the time of Alexander the Great" and, even more remarkably, still to be found "fighting for the remnant of his life and language . . . in the huts of Connemara and Donegal."[4] O'Neill then took on the role— and, possibly, even the identity—of that "ancient Celt," convinced that beneath the facade of his own "modern self" lay several ancient and heroic pre-Christian souls. As he had fabricated his origins, he also Gaelicized his name and asserted that his appear-

ance—tall, lanky and rubicund with huge hands and feet—ensured
his descent from the ancient race of Hebridians.

This belief in past-life experience had at least a ten-year history.
When he moved to Dublin in 1907, his wife was still a student at
the National College of Art, and the O'Neills immediately fell in
with the literary and artistic avant-garde. The end of the Celtic Twi-
light was a period of intense interest in and exploration of mysticism and psychic phenomena. The Tarot deck, seances, and
visualizations were common fare at the houses of the literati. At
first, this preoccupation had a nationalistic intent—a way to find
the source of Celtic mysticism and magic which these women and
men felt was long buried under the strata of British governance and
the Roman Catholic Church.

Here, at any rate, were a group of young artists devouring Jung's
*Archetypes and the Collective Unconscious, The Integration of Per-
sonality*, and *Modern Man in Search of a Soul* which explored his
theory of the Ancestral Past and collective unconscious. Eastern
philosophies such as the teachings of the Indian mystic Rabindran-
ith Tagore, and A. P. Sinnet's two curious little volumes on the rein-
carnation of the soul, *Esoteric Buddhism* and *The Occult World*,
were also standard matter.

It is important to understand that the study of these theories was
more than a passing fad. For many of these young men and women,
these were lifelong beliefs, which formed the basis and served as
the source of theories as sophisticated as Yeats's preoccupation
with the Mask and his "automatic writing" experiments which
formed the basis of *A Vision*.[5]

Throughout his life, O'Neill was encouraged in his mystical pur-
suits by the company he kept, particularly by his best friend and
mentor, the infinitely gentle AE. He wrote O'Neill upon the publication of his first novel, *Wind from the North*, which was set in
Norse Dyflin in the eleventh century:

> I think your story of the Norse is a personal memory breaking through.
> . . . This is the Ancestral Wisdom Keats said was in every man, and if
> we wished, we could turn in "drunk with that old wine of heaven." You
> tap your most ——— memories, my friend—what wells up in you as
> imagination. And you will well up stories innumerable. You have doubt-
> less killed and gone adventuring with the Vikings, and hunted . . . and
> worshipped strange gods on the mountains, and had more affairs than
> would go into a library and you walked the stars with the Chaldeans and
> remote Aryans . . . and crucified your enemies and tilled your fields,
> and taught your tribe wisdom. (You are reaping the Karma of this now!)
> Don't be afraid to think greatly about these things. Your will and your

immortal soul are ready to pour their wisdom into you if you are ready to listen to them.[6]

These words must have brought comfort to O'Neill, who lived in a dichotomous world. Trapped in a routine bureaucratic job, deploring the events and banalities of the present, O'Neill longed for a world in which he might be given the opportunity to heal his disintegrated personality and find a "lasting" self. Nevertheless, he endured this dichotomy until 1934, his fifty-sixth year, when he began to write.

Careful and tentative at first, O'Neill's novels, from the very start, are a spiritual autobiography of a tortured soul gazing into a mirror, seeing his "other" self and longing to merge with it. Equally important is that O'Neill also examines his national identity, the malaise of his country and that of the modern world. However, O'Neill was careful about exposure. His personal confusion, criticisms of Ireland, and general despair are cloaked in the metaphor of historical romances, until he elucidates his former subtext clearly and unequivocally in *The Black Shore*.

III

Besides an early play, several poems, and some serialized fiction, O'Neill's reputation rests on five novels, three of which are historical and two, science fiction. Despite the differences in the genres, all are responses to the deep pessimism that engulfed the West in the wake of World War I. The historical settings, however, have a distinct similarity: eleventh-century Norse Dyflin, Jerusalem of 33 AD, and the last years of Elizabeth I are all single moments in history when the world hung on the edge of profound change. In each setting, O'Neill's protagonists have a choice to act and effect a change for posterity. In each novel, however, the protagonist is prevented from participating in this change by a powerful father or father-figure, who represents a generation for whom the assertion of identity was a simple Nietzschean will-to-power.

The focus on the father-son struggle also shows the direct influence of Freud, but, for O'Neill, the Oedipal conflict merely offers a way to confront and deplore the violence inherent in a strongly patriarchal culture.

As early as 1917, O'Neill had tried out some of these ideas in his verse play, *The Kingdom-Maker*. Set at the beginning of the Christian Era in Ireland, when the two states of Connaught and Ulster had reached a "comparatively high degree of primitive luxury,"[7] the play explores the dangers of patriarchy. Thuahal, the "king-dom-maker" of the title, who has recently risen above a squabbling mass of chieftains to give Ireland some semblance of unity, has tol-erated the coexistence of the semi-hostile race of Firbolgs. Intent on creating a patriarchal line of succession, and expanding his kingdom, Thuahal arranges a marriage between his elder daughter and Eochy, the young king of Leinster, unaware that Eochy and his younger daughter are lovers. At first resistant to the marriage contract, Eochy is naively persuaded by the Firbolg to marry the elder daughter, send her away and report her missing, then take the younger daughter to wife.

Eochy agrees to the scheme, but at the second marriage feast, a Firbolg saboteur enters Thuahal's Hall with the first wife. The two women die of shock and Thuahal, despite Eochy's offer of his own head in payment for his misdeeds, orders his armies to attack Leinster. Both civilizations crumble in the ensuing conflict, while the Firbolg, crouched on the brow of the hill overlooking the battle-field, smirk and wait until their victory is assured.

Although Gael and Firbolg represent the conflicts of reason and passion, political maneuvering and primitive savvy, these opposing forces also are present in Thuahal himself. For all his talk of creat-ing a kingdom that is civilized because it values peace and compro-mise, Thuahal reverts to war the moment his authority is challenged and his scheme for establishing a patriarchal hierarchy thwarted. If, as *The Kingdom-Maker* suggests, impulses toward vio-lence and revenge lurk so close beneath the surface of what we call "civilized" behavior in human beings and in entire nations, endur-ing balance and peace are futile dreams.

The Kingdom-Maker, however, only hints at a skepticism about what Western culture traditionally defines as "civilized," and it is not difficult to see the play as a direct response to Ireland's chaos after the Easter Rebellion and Europe's, in the throes of World War I. To make the play topical or historical alone is to understand only partially the obliquity of O'Neill's points of reference and its counter-utopian avowal that unless we reinvent our cultural myths, we are doomed to repeat the mindless violence of the past.

Seventeen years later, O'Neill's first novel, *Wind from the North*, developed these same themes even further. Generally perceived as a historical novel, and awarded the Harmsworth Prize of the Irish Academy of Letters in that category, ironically, *Wind from the North* challenges linear time, Christian "history," and the secular notion that civilization is somehow progressing. After an accident with a tramcar on Grafton Street, a nameless Dublin clerk finds that he has been transported to eleventh-century Norse Dyflin. As Olaf, only son of the Norse headman, he is forced to participate in the violence, bloodshed, and political intrigue that permeated the high courts of Norse-dominated Ireland in the months preceding the Battle of Clontarf in 1014, when Brian Borumha crushed the Norse bid for kingship of Ireland.

Although the events are scrupulously researched and their evocative settings are, without doubt, "historical," O'Neill's focus is less on these events than on the protagonist's response to the conflict posed by his transmigratory experience. Although Olaf cannot specifically remember his twentieth-century existence, it nevertheless blocks his ability to assimilate himself into his new, but ancient, culture. Caught between the Hammer of Thor, embodied in the figure of his violent Norse father, and the Cross of Christ, embodied by the figure of his Celtic mother, Olaf soon discovers that when he is called on to act, he can only think; called on to decide, he can only speculate. In the final scene of the novel, as Brian Borumha batters down the walls of his tun, Olaf, weakly holding a battle-ax in his hands lets it drop to the ground. He awakens abruptly in a Dublin hospital, a man changed irrevocably in his knowledge that the modern world, which works so hard to repress conflict, is no place for him:

> I have no great wish to share my memories with other people who may not understand them or sympathize with them. What I desire most and above everything is to go back to Dyflin away from this twentieth century world that has grown so strange and lonely to me, but until I can get back, if I ever do get back, there is no happier way, that I can think of, to spend the time than by remembering my life in Ulf's hall. . . .[8]

Wind from the North's Olaf is the first in a series of similar protagonists. Coming into direct confrontation with their primary and ancestral selves, they encounter the chthonic and male sides of their natures. Olaf, like all the others, is never given a choice to assimilate, only a choice to choose: either he succumbs to the nearly irresistible pull of his maleness, or he resists it. Invariably, he chooses resistance and, in resistance, allows his female side to rule his nature.

It is within the realm of conjecture that, beginning his literary career at fifty-six, O'Neill may not have felt he had the time to research another work set in the past. The terror of the European situation in 1934 and 1935 probably provided the urgency O'Neill felt and voiced in his next two works—*Land under England*, a science-fiction thriller, and *Day of Wrath*, a futuristic enactment of a second world war O'Neill predicted would begin in 1952. Thus, *Land under England*, his most popular novel and the book by which, ironically, he is probably best remembered, cannot at this point in O'Neill's career be called a "departure" from historical fiction. It and the novel that followed show two years of experimentation in other genres before he returned to history with renewed vigor and confidence.

Written in the tradition of the counter-utopian thriller of the 1930s, *Land under England* recalls the protagonist's journey underground to a land of strange and horrifying automatons, descended from the last Roman legionaries to occupy England. He makes this journey in order to find his father who, deranged by his experiences in World War I, has disappeared to find his Ancestral Past, which he has read about in family archives.

Descending through an opening in the ground, the son enters a Dantesque region of sunless cliffs and phosphorescent caverns covered by a trailing fungoid growth and peopled by toads, spiders, and other masterpieces of the imagination. Reaching the center of this underground world, he finds a city ruled by a Master of Will and Knowledge, where human speech has been replaced by telepathy and where his father has been absorbed by the Will of the State. The ensuing struggle is between the father, who wishes to coerce the son into providing this underground race with the technical knowledge it will need to ascend and conquer the upper world, and the son who finds himself locked in a life-and-death struggle as the self-appointed guardian of civilization, such as it is. As in *Wind from the North,* the mother-preserver principle, associated with civilization and historical continuity, prevails.

Though clearly a political allegory, *Land under England*, like *Wind from the North,* also is a hair-raising psychodrama as the protagonist-narrator, who also despairs of the banality of his workaday world, revels in passing through the "doors by which my father escaped from the upper world of dreary twentieth-century realities into kingdoms that were lit by the suns of other days."[9] Although O'Neill chooses not to regress in time but in consciousness, the goal of the protagonist, once again trapped in an alien world, is to choose between absolute absorption into a culture and absolute isolation from it.

The primitive instincts of Ulf reside in the father-figure. With the absence of the mother-preserver, the struggle between father-destroyer and son is only tangentially Oedipal and seems to be more deeply consonant with the world of Northern mythologies, plunging us into the dark wood where father and son engage in the primitive battle of sexual dominance and survival. O'Neill expands the metaphor of this conflict further, once again turning the struggle between generations into a struggle between past and present, depth and superficiality, barbarism and civilization, male and female.

As the novel progresses, the son discovers that, rather than possessing a separate identity, his father lives horribly within him and that his salvation depends on destroying his father or being destroyed. Incapable of the act, however, he, like Olaf, lets his weapon drop and allows one of the slobbering two-headed horse-like creatures of the underground world to do his work for him.

In both *Wind from the North* and *Land under England*, there are obvious sexual overtones. Looked at from a Freudian perspective, it is easy to say that O'Neill had less than repressed disgust with paternal figures and patriarchal values. The message is more complex, however, and carries cultural overtones as well as purely personal ones. The younger man is thoroughly "modern," in that—cut off from parental moorings (like Olaf, he is the last of a line) and increasingly aware that traditional values are not innate but evolved—he is trapped in the tight cell of the ego where choice becomes impossible and where leaps of faith are conspicuously awkward. Fated to live this life of continuing frustration, he must either pursue some proactive course and run the risk of distortion or, at worst, madness, or return to a life of calmness and daily routine, which, in fact, he does.

These ideas informing *Wind from the North* actually are in sharper focus in *Land under England* because O'Neill, unencumbered by the need to develop and evoke a historical setting, concentrates primarily on the complex and opposing value systems of the two male characters.

The potboiler that followed, *Day of Wrath*—a quickly written, ill-conceived narrative owing much to O'Neill's fondness for American pulp westerns—joined other popular science-fiction thrillers such as those of H. G. Wells and Balmer and Wylie's *When Worlds Collide*. Nonetheless, *Day of Wrath* adds a second important element to the theme of identity confusion in its outward expression of racism and the fear of mixed origins. With the same kind of horror with which he viewed the dark-skinned, almond-eyed race below the surface of England, O'Neill trembles at the possibility that the result of a second world war might be a non-white Europe. Fearing a Japanese invasion of the West, O'Neill prefers a German victory, since

Cartoon by H. G. Wells, among the O'Neill papers at the National Library of Ireland, MS 110003.

nothing would be changed fundamentally. The white man would remain the dominant factor in world affairs.[10] If, however, Western countries weakened one another enough so that Japan could march West that would mean the end of Europe, and all she stood for [would disappear] from the stage of world history, that what the Persian, the Carthaginian, the Hun, the Tartar, the Turk, all the Asiatic hoards, had failed to do, had at last been done by the Jap.[11]

This fear reaches pathological proportions in the "African episode," where O'Neill cannot even bring himself to picture a black, but only the carnage in the wake of a black revolt seeking to avenge

Africa by crucifying and plunging into boiling oil baths the white imperialists who have had the misfortune to remain.

In this expression of the deep doubts and fears lurking in the imperialist mind, *Day of Wrath* falls into the genre of much popular British science fiction between the world wars, in which Martians and other intergalactic (that is, non-white) invaders threatened the fabric of the civilized imperialized Western world.

For O'Neill, however, who was not British and whose own country had suffered as greatly as many non-white nations under English dominion, the racism in *Day of Wrath* stems from a deeper, more personal fear that permeates O'Neill's works—most obvious in this novel because it is O'Neill's most careless. All O'Neill's protagonists are in anguish because they are of mixed origins: in *Wind from the North*, the Norse and the Celtic; in *Land under England*, the Roman and the Anglo-Saxon; in *Philip*, the Gentile and the Jew; and in *Chosen by the Queen*, O'Neill's final complete work, the feudal and the Renaissance. In each tragic admixture, the Norse, Roman, Jewish, and feudal components war with the Celtic, Anglo-Saxon, Greek, and Renaissance ones in such a way as to render the character caught in one of these conflicts a split personality incapable of assertion and will.

What evolves is a nearly textbook definition of the marginal man—one poised in psychological uncertainty between two or more social and ethnic worlds, reflecting their harmonies and attractions, their discords and repulsions. Marginal man's implicit belonging is based on race or nationality, birth or ancestry. Exclusion from or confusion about these external emblems of identity removes such an individual from complete participation and precludes complete understanding (and acceptance) of self. Thus, the basic fear of each of these characters is the ancient fear of miscegenation.

IV

Once O'Neill had expressed his fear of miscegenation directly in *Day of Wrath*, he was free to explore it more carefully in his best work of fiction, *Philip*. Using Dostoievsky's Prince Myshkin as a model for his protagonist, Philip Bar John, an epileptic physician and last descendant of an ancient family of Sadducees, O'Neill sets this novel at the time of the Passover in 33 AD. Gentile on his Greek mother's side, he has lived and worked in the courts of Athens, a respected and successful physician until, at the age of thirty-three, the longing to find his spiritual home in Jerusalem.

As a marginal man, Philip could not have come to a worse place at a worse time. Jerusalem seethes with fear, tumult, and fanaticism. Religious and political power struggles among the Sadducees, the Pharisees, and the occupying Roman legions grip the city and revolution rumbles in the poorer sections, exacerbated by the seditious preaching of a madman calling himself Jesus of Nazareth.

In his attempt to find a psychologically comfortable perspective in this strange, yet familiar, environment, Philip briefly joins the revolutionary movement of John Bar Hillel, but cannot countenance violence. At home, in the house of his father's family, he is equally uncomfortable. Step by step, he is drawn toward Jesus, who represents a refuge and an ideal of otherworldly disregard. In the final stage of his commitment to the ways and teachings of Christ, Philip is betrothed to a mild Galilean woman, one of Christ's followers, and concentrates on ministering to the poor, helpless, and outcast of Jerusalem's Old City.

Neither marriage—to his betrothed or to Christ—is destined to happen. A Passover, a crucifixion, and an earthquake intervene. Philip gives up all his earthly possessions and descends to the Old City to help the earthquake's victims and is there murdered by a mob who, because they cannot fathom his intentions, fear him. The first of O'Neill's protagonists to die, Philip dies unresolved and uncommitted "with a look of amazement on his face."[12]

Throughout Philip's search to integrate his personality, he is drawn ever closer to Christ but cannot reach him. He is the doctor who attends Lazarus but cannot save him; a Jew betrayed by a friend for twenty pieces of silver; a suspected political agitator brought before Pilate but freed. Philip just misses seeing Lazarus walk out of his tomb and returns from Bethany to face the irreversible deaths of his grandfather and grandmother, whose tomb is sealed with a rock that stays where it is placed. He meets Judas the night before the betrayal, obsessed with the idea of murdering this man who would ultimately betray Jesus, but dismisses his impulse as irrational. At dawn, wandering the streets, he hears a cock crow three times and a hesitant voice denying something.

Christ never appears, but remains a force and an unseen presence, which further complicates Philip's search for transcendence. That, of course, is O'Neill's point: neither inspired nor divine, Philip can rely only on his intelligence, reason, and goodwill. The moments of clarity, exultation, and vision he experiences are but the fleeting, euphoric preludes to one of his epileptic seizures. He does not transcend, he is not heroic; he is simply disabled.

Most of Jerusalem's citizens are in the same predicament. Like Philip, they live to a greater or lesser degree in the hazy realm of the ego—for O'Neill, a trap of inconsistencies and specious rationality. Here are those who, rejecting a greater authority and fearful of relying on instinct, are incapable of making a decision. Pilate, of course, is the stunning example; but so are most of the less historically maligned "decent sorts" of the city. And then, on the level of the id, live the self-gratifying personalities embodied in O'Neill's portrait of Barabbas, a thorough moral degenerate.

If the human mind is an admixture of these forces, the admixture is tragic, in that it represents two irrational levels of consciousness, the source of the protagonist's entrapment: lacking divinity, he cannot be Christ; possessing humanity, he cannot pursue equally self-gratifying revolution and sexuality. Although the Freudian structure is there, once again, O'Neill lacks the Freudian optimism in the basic health of the instinctual life.

Philip is a further exploration of the father-son relationship in a patriarchal society, but far more sophisticated in the unmistakable inference that the conflict is deeply rooted in Western culture. Because Philip's father is dead, he poses no actual physical threat to his son; therefore, rather than being the source of fear and hatred, he is the source of guilt. Before his death, the father had been the pariah of the tribe for having married a Gentile. Thus, when Philip arrives, he, like Christ, is the embodiment of the father in flesh, mistaken for him by the family, given the father's room to sleep in and his old clothing to wear. Although Philip is perceived as his father's "second chance," he is incapable of rectifying his father's mistakes in spite of his will to do so.

The mastery of form in this novel is apparent in this skillful convening of the historical setting with the psychological drama and religious theme. In *Wind from the North* and *Land under England*, the settings and backdrops, skillful as they are, remain relatively random places where life and death struggles for ascendancy are worked out. In *Philip*, however, the setting itself is the point. God is dead: there is no father and thus no divine imprimatur for patriarchal authority. To attempt meaning within the patriarchal value system is an exercise in futility and frustration, and the agony of Gethsemane is purely personal and existential. Philip's father's non-appearance, in fact, emphasizes O'Neill's existential point. No longer able to "blame" an outside force, Philip must acknowledge his conflict and accept the sole responsibility for its existence.

In *Philip*, O'Neill establishes a clear line leading from the remote Dyflinskidi to the reality of himself. Moving from the esoteric and the fantastic into the historical mainstream, O'Neill had only two steps left before facing his own image squarely. The first step he takes in the last published novel, *Chosen by the Queen*, in which the conflict resides in an actual flesh-and-blood being, Robert Devereux, Second Earl of Essex. The second step he takes in *The Black Shore*.

In the famous and ill-fated Essex, O'Neill saw another human being in conflict, one who lived in an age no less fraught than his own with inconsistencies and contradictions. The most perfect Elizabethan courtier since Leicester, Essex's behavior betrayed a man uncomfortable with the age in which he had been born and the roles he was asked to play. Although he stood at Elizabeth's side as a protector and, presumably, the protector of the nationhood she had striven so hard to achieve, he also was the last of the great feudal barons, fiercely independent and resentful of monarchy. Ironically, his final days stood not only as a metaphoric end to vestigial feudalism, but to the Elizabethan world itself—a fact of which Elizabeth, in ordering his execution, seemed painfully aware.

Nevertheless, in this most "actual" of his novels, among whose characters are a host of historical personages, O'Neill continues to cloud issues and obscure his theme by placing the responsibility of the narrative in the hands of a fictional character, a Wycliffian brachiographer whose journal entries comprise the text of *Chosen by the Queen* and who is himself so overwhelmed by the intrigues of the aging Queen's court that he can see but confusedly. The problems O'Neill creates by choosing a random-entry journal technique are manifold. So often is the narrator incapable of understanding what is happening that, unless a reader is familiar— almost intimate—with the Elizabeth and Essex tale of woe, the novel makes little sense.

It does, however, make much better sense as metaphor than any of the preceding works. Essex was, after all, real, and the English Renaissance closer in time and place to O'Neill's contemporary Ireland. Together, character and setting provide O'Neill with a ready metaphor for his own despair. *Chosen by the Queen* rings with disapprobation and a nearly palpable sadness that the great days of the Renaissance are over; that the good queen, ill and brooding, and her last courtier Essex alike, are being manipulated by the cynical, the unscrupulous, and the power-hungry. Only Sir Christopher Blount, Essex's last retainer (who had reached his sixty-ninth year in 1600, as O'Neill had reached his in the year of this novel's publication), preserves any of the dignity and high idealism of the past. When he marches with Essex in the abortive attempt to usurp the throne, he does so to make one last stand to preserve the glories of the past and to prevent the consequences of a Stuart reign.

Physical decay is epitomized by the now-hideous old queen and the deformed body of Anthony Bacon, and moral corruption, by Henry and Elizabeth Wriothsley who have turned in old age from lovers into libertines. *Chosen by the Queen* is, in this way, as much a statement about the moral collapse of postwar Ireland and the tarnishing of once bright dreams as it is about the "other" Renaissance. In a letter to Colum, written after the novel's publication, O'Neill expressed dismay that he had not yet been able to purchase a copy of Mary Colum's *Life and the Dream* (1947), the romantic view of the Irish Revival, seen from the perspective of a student in the first decade of the century. "It gladdens my heart," he wrote, "that the story of the age of golden dream will be preserved."[13] This nostalgia had also been exacerbated by the death, a month earlier, of Ernest Boyd, O'Neill's friend for nearly half a century and one of the most lively and passionate chroniclers of the Irish Renaissance. Boyd's death from general dissipation was emblematic as well. Ireland had once had a chance and let it slip by.

V

That O'Neill meant *The Black Shore* to be his final novel, a capstone work drawing the others together, suggests that it would complete a pattern in the oeuvre. With each novel, O'Neill draws himself more closely and courageously into the work; with each successive venture into fantasy or into the past, he limits his peripheral focus and concentrates on the predicament of the protagonist. With each successive work the protagonist becomes more real, until he takes the shape of a historical character.

Yet, until *The Black Shore*, O'Neill generated frustration in the works. Reading them was often like having a conversation with someone skirting the real issues, however compelled he might have been to talk about them. The final novel, far more direct, suggests that whatever their time or place, all O'Neill's novels have been metaphors for what he perceives as the predicament of being Irish.

The Black Shore is set in the fictional West Ireland coastal town of Lochnamara, "a lunatic land . . . where no human being could keep sane, except those who were already outside the bounds of sanity."[14] One issue merely hinted at in his earlier works and

brought fully to light in this novel, is Irish sexuality—either the lack
or the plethora of it. The fact that the protagonist in this novel is
two people—the rational Dr. Philip Ederney (another Philip and
another physician who cannot heal himself) and the spiritual Fr.
James Clogher (another epileptic prone to euphoric visions) who
are both in love with the same woman—suggests that O'Neill's
search for personal integration has ended in futility or been abandoned in the recognition that both sides of the same personality
suffer exactly the same agonies and that only the source of these
agonies is different. Both men, for example, are self-flagellators:
Ederney in his ceaseless work to clean up the bacteria-infested
cesspool that is Lochnamara; Clogher by more conventional hair-
shirt methods. Ederney is punishing himself for his nearly fanatic
denial of the spiritual life, Clogher for his hatred of his physical
feelings. Both are equally prudish. Both are equally frustrated in
their prudery, and both naturally consumed with guilt: Ederney
because he does not sleep with his wife; Clogher, because he
wants to.

The Oedipal theme in *The Black Shore* is more open and more
complex than in the previous works. Both men's sexual dysfunc-
tions are directly related to their mothers and their religion. Ederney's denial of religion has its source in the jealousy he felt when
his mother began paying undue attention to the new Monsignor in
their parish when he was a boy; Clogher's vocation, its source in
the smell of his mother's hair when she returned from Benediction.
When hatred of or love for religion, as they are associated with love
for the mother, affects sexuality, all havoc breaks loose. If, as is true
in the patriarchal scheme, the "Father Almighty" is the ultimate
source of sexual power (as he certainly has been in all O'Neill's
works), denying the father is denying the source of one's own sexuality. In this, lies Ederney's problem. Accepting the father, however, does not result in the opposite effect. Clogher's problem is
complicated by his acceptance of the father's omnipotence and his
own powerlessness in the face of that omnipotence; thus, although
he has strong sexual feelings, he cannot act on them, because to do
so would pose a challenge to the Father Almighty. Institutionalized
celibacy ensures the sexual obedience of God's servant as the con-
cept of the Trinity ensures that the son, never a separate entity, can
also never become a sexual threat to the father. Thus, sexual dysfunction lies in both the acceptance and the denial of a religion
founded on patriarchy.

There is much of O'Neill in these two men—particularly Ederney, whose life reads like an O'Neill autobiography. Born on Aran

in a "boma hedged round by the Gaelic language and the rites of the Church,"[15] Ederney, like O'Neill, matriculated at Maynooth, but left soon after reading Gustave Lanson's violently anti-clerical *History of French Literature*. And, if Ederney's doubts are also O'Neill's, *The Black Shore* explains O'Neill's self-imposed intellectual exile and counter-utopian skepticism:

> Why was the pretense of faith not killed that Sunday when doubt first came, the evening I spent immersed in Gustave Lanson's *History of French Literature*, the book that blew our *boma* to shreds for me. That Sunday evening devoured whole years. Did it transform the ambitions bred on them? Was it then I filled the sudden emptiness of my world with another image, the image of myself as a liberator, the man above all beliefs?[16]

Cultural "fit"—that is, assimilation—is impossible at each extreme of denial or belief, and so Ederney and Clogher come together *in extremis* to form O'Neill's final marginal character.

In rejecting spirituality, O'Neill may also have rejected his sexuality. It can also be speculated that if, according to O'Neill, women did not suffer from limited choice in character and behavior, their marginal men might be saved. O'Neill had some difficulty in creating women characters, who appear in his works often by narrative necessity. Having inherited a Victorian sensibility about female gender roles and sexual expression, O'Neill's women are either hopelessly pallid housebodies or manipulative seductresses exciting male sexual passion, jealousy, and killer instinct.

In *The Black Shore*, O'Neill has reversed his usual pattern in which the single male protagonist is possessed of an irreconcilable double nature and the women are either drudges or Delilahs. In fact, in this novel, he admits, albeit tacitly, that hitherto he had been so obsessed with the problems of males that he had been unfair to females. *The Black Shore* shows O'Neill to be surprisingly sensitive to the sexual predicament of Irish women. Ederney's sexual dysfunction does not prevent him from convincing the women of Lochnamara that they are not the sexual possessions of their husbands and that "No" means "No." Bid Faherty, truly a marvelous character, claws the eyes of the parish priest who has come to her home with the argument that if she does not give her husband sex, he will be driven to committing mortal sin. She replies:

> Aye, rowl in the dunghape of mortial sin with the divils in hell, wan afther th' other till his belly burshts, that's what Pat Faherty can do if he want it, down in the pit o' hell, but my life he won't take for his

shport; becripes, he won't, your holy Rivirince, not even with your Rivirince's blessing, not if I have to brain the bloody divil with the tongs to
keep him off.[17]

This assumption that sex with his wife is the salvation of men is
at the core of Nan Ederney's anguish. Urged by her uncle, the parish priest, to marry the atheist doctor as an "instrument of his salvation," Nan's marriage is a sham, and O'Neill makes no pretense
about it. As she is listening to her husband's nightly litany of cases,
her mind wanders to her role as his wife:

> "Still playing a part," she thought, "always the grand little part. . . . I'll
> probably fall into flesh, become a stout and comfortable woman hunting
> for gossip. . . . I'm not doing my job now, going on with the play-acting.
> I must listen to what the man is saying, get the habit of listening. My
> God, what a bore it will be, not the grand uplifting tragedy I've been
> pretending. Just a crashing bore."
>   "What an interesting case, Philip. Do you think the woman will sur-
> vive?"[18]

Nan is O'Neill's "Nora," creating dollhouses wherever she goes for
lack of any self-fulfilling role. Marrying Ederney to save his soul,
she nurtures him as though she were his mother and behaves like
a kind of demented Virgin Mary. Frustrated in her attempts to effect her husband's spiritual salvation—frustrated in sexuality, frustrated in motherhood—she turns her attentions to poor James
Clogher. Here, she attempts to effect a secular salvation by curing
Clogher's neuroses and in this attempt succeeds in pushing him
entirely over the edge.

For O'Neill, sexuality, limited and defined by the Roman
Church, which has not changed significantly since the days of Saint
Jerome, lies at the heart of an unnatural, humiliating state of affairs. Women in good Catholic marriages are either the objects of
their husbands' sexual needs and baby factories or, lacking sex entirely, become their husbands' mothers and feed into the Irish Oedipal fantasy in a nearly unending neurotic pattern. More
important, the sexual obtuseness of Irish males, who, if they are
sexually functional, are often their wives' rapists, excuse their behavior by equating coupling with cultural survival:

> They want us with our dwindlin' population to go down like the deca-
> dent countries round us, England, France, with their birth control,
> slidin' down the slippery slope into hell until they're eaten up by the

Bolshies, the yellow men, the Indians, the Blacks, all them fellows that's breedin' like rabbits.[19]

This cultural lunacy issues from the mouth of a Mr. O'Roarty, the village schoolmaster. It is probable that O'Neill took great pleasure in satirizing a member of a profession that had given him no end of grief for most of his working life.

The Church comes in for more than simple criticism of its misogyny and its responsibility for dichotomizing spirit and flesh. The one institution that could lead in establishing some program for reform and social justice turns away from the squalor, drunkenness, and despair of its parishioners, mouthing instead platitudes about the glorious creation and the inscrutability of the Divine Plan. At worst, the shepherds are actively damaging the flock; at best, they are in a state of remote otherworldliness. Fr. Ned, the parish priest, may appear outwardly benign, but what of this mellow and self-satisfied reverie:

It was pitiful the way people took life, pushing aside the real things, hankering after the shoddy. Here was today's dinner, a joy; for even if Kate's hand in pastry was a little heavy, the rest was delicious, the ham had melted in his mouth, the cabbage never so good with anything else in the world as with a bit of Irish bacon, done by somebody who knew how to do it, and Kate certainly did. Even the pastry, if a bit on the heavy side, was good solid food. The apples in their sweetness were a treat after the bacon and cabbage. The sun was shining outside; the day calm and sweet as a heart could wish, without any of the strain and stress of a town, and surrounding it all was that Catholic faith that made prayer such an easy ascent of mind to God.[20]

Tender as this might be, the thoughts are irresponsible in one who is the spiritual leader of a community living in hunger, abject poverty, and disease.

Fr. Ned joins a host of other stage Irish, rivaling each other in tawdry taste and weak intellect—the Gaelic Revivalists, the blood-sucking shebeen men, and fanatic schoolmasters who people this novel, owe what they are and have become to their religion, the fears it has instilled in them, and the excuses it has given them to engage in thoughtless, selfish, and lunatic behaviors. In fact, clarity and reason reside in only one character—the libidinous, perpetually drunk former doctor of the village whose only religion is irreverent disregard for those who worry about it.

Possibly aware in his seventieth year that he would not write another novel, O'Neill wrote *The Black Shore* to get off his mind what had been on it for a lifetime. The institutional, cultural, and personal neuroses encountered in this novel are primarily those of a people forced to live a life and adopt a religion inimical to their ancestral identity. The fear of miscegenation takes on a particular clarity when it is seen in this context: in every one of its ugly guises and manifestations, it is the most obvious expression, and at the core, of cultural insecurity. *The Black Shore* can certainly be read as O'Neill's disclaimer, an obvious retreat from his former belief in the purity and decency of white imperialist Europe.

The Black Shore offers us something in the way of a theory: The ancient pagan Celt, now become the neurotic Irish, have been made so by being forced to participate in an empty ritual. Although they can out-talk the wind, they are basically incapable of self-generated change because they are not in charge of themselves. These Irish, O'Neill seems to be saying, have become the principals in a mime show, and, less fortunate than most puppets, unconsciously sense that what they are is not what they are. Whether in the guise of the Norseman, the Chaldean, the Elizabethan, all O'Neill's protagonists have been such puppets—but with souls and ancestral memories. They have longed for an ephemeral past, unable to call it back except in fleeting moments of epiphany. Pre-Christian Celtic culture, like the high civilization of the Sadducees before the advent of Christianity, like the Renaissance before the reign of the Roman Catholic Stuarts, like Norse Ireland before the crushing victory of Brian Borumha, fought furiously to resist it and fell to the overwhelming power of religion.

In an assessment and understanding of Joseph O'Neill, the novelist, *The Black Shore* makes his easy dismissal as a romantic posturer and an idealist difficult to argue. Although his dreams of a return to the heroic past may have been as directionless as strands of milkweed in October wind when compared to the grim realities of a traffic jam on Grafton Street, to disregard these dreams because they are impossible to realize is distinctly unjust. Equally "unjust" is to "explain" them as quirks of time, place, and influence.

O'Neill, I believe, saw himself as an emblem of his race, trapped between a cultural reality and a cultural dream. It is a condition explaining most of the paradoxes surrounding him—his yearning for an ancestral self; his obsessive disavowal of the country on-its-surface; his restlessness; his anger at the mundane work he had to do and his compulsive need to do it as a refuge; his curiosity about the lives of others and of his fictional characters; and his secrecy about his own.

The Black Shore offers no solutions for either O'Neill or the plight of human beings like him in the modern world. The narrator has disengaged himself entirely from this work and stood outside it, and in doing so, disengaged himself from any hope of resolution or salvation. In this sense of sheer helplessness, O'Neill must be categorized as a "modern" writer and included among a host of his contemporaries tormented by the anguish of living in this century, searching for a New Eden, and cut off from the past and the meaning of the past by a chasm the legs of Atlas cannot bestride.

As an Irish writer, in particular, O'Neill joins many of his contemporaries in his exploration of what it means to be Irish, and of this we are unerringly assured by the existence of *The Black Shore*, the one work which gives all his words credibility, consistency, and integrity.

Notes

1. Letter from Joseph O'Neill to Padraic Colum. 9 September 1948. The rest of the text of this letter may explain in part why O'Neill had chosen Colum. At the time, seventy years of age and saddened by the loss of many of his friends, O'Neill seems to have made out of Colum a friend he never was:

> That first meeting of ours and your reading of *The Land* was such an epoch for me that it remains as vivid as if it was yesterday. Years afterward . . . I was never able to forget that it was you who had given me entrance to a country of visions. I do not think you could have known how much your company and your work meant to me in the old days. . . .

2. Letter from Joseph O'Neill to Richard I. Best, n.d. (National Library of Ireland MS #11003).

3. In *Red Roses for Me* (1942), Sean O'Casey includes the following dialogue between the hero, Ayamonn Breydon, an Irish Catholic in love with a Protestant woman, and his mother:

> *Mrs. Breydon*: There's worse still than that in it.
> *Ayamonn*: Worse, is there? What may be worse?
> *Mrs. Breydon*: She's the child of a Sargeant in the Royal Irish Constabulary, isn't she?
> *Ayamonn*: Well, she can't help it, can she?
> *Mrs. Breydon*: I know that: but many have murmured agin' a son of mine goin' with a man crouchin' so close to their enemy. (*Collected Plays*, vol. III, 169).

4. Seósámh Oneill, "On Living up to One's Income," *The Irish Statesman*, Vol. I (27 October 1923), 200.

5. Austin Clarke remembered Yeats at these evenings with the O'Neills:

> I saw [Yeats] every Thursday evening during the following winter at the house of Joseph O'Neill. . . . Yeats was then writing *A Vision*. Women crowded around him in the drawing room, listening eagerly as he discussed the book with them. . . . (*A Penny in the Clouds*. London, 1968, 201–2.)

6. Letter from AE to Joseph O'Neill, 4 October 1934 (National Library of Ireland, MS #11003).

7. Seósámh Oneill, *The Kingdom-Maker* (Dublin, 1917), vi.

8. *Land under England* was brought out by Simon and Schuster in the United States; translated into French and published by Gallimard; translated into Italian and suppressed by the Mussolini government. Much to my astonishment, while browsing through a New Age book store in the East Village looking for books dwelling on the fantastic for a young reader's Christmas gift, I saw that a new paperback edition of *Land under England* had been published in 1984 by Overlook Press, a press specializing in the occult.

9. Joseph O'Neill, *Land under England* (Gollancz, 1935), 40.

10. Joseph O'Neill, *Day of Wrath* (Gollancz, 1936), 37.

11. *Day of Wrath*, 40.

12. Joseph O'Neill, *Philip* (Gollancz, 1940), 447.

13. Letter from Joseph O'Neill to Padraic Colum, 30 April 1947.

14. *The Black Shore*, 205.

15. *The Black Shore*, 212.

16. *The Black Shore*, 212.

17. *The Black Shore*, 157.

18. *The Black Shore*, 105.

19. *The Black Shore*, 83.

20. *The Black Shore*, 69.

Annotation of Private Archives, Sources, and Collections

Archives of the Irish Department of Education. Documents pertaining to the Secondary School Inspectorship of Joseph O'Neill.

Archives of *The Dublin Magazine*. Six letters of literary interest from Joseph O'Neill to Seumas O'Sullivan. Dublin Library, Trinity College, Dublin.

Archives of *The Irish Independent*. Two letters of literary interest, 1906.

Archives of the publishing house of Hodges & Figgis & Co., Ltd. Documents pertaining to the publication of the school edition of *Wind from the North*.

Archives of the publishing house of Jonathan Cape, Ltd. Letters of literary interest.

Archives of the publishing house of Victor Gollancz, Ltd. Letters of literary interest; transcript of a review of *Chosen by the Queen* by Benedict Kiely, Radio Eireann, 14 July 1947.

Manuscript Collections in the National Library of Ireland:

MS #8184. A collection of letters addressed to Joseph O'Neill on literary subjects from George Russell (AE), Francis Stuart, Francis Hackett, and Sigrid Undset.

MS #11003. The Richard I. Best Papers. Letters from Celtic Scholars, including Joseph O'Neill.

MS #13576 (pp. 20ff.) Handwritten notebook by W. B. Yeats prepared for Mary Devenport O'Neill.

A Selected Bibliography of the
Works of Joseph O'Neill

Articles

Joseph O'Neill, "Irish for the Irish," *Irish Statesman*, vol. 9 (24 December 1927).

Seósámh Oneill, "Education and Its Varieties," *Irish Statesman*, vol. 1 (13 October 1923).

———, "Educational Aims," *Irish Statesman*, vol. 1 (20 October 1923).

———, "On Living up to One's Income," *Irish Statesman*, vol. 1 (27 October 1923).

———, "Education as Fusion," *Irish Statesman*, vol. 1 (3 November 1923).

———, "Celtic," *Irish Statesman*, vol. 1 (10 November 1923).

———, "Should We Let Irish Die?" *Irish Statesman*, vol. 1 (24 November 1923).

———, "Should We Let Irish Die?—II," *Irish Statesman*, vol. 1 (1 December 1923).

———, "Should We Let Irish Die?"—III," *Irish Statesman*, vol. 1 (8 December 1923).

———, "The Opening of the Dykes," *Irish Statesman*, vol. 1 (2 February 1924).

Translation:

Seósámh Oneill, "Cath Boinde," *Eriu*, vol. 2 (1905).

Play:

Seósámh Oneill. *The Kingdom-Maker: A Verse Play in Five Acts.* Dublin: Talbot Press, 1917.

Poems:

Joseph O'Neill, "When Carthage Was Falling," and "Timeless-ness," *Dublin Magazine,* vol. 25 (Summer 1950).

Short Fiction and Historical Sketches for the *Dublin Magazine:*

"Dyflin Days," vol. 19 (Fall 1944).
"The Outlaw," vol. 20 (Winter 1945).
"An Evening with Ben Jonson," vol. 20 (Spring 1945).
"An Audience with Gloriana," vol. 20 (Summer 1945).
"Pages from the Journal of Edmund Shakespeare," vol. 25 (Summer 1951); vol. 25 (Fall 1951); vol. 26 (Winter 1952).

Novels:

Wind from the North. London: Jonathan Cape, 1934.
Wind from the North. Dublin: Talbot Press, 1936. School Edition with glossary and maps.
Gaoth Adtuaidh. Dublin: Tomas de Bhial d'aistrigh on mBearla, 1940. Translation of *Wind from the North* into Gaelic for the Gaelic Language Irish Texts and Translations.
Land under England. London: Victor Gollancz, 1935.
Land under England. New York: Simon & Schuster, 1935.
Land under England. New York: Overlook Press, 1984.
Le Peuple de Tenebres. Paris: Gallimard, 1935. French translation of *Land under England* into *The People of the Shades.*
Day of Wrath. London: Victor Gollancz, 1936.
Day of Wrath. London: Victor Gollancz, 1940. Second paperback edition.
Philip. London: Victor Gollancz, 1940.
Chosen by the Queen. London: Victor Gollancz, 1947.

A Note on the Text

O'NEILL READ AND EDITED THE TYPESCRIPT OF *THE BLACK SHORE* before his death. I have incorporated all his changes in the current edition and corrected only the typographical errors he missed. I have retained the British spellings (for example, "traveller," "realised") but changed certain conventions of British punctuation into those adhered to in the United States (such as placing marks of punctuation within quotation marks). O'Neill's strange habit of omitting "and" as a conjunction between two separate but equal actions—"Nan sat down, poked the fire"—frequently causes confusion when the second element can ambiguously be read as a subordinate of the first. In these cases, I have supplied an [and].

Further, O'Neill was a voracious reader whose retentive mind was like the lady of Ezra Pound's poem, a veritable "Sargasso Sea" of information. Sometimes words and phrases were so deeply imbedded that O'Neill was unaware he was quoting someone else. An example of this is his use of the phrase from Matthew Arnold's "Dover Beach" to describe "the long withdrawing roar" of the sea in Lochnamara. For arcane references and quotations, I have provided footnotes.

I have also provided a glossary of Irish words and Irish slang.

O'Neill's rendering of English as it is spoken by the West County peasant through phonetic transcription is not meant to poke fun. In fact, he refers several times in the text to their "soft, Western voices." He is attempting to give a reader who is unfamiliar with English as it is spoken in Connemara a clue to how it sounds. In the craggy, harsh west of Ireland, particularly, English was not as quickly assimilated as in other more fertile and productive areas where the English were a more frequent presence. English did not spread to the remoter districts of Ireland until well into the nineteenth century. In fact, in 1801, although the English had been in Ireland in large numbers since 1550, of the 5.2 million Irish inhabitants, 4 million spoke Irish as their first language, and, of those, 2 million spoke no English at all. (A. G. van Hamel, *On Anglo-Irish Syntax*. University of Chicago Press, 1977). When they learned

34

English, the Irish peasants learned it imperfectly and experienced great difficulty in pronouncing sounds very different from their own and in adopting English idioms and constructions. The result was a strange and rather musical/rhythmic combination of Irish syntax and idiom and English words, which we call Anglo-Irish. O'Neill, a native Irish speaker and former philologist whose second language was English, understood this all too well.

An exhaustive analysis of the survival of native Irish in English seems pedantic in this context. A few examples will make the point. For example, when we read " 'Tis dhrowned you'll be altogether," instead of "You'll be drowned," we are following a rule of Irish syntax. Irish sentences begin with the verb and if that verb carries the emphasis of the sentence, well and good. However, if another word is to be emphasized, it must follow a form of the verb "to be." The "It is" construction is very common in Anglo-Irish.

Another common construction is the use of the word *after*, a literal Irish construction of the present perfect tense. Thus, instead of saying, "The young doctor has gone," we read, "The young doctor is after going."

Irish has no conjunctions to introduce time, cause, adjectival, or other subordinate clauses. So, instead of "The sun was setting as she walked down the strand," we hear, "The sun was setting and she walking down the strand." And, finally, in the character Owney Foran's " 'Tis a bad day for Lochnamara, a bad unlucky day whin the likes o' that cud happen in a house in it . . ." the seemingly superfluous "in it" is a literal translation of the Irish *ta ann*, or "extant," "in existence."

I offer these few examples to illustrate that the language of ONeill's West County peasants is not some sort of invented, "stage Irish," bog-trotter's argot, but an accurate rendering of how native speakers of Irish adapted English when they adopted it.

The Black Shore

"Why don't you leave Maynooth if you feel that way?" he had asked Anthony Cloyne after one of those pitiful confessions you sometimes got of nights up in the beachwalk in St. Mary's.

"It's easy for you to talk, James," was the answer. "It's easy for you with your brains to talk like that; but if I went, what would there be for me but the police or a chucker-out' job in Liverpool or New York with the old people at home hanging their heads when they met the neighbours?"

They were humble, unsure of themselves. When they were ordained they had suppressed their hungers [and] been good priests, while he had let the sin of pride possess him, the sin for which Lucifer fell. When he left Maynooth, an ordained priest, he had known no fears. He had felt himself alone with God, at one with Him. He remembered still the ecstasy of that first Mass, the moment when he held God's body in his hands, God's body created by himself from the wafer that had been nothing but bread a moment before. All that day he had walked on air. Day after day he had been lifted above the earth. When he had looked into the faces of the others, he knew that they had not that overwhelming sense of God, that they could never grasp the mixture of joy and dread that seized him afresh every day at the Consecration of the Host.

When Nan had come into his life, the ecstasy had become greater. He had not understood that quickening. He had taken it as proof of his growing union with God.

"Oh God," he cried, "Oh, God! What a sinner I have been, proud and blind, looking down in my pride on Paddy Murphy and Anthony Kelly and John Maurice and Jack Nolan, those humble souls that have entered on God's service in true humility, taking back seats, never opening their mouths, God's true children in their feeling of their unworthiness."

Nan's face came before him, the golden eyes in the small pointed face, the gaiety. It was the act of God to choose such a one to bring him back to his senses, but perhaps it was the only way. If it had been a woman of the flesh with fleshly glances, he would have been on his guard from the first. He would have been repelled.

"Oh Nan, Nan—" he cried, "how could your pure eyes have snared my soul!"

He stiffened. That was she coming in by the sea-road. Soon Michael Leland would appear from the other end of the village.

A shiver went through his body. He turned away. What was it to him? God forgive him, if those two met up on the crags to say goodbye? It would be farewell, only that, a final farewell. The innocent child in her had been caught by that man's flashy glitter, the talk of

Dublin days, London days, Paris nights. That would pass. Even if it didn't, it was none of his business. His duty was plain, to drive out those longings, to humble his heart before God who had let the adversary trap him in punishment of his foolish pride. The permanent doctor would come tonight or tomorrow. He was hoping that Nan would attract this new doctor as she attracted everybody, that it would be a match, a natural match—the parish priest's niece and the brilliant young doctor from England with all the degrees and special qualifications. It was the hand of God.

Why should a doctor with such a record choose to come to Lochnamara if it weren't the hand of God?

It would be easier to give her up to a man like that, an earnest, serious man who chose a place like Lochnamara when he could have had the pick of the Irish or English dispensaries.

"'Give her up!' God forgive me," he thought ruefully. "There I am again with my 'give her up.' I have let my sinful thoughts get embedded in me."

He began to pray silently.

From the village below, a roaring voice began to bellow a song. He stopped his prayer, stood glaring angrily at the huddle of houses. Tony Culkin was drunk again, a source of scandal and gross disedification* to the village.

He began to hurry down the boreen* that led to the cabins. This at least he could deal with and should deal with

> Hi foloo, tiddy foloo,
> Hi—full—hi—full—tiddy foloo

The deep bass was booming through the village, coming up to him with its note of mockery.

When he reached the houses he was white with rage. Dr. Tony Culkin caught sight of him, left the group of villagers he was singing for and came towards him swaying a little.

"The saint, begob, our Lochnamara saint! How goes it, Fr. James, Fr. James, the sweetest soul that ever sang before the eyes of God! Sound the loud timbrel o'er Egypt's dark sea!"[4]

The priest stood in front of him, almost speechless with rage. If it was drunkenness alone, he might have let it pass. It was all the other things, the tampering with the girls of the parish, the fact that Tony's father, the "gombeen" man,* had his noose of credit round the necks of nine-tenths of the people. Father and son were the curse of the parish in their different ways, scoundrels who took advantage of the people's miserable poverty to make them slaves, the father of his greeds, the son of his lusts, and here was this fellow ridiculing him for his piety.

"A disgrace," he shouted, "a scandal and a disgrace—that's what you are, Dr. Tony Culkin."

Tony laughed joyously.

"And the devil a truer word you ever said, Fr. James," he agreed heartily, "the devil a bigger scandal than myself is to be found in this diocese nor in any part of the county west of the Shannon."

He stretched out his hand.

"Put it there, Fr. James. 'Tis you and me are the opposites, on the see-saw between God and the devil, you always up to heaven and me down. You won't shake—well—well—now. There's a lack of charity for you."

He turned toward the grinning faces.

"What the hell are ye grinning at?" he yelled. "Don't ye know how good God has been to ye? Ye get a saint for a priest, the greatest saint in Ireland, and tonight you'll be getting other sort of saint for a doctor, an atheist, they say, aye, faith, a grand devil of a saint of an atheist who doesn't believe in Heaven or Hell, Purgatory or Limbo, God or devil, nothing but the poor and the distressed. He wants to serve the poor, save your rotten bloody carcasses while Fr. James is saving your rotten bloody souls."

He turned back to the curate.

"Well, no hard feelings, Fr. James. You haven't a greater bloody admirer in this parish than [me] if only you had the sense to see it. From everything I hear, you mayn't get as much respect and love from the new fellow, not by a long chalk, Fr. Saint James. However, 'twill be all the more chance for holy mortification, the grace of God and the turning of the other cheek, so

> Hi foloo—tiddy foloo
> Hi—full—hi—full, tiddy foloo
> There was an old lady who lived in Glencree;
> Hi—full—hi—full, tiddy foloo
> When her heart went against her,
> She went on a spree
> With a hi-foloo, tiddy—foloo.

He did a couple of steps of a jig, went dancing between the green pools in front of the cabins. The crowd of men in woolen bawneens* and flannel drawers opened to let him pass.

"Sure, 'tis no wondher the crathur is mad with the dhrink today and thim fellows up in Dublin doin' him out of the dispensary his father and ould Joe wor keeping warm for him till he'd be ordained," an old man with a grey beard said softly.

He wagged his beard like a wise old goat.

"Ordained! 'Tisn't how they ordain docthors, Martin Faherty," said another.

"Thin, what do they do with thim?"

"Divil a wan o' me knows, but it isn't ordainin' nor consecratin' ayther, though, if I heard that Pat Culkin's son was consecrated by the divil, it wouldn't surprise me, no nor anyone in this village. Look at the way he's after downin' the poor preesht, God help him, as innocent an' holy a man as ever walked the street of Lochnamara. 'Tisn't much luck he'll iver have, nor any of his dirty breed, if there's a God in Heaven—"

"Aisy there now—aisy there," said a young fellow in shoddy English clothes. "There's many a worse man than Dr. Tony Culkin, whatever his dirty dog of a father may do. A dacenter lad with the dhrink there isn't in the wesht nor with anything else, God help him."

" 'Tisn't much o' God's help he'll ever get, downin' preeshts the way he does—look at poor Fr. James draggin' himself up the hill with all the heart taken out of him be that blaggard."

The priest was climbing the boreen wearily. The world was dark. His own mind was dark and sad. It couldn't be that God would hurl him into the pit, yet here he was envying Tony Culkin, Tony the drunkard, the debaucher of women, the shameless scamp devoid of grace, of contrition, of the slightest twinge of conscience for the mortal sins he was committing daily.

Chapter III

MICHAEL LELAND WATCHED THE NEW DOCTOR WITH MORE AND MORE distaste. What a disaster this lunatic would be.

He hadn't expected the Dublin sort of boy, of course. Even the ordinary English medico was different and a fellow with this chap's string of qualifications who chose to take a dispensary at the back of God speed must be madder than most, the sort you got amongst

Protestants [or] atheists—fellows who must follow some sort of crazy dream to give life meaning the true faith would have given them if they were lucky enough to have it, but this man who thought he could begin a dispensary practice in the west of Ireland by insulting and ignoring the local P.P.* must be the worst brand of lunatic of all lunatic brands. What a disastrous bloody thing to happen.

Still, it wasn't his business. Even Nan wasn't his business—poor Nan—depending, now that he had left her, on this gentleman to bring her salvation! Not that she had any cause to blame him. From the start he had been honest and above board and dammit this chap wasn't unpresentable, quite good-looking, in fact, if he hadn't that cracked look. He kept reminding him of a fellow he had seen in some old picture. Roman soldiers were scourging him and he was looking into space with the look this fellow was giving him now as he talked about priestcraft. The same brand of madness, mental distortion, though of course the fellow in the picture was a martyr. Still, even martyrs—

Leland knocked his pipe against the grate.

"Well, doctor," he said, "it's a pity you feel so strongly about it. Fr. Ned is one of the decentest old souls you could meet, none of your bossy parish priests but just a kindly old man who is sitting up there in his parlour with the whiskey and the sherry and the cigars ready, waiting for you to call."

"Aye, the whiskey and the sherry paid for out of the sweat and misery of the poor dupes he's fooling. Hardly the best bait to make me give up my principles. There's no reason for my calling on him anymore than on the police sergeant, the keeper of the local store, or any of the other prominent people, less from my point of view, since the man is for me the representative of the greatest poison agency in the country."

"As a good Catholic, doctor, I can hardly accept that description of our faith; but I don't want to argue. If you won't come up to Fr. Ned, well, you won't. I'm sorry. I feel that, if you would only work hand in hand with the clergy, a man of your qualifications could do a lot in a place like this, rotten with TB, infantile cholera, enteric, with typhus endemic."

The other scowled.

"A nice commentary on the work of Fr. Ned and his breed. His kind have been running these people for centuries, the only educated men amongst them, if what they get at Maynooth could be called an education. They have nothing to do but eat and drink and sit on their backsides from Sunday to Sunday. Typhus means filth.

Don't you think, doctor, they may have done a little to clean up the filth, given the poor devils they batten on some little return for the money they squeeze out of them?"

Leland got up.

"No use quarreling, doctor. Being a good Catholic, I know what the priests give their people perhaps a bit better than you could, and, as for laziness, I'm not so sure there are many harder workers in this county than the curate, Fr. James Clogher. I've had to warn him against overwork. However, better for you to discover all this for yourself. As you're not going over to Fr. Ned, we may as well get down to business if you're not too tired from the journey."

The new doctor's eyes brightened.

"You spoke of typhus. Have you any cases at the moment?"

"Unfortunately I have, three clear cases and a couple of others that look the thing. Here are my notes."

An hour later Leland knocked at the parish priest's door. Kate, the middle-aged maid, peered into the darkness behind him.

"Where's the other gentleman, docthor? His riverence has been waitin' for him over an hour. The kittle's bilin' the head off itself in case he'd like a dhrop of something strong. Miss Nan herself made a sweet cake, with a pint of cream and a half dozen eggs in it."

Leland smiled.

"That's the stuff, Kate, but I'm afraid he won't be able to come tonight. There was a call from one of those black fever houses. Tom Flaherty is in a bad way and he insisted on going with young Tom. He won't neglect the sick even to come to see his reverence, so I've come to make excuses."

Her face fell, but she said comfortingly, "A grand man he must be surely to face the fever after his day's travelling. If his Reverence knew about it, he'd have gone down himself to welcome him instead of asking him up. As for Miss Nan, I don't think she'll be worrying. It wasn't of him she was thinking I'll be bound when she was putting all the cream and the eggs in the cake."

She smiled up at him.

"We all wish it was you comin' to us for good, docthor."

He patted her on the shoulder.

"You'll feel the same about the new man in a couple of weeks, Kate. He's a great man. There isn't anything he wouldn't do for the poor and he has the honestest face you ever saw. Too honest, the poor man is, I'm afraid, as open and simple as a child."

"We could do with a little more of it 'round here, docthor."

"Well, I'll warrant you'll get it from the new doctor, Kate, plenty of it, foolishness, perhaps, along with it, the sort of innocence of a child that doesn't know much about the world, God help him."

"Fr. Ned will like that. Fr. James, too, an honest straight gentleman like that."

"Perhaps, Kate, perhaps. Children can be very troublesome at times in their simple foolishness. They're always so sure they're right, but he's a grand doctor, a grand one altogether. I'll say that much for him. The way he hurried off with young Tom tonight and he dead beat with all that travelling—there aren't a lot of doctors going who would do that, Kate."

"You're right there, docthor, though thanks be to God we've been very lucky in the grand docthors we've been having."

Fr. Ned Clooney rose from his chair, came forward with a smile of welcome. The smile faded somewhat when Leland came in alone, shut the door behind him.

"He's not coming, Michael?"

Leland shook his head.

"No luck, Fr. Ned. Tom Flaherty is in a bad way."

Fr. Ned nodded.

"Yes, the man's dying. Fr. James is gone down there with the holy oil."

Leland shrugged his shoulders.

"I hope they won't clash over the dying man," he muttered.

Fr. Ned gave him a shrewd look, pulled an armchair in front of the fire.

"Sit down and have a drink, Michael," he said. "No use offering you a cigar. You have your pipe, I know."

Leland sat down, watched the priest while he poured out the drinks.

"You know, Fr. Ned," he said, "you could pass for Eisenhower's brother if the photos of him are anything like the man himself."

The priest smiled.

"Well, here's how, Michael. Looks as if I'll need all Eisenhower's gifts to handle this new man."

Leland nodded.

It's lucky it's here he's coming, Fr. Ned; only I wish you had had a talk with Fr. James before those two met."

"As bad as all that?"

"Couldn't be worse. No use trying to hide it. It isn't only that the fellow is an atheist. He's a bloody fool, one of those stark staring lunatics when you touch religion, raving, crazy mad. I hope in God there won't be a scene over poor Tom Flaherty's dead body."

Fr. Ned looked at the picture over the mantelpiece, a little ship heavily laden with apostles trying to negotiate the Sea of Galilee.

"Our Lord will help us," he said.

Leland looked across at him doubtfully.

"I told him there wasn't anything more a doctor could do for poor Tom, that 'twas a case for a priest only, but he would go, no matter what I said. If I'd known Fr. James would be there before him, I'd have insisted on going myself, but somehow the thing caught me all unprepared."

He got up. The priest put over his hand and pulled him down.

"No use worrying, Michael. If they've met, it's over by now, whatever happened. So you think there'll be bad trouble?"

"I know it, Fr. Ned. There's no chance of the man going to Mass or to his duties. Worse still, I'm afraid he'll consider it his duty to preach what he practices. What you're going to do I can't imagine. If it was only yourself I feel that you'd manage him somehow or other, but with Fr. James squaring up to him—"

He grinned.

"You won't think me irreverent, I hope, Fr. Ned, but do you know those two are birds of a feather, one of them on God's side of the fence, the other on the devil's. No disrespect, of course, but the fellow kept reminding me all the time of the picture of a Christian martyr in my mother's bedroom. If only the grace of God had come to him, he'd be being flayed alive by the Bolshies or Chinese right now if he wasn't in some leper settlement."

The priest took a letter out of his pocket.

"You know, Michael, I wrote to Manchester to Fr. Carmody, asked him to find out as much as he could about him. Here's the answer, the same thing you're saying, only in different words and full of hope."

He wiped his spectacles, put them on.

"Here it is—"

" 'I look upon it as the Grace of God that sent Ederney to you, Fr. Ned. I've long been praying God to take him out of this environment, send him amongst truly Catholic people. He's too good to lose. When I heard he had applied for the dispensary at Lochnamara I felt that God had answered my prayer. There's no need for me to beg of you to take him softly, let the Grace of God come to him from the souls of your flock, their piety, all the beauty of our Holy Faith that's revealed in your Western parishes more than anywhere else in the world. Poor Philip is God's child, a child struggling against his Father.' "

Leland's face took on an expression of piety.

"Perhaps it's God's will, Fr. Ned. Looked at in that way, it becomes intelligible. Only God's direct intervention surely could make a man with his qualifications leave a job at an English university that might lead to anything for two hundred and fifty pounds a year at Lochnamara, and, if I might say so without impertinence, the Divine Will has made a grand selection for its operation here in yourself, Fr. Ned, a divine representative such as could hardly be found in any other parish in Ireland. I only hope your parishioners won't find him too much of an experience after Dr. Joe. Even the old clothes this fellow wears, a soft hat that has seen many a better day and an old sport's jacket that won't help with your people after Dr. Joe's pomp and ceremony."

Fr. Ned sighed.

"Yes, Dr. Joe is a loss. That Father Christmas beard of his and the fur collar and the half-deck hat and the omniscience, the confidence they inspired, were half the battle. They'll think our new man very ignorant if he turns up in old clothes and tells them he doesn't know what's wrong. I expect he won't be satisfied either with pouring some ether into a gauze mask and clapping it over a patient's nose and letting him or her come to when they turn blue—"

He shook his head.

"He'll upset them undoubtedly in more ways than one. When one of them said to Dr. Joe, 'Mary has a pain in her back, Doctor,' Doctor Joe promptly answers, 'kidneys,'' or 'lumbago' according as the mood took him and gave a bottle. It was very satisfactory."

Leland grinned.

"Ederney is more likely to tell Mary she's holding herself wrong or some other nonsense from their point of view. He doesn't understand that down here the doctor is still the wizard, the hoodoo man who knows everything, can cure everything. There again, Fr. Ned, I think he's lucky in having come to you for you're the greatest scientist he has yet met. You don't treat people as if they were lab specimens. You know them as they are, poor devils."

He got up.

"Well, cheerio. You've no idea how much I'll miss you and Nan. Sometimes I wish I could stay here and forget Dublin and Marge and the rest of it; but you know how it is, Fr. Ned. A man rushes in before he knows where his life ought to be. Then there's no turning back."

Fr. Ned put his hand on his shoulder.

"I understand, Michael. Nan is suffering. There's no use denying it, but that will pass. Young hearts heal quickly. You've nothing to blame yourself for at any rate. From the first night you came to see us you were completely honest and above board."

Leland caught his hand, wrung it.

"You've no idea what a comfort your words are, Fr. Ned. Nan is sore with me, very sore, I'm afraid, but God knows if I had met her before I entered into those commitments—"

Father Ned pressed his arm.

"Don't speak of it or think of it any more. Who knows but Nan may be reserved to be God's agent in saving this man's soul. God's ways are inscrutable. Through suffering He purifies us, saves us. Nan had one gap, that she had never known grief or sorrow or pain, the sufferings that deepen the soul. Don't trouble yourself any more, Michael. All these things are in the hands of God."

Chapter IV

Pat Culkin stood at the door of his pub-hotel, his thumbs in the armholes of his waistcoat. A heavy gold watch chain went from the left hand pocket to a button hole that lay comfortably on the summit of his stomach. His curves, the thickness of his gold chain, the heavy boots and the homemade woolen clothes were symbols of a most satisfactory prosperity, yet the look on Pat's face was not one of satisfaction, still less of exultation.

A stray dog sneaked down the road, came to a diffident halt in front of the hotel. It was the only house where a dog could hope for scraps.

The sight of his starved body, his hungering eyes, blew the spark of rebellion in Pat Culkin's heart to a flame. He ran at the cur, picked up stones, hurled them venomously after its flying carcass.

At the corner of the nearest hovel it turned, watched him, its miserable body tucked away 'round the corner.

Pat stared malevolently at the watching head. It was no use pursuing the matter. In spite of its condition the brute had a turn of speed that would have left him far behind even when he weighed four stone less than he did now, and, anyway, it was only a millionth part of the malignity that was getting him down.

This bloody doctor! What the hell could have brought a fellow with [such] big degrees to a Godforsaken hole like Lochnamara?

He gathered the phlegm that was swabbing round the back of his throat, spat it viciously at the road.

It looked as if the devil himself was taking a hand in the game. Old Dr. Joe had done everything, everything, had kept on doddering about, waiting until Tony would be qualified before retiring. The dispensary would have been in his pocket if this lunatic hadn't turned up; for who the devil in his senses would compete for a dispensary in Lochnamara if he had anywhere else in the wide world to go?

The dispensary was Tony's by nature's act, the graces of Dr. Joe and God, every natural law; and then up comes this lunatic from England with degrees and medals that would have got him to be the King's doctor and nothing would satisfy him but to apply for Lochnamara.

Pat sat on the case of empty porter-bottles that was waiting outside for the Roymore lorry that collected along the shore of the bay.

He stared at the bleak shore exposed by the ebb, the figures of the men up to their thighs pulling the sea-weed.

One of them came out of the sea with his load, water streaming from his flannel drawers. One of the first things this crazy doctor would do would be to try to get them not to walk in the water with two or three flannel drawers on, to change their wet clothes. He wouldn't even know that they had no others, that all the clothes they had they wore winter and summer, in sea or on land. No; he wouldn't know that or anything else.

Pat's face brightened. The fellow wouldn't last. He couldn't. He'd go round talking against the priests, against the women having babies until they died of them, against every bloody thing these benighted natives held on to. Tom, the driver who brought him out of Roymore the night before wasn't exactly a troteen,* but even Tom was shocked by the way the fool talked of the Holy Sacrifice and the marital rights of the husbands.

Pat's face relaxed. The starved cur, surveying it from the corner, decided that the worst was over. He advanced cautiously, his eyes fixed on the face. There were times when the look on that face was good for a bone. It seemed to be setting in that direction now. He cocked his ears. The man was talking good talk though he couldn't follow the words.

"Six months, less with Fr. James here, it's bound to be less. Even Fr. Ned couldn't want to keep him, much as he wants to get that

girl off his hands and anyway this sort of gentleman is hardly the
choice he'd pick—hardly. No, it won't even be six months."

He rubbed his hands. The dog came nearer.

"A boneen, you poor starved misery? Well, there might be one."

He jerked his thumb in the direction of the door.

The dog wriggled his body. He might have been "man Friday"
doing his bowings to Crusoe. He slipped past, still doing his cere-
monial convulsions. If he could get to the woman inside, she'd give
him the bone, anything else she had to spare. If he could have
reached the simile, he would have thought she had a heart of gold.

Pat Culkin's face was grinning. If the devil was in the game, he
might make a full flush.

Nan Clooney was a standing menace. As long as she was there,
Mary would never have a chance of picking up a doctor or a school
inspector or a police superintendent, not with Nan shining so bra-
zenly on the sacred mount of the Presbytery. Nan was a contrary
piece. What if she fell for the new man in spite of his atheisms and
his denial of the marital rights of a Catholic? She must be longing
to get out of Lochnamara, particularly after that bad knock she took
from the locum. If she caught the new fellow, skedaddled with him
when he went back to England, the coast would be clear for Mary
as well as Tony.

Pat Culkin got up, the Roymore lorry was coming.

The lorry driver got off.

"A grand day, Mr. Culkin, makes a man feel drouthy. That's the
only fault I have with it."

"Aye, Tom. Come in and have a wet."

"God and His Blessed Mother give it back to you, Mr. Culkin. It's
yourself is famed far and wide for the free hand."

Dr. Tony Culkin's face came round the corner the dog's face had
negotiated a while before, round and shining with two little blue
eyes that surveyed the hotel with a caution that was carefree in
spite of its wariness.

"Be-God!" he said, "Be-God; who'd ever have expected it, dad in
a good humour this morning of all the days."

He stood at the corner to consider the implications of his discovery.

"Damned if it makes sense," he concluded.

He scratched his ear.

"No, damned if it makes sense," he repeated.

He took a bottle out of an inside breast pocket and took a swig.
The fiery raw potheen˙ made him grin violently, but, when he had
mastered the attack, he took another swig.

"Great stuff, be-God. Nothing like it," he chuckled. "Proves there's a God, too. Who else would have tempered this bloody country to the shorn lamb with hell-fire stuff like potheen but an all-seeing Providence?"

He took another swig. The forlorn landscape had brightened, taken on that light that never was on land or sea that only the pure native potheen could give.

He lounged down to the shore. It was raw and harsh like the land behind it, a bleak brown that stretched drearily until it curved away out of sight north and south, dotted with rocks, scrawny with sea-weed and pools left by the tide.

"Be-God," he chuckled, "the new man is welcome to it, welcome and be-damned. A grand no-man's land he'll have, made by God Himself for the cormorants and the curlews and the bloody shrimps that don't know any better."

In front of him the Atlantic stretched to the horizon. It was hard to believe that beyond that empty desolation there could be the life of New York, Philadelphia, all that heaven.

"Cripes," he said, "what a bloody funny world! The Creator ends th' ould world with this, throws in His hand, be-God and then, be-yond, over there, He starts with the biggest thing ever, all over again, and dad was in it and he leaves to come back to this bloody awful hole—begor."

He chuckled.

"And expects me to settle down in it with him and my wife, when I get one, as if there was a bloody woman in the world, worth a damn, that'ud settle down here, any bloody female that was ever hatched under fur or feathers outside of a cormorant's nest or a curlew's."

He threw up his head and began to sing.

> In Lochnamara for to plant
> You'd need to be a cormorant
> A bloody ant, a bloody plant
> A fuzzling, guzzling cormorant
> Halloo—halloo—halloo.

The sea-weed pullers nodded to one another.

"Faix' 'tis fine an' early the young docthor began the booze this blessed morning."

"No wondher in that, no wondher at all in that an' him afther been put out o' the job his dad and old Docthor Joe was keepin' warm for him since he came out of the cradle, God help the cra-thur."

"Divil a much help God'll ivir give Pat Culkin's son, if there's a stim o' pity in His heart."

Tony Culkin surveyed their bent backs with exultant eye.

"At one with nature," he chuckled, "and lucky for them. Just down on the level of seaweed, enough above it to pull it instead of it pulling them."

The contemplation of their home-spun flannels suddenly filled him with a flood of joy.

"And it's down there with them I'd be, if God or the devil hadn't put it into dad's nut to go to Chicago and make his pile. Aye, begor, down there with them I'd be, a bloody weed."

He took the bottle out of his pocket, took a swig, held it up to the light.

"May as well finish it. Heart o' the wild—" he said, [turned] the bottle on [its] head, glanced at it and let it fly.

It landed with a triumphant crash on the rocks, making the sea-weeders' jump.

"Let them stay here that damn well want," he roared

> I'm not a bloody cormorant
> A bloody ant, a bloody plant,
> A feedin' bleedin' cormorant.

He turned his back on the sea and the coarse shore, waved his arms and strode along the road.

> 'Tis anywhere but here for me,
> The noble land, the foamy sea,
> 'Tis God's own gift of liberty
> I'm after, be hoakey!

The lorry outside the pub door caught his eye.

"And what's wrong with Roymore for a good binge?" he mused. "An' what's wrong with Roymore? Never look a gift horse in the mouth. If I just mind the corner of the road till the lorry heels round with thee empties—aye, faith, the biggest empty of the lot'll be waiting for Tommy an', inside an hour, I'll be in the grand town of Roymore with no one to question me, devil a one an' the boys all waitin' with throats as dry as lime-kilns."

He smiled happily. The thought of Roymore, of the faces of the boys, the pub-crawl that could last round the twenty-four hours if you knew the ropes—

"I can drop a note to the dad saying I came to Roymore to consult the new medical books Jack Melia got last week, wonderful new books with the new genito-urinary surgical methods—genito-urinary! —that's a grand one— tooral—looral—urinary—"

He stood, threw out his chest, extended his right arm toward the sea.

"Man should discover for himself the circumstances that lead him back to health," he perorated, 'rest, attention to diet and nutrition, friendly sympathetic faces, the ministrations of gentle hands, flowers—' "

He did a quick-step in the road with an imaginary partner. "Darling—darling," he gurgled, "my own sweetie. Flowers, kisses, the little attentions and the little drinks in between. In the proper timing and encouragement of these processes lies the art of cure."

He cocked his ear. The lorry engine was warming up.

Chapter V

Fr. NED WAS WATCHING NAN ACROSS THE BREAKFAST TABLE WITH TROU-bled eyes. The pain and bewilderment in her face were so unusual with Nan that it frightened him. He had never dreamt that she could suffer like this, least of all for a fly-away like Michael Leland, a nice fellow enough, to be sure, but with nothing to him beyond that easy charm and good-looking face that would be gone in a few years.

If he could only talk to her about it, he might help her as he helped everybody else in the parish, but the way she was holding herself, the ragged stiffness of her face were warning enough that the last thing he could do would be to help her by any sort of talk about Leland.

"The rashers' are worse this week, Nan," he said. "Do you think if you ran in to Roymore and had a talk with Galvin you might be able to ginger him up to send us center cut instead of this stuff?"

She started, looked wildly at him for a moment as if she had been wakened from sleepwalking. He shifted his glance from the trembling upper lip.

"Poor child," he thought. "It's as bad as that with her and for that boyo—God help her. That empty tin can!"

"I think I will, uncle. They've been getting worse every week."

Her eyes went to the window. In a few minutes Michael would be passing, calling in to say goodbye. Last night she thought she had got a grip on the pain, that she could hold it while under her uncle's eyes and the eyes of the neighbourhood, but here it was, tearing her apart at the moment above all others when she must hold it back from the eyes of the world.

A car was coming down the road from the doctor's house.

"Michael is making sure he'll get that Dublin train," Fr. Ned remarked softly.

"Yes, uncle. He mayn't have booked a seat."

Her voice was under control now. If only she could hold it while Michael was with them.

The car stopped. His voice came to her from the hall, easy, jocose. If she had been keeping a little remnant of hope, that soft, careless voice was dispelling it. She could see the smile in the grey eyes as he joked Kate about Peadar Conneely, the old widower, the same smile that would be in his eyes when he talked about her to his Dublin friends, telling them about the country beauty who kept house for Fr. Ned, simple, innocent, and sure that she was the world's choice, completely charming. He'd insist on that, how charming she was, not like the city girls with their pretense at modernity.

She didn't turn around when the door was opened. For a minute she toyed with her plate while her uncle was going to meet him. Then she got up easily, naturally. His voice was making her heart beat, but she could hold it now.

"We'll miss you, Michael," her uncle was saying in that easy, friendly voice of his that pretended he knew nothing, knew there was nothing to know. Michael was handing him back the same pretense. They were pitying her.

Her head went up.

"Michael will be anxious to be off, uncle, to make sure of his seat on the train."

Leland gave her a curious glance.

"I'm not in that [much of] a hurry, Nan," he said.

The bitter little laugh had squirted from her lips before she had been aware of it. It was like him to think he was making up for what he had done by not being in a hurry to go.

"When you're up in Dublin, Fr. Ned, I know you'll spare at least one evening for me. Only be sure to write or phone so I won't miss you."

They were getting to the door, through it to the bright vacancy outside, the sea that stretched away to the sky and as empty as life.

Michael's soft voice was going on and on through the emptiness, thanking her uncle for the delightful time he had given him.

"When I was coming here, Fr. Ned, I confess to you now that I was looking forward to it with horror. If it wasn't that I needed to be able to say that I'd spent some time in a native-speaking Gaelic place I'd never have faced it and now I can't bear the thought of leaving. Hello! there's Ederney—the lucky man."

A man was coming along on a bicycle, his head down.

He didn't want to see the group at the Presbytery. His head, his shoulders were saying it. He wouldn't stop if he could help it, but he was a providential happening to Michael Leland.

He moved across the road and stood in front of the bicycle.

"Ederney, there are friends here I want you to know, the best friends a doctor could have in Lochnamara."

A rigid face was turned toward them. Besides Leland's cool grey eyes, the stranger's looked like circles of pale fire.

Nan watched them across the road. It was a transaction. She was being handed over to the new man, with her uncle silently blessing the transfer.

She switched the rage that had been eating her heart on to the other fellow. It was a relief to have him there to hate, this boor who had insulted Fr. James over Tom Flaherty's deathbed.

Whatever poor James was in the way of a simpleton who thought he had a private share in God, he was pure-souled, honest, and decent, a man who would give his life for his flock—miles above this cocksure prig who knew so surely that there was no God.

Never had she thought so much of James as she did when he came back from Tom Flaherty's the night before, full of praise for the new man, of excuses for the insulting way he had cold-shouldered him before his parishioners.

The ice-blue eyes were on hers. They seemed to be drinking her up, venom and all. The old battered Trilby, the worn sports jacket were appealing to her. A cocksure prig? He was something more than that. Those eyes held something compelling, a fire that seemed to be burning in the man. Suddenly she pitied him. He too was a fool and defenseless.

She turned to Michael Leland. The grey eyes were on her face, wary, watching. No defenselessness there, nothing to pity or protect. She gave him her hand and smiled as he pressed it. When he looked back at the turn of the road, she waved along with Fr. Ned.

Beside him, the new doctor was riding slowly, glad of an excuse to get away from the priest.

❄

Philip Ederney stood at the door of the doctor's "residence" looking down at the raw shore that began across the road.

A sour smell was filling the air, the stench from the heaps of the rotting seaweed and dog fish and rays that had been thrown out by the fishermen.

The shore was empty. The flowing tide had driven the seaweed cutters home and there was nothing to do on the beach. The heaps of rotting weed would keep, rotting and ripening until the spring sowing.

Seaweed is worth its weight in gold and ray could be sold for four shillings a pound on the English market.[5] Waste and starvation [everywhere] and that fat parish priest sits there, watching it all, giving no help, nothing but lies and superstition—his return for the livelihood he wrings out of these unfortunate devils with his hellfire.

He glared at the shore. The old hatred was shaking him, the remembrance of the Monsignor's self-satisfied smirk as he talked to his father while his mother brought out all her little delicacies for His Reverence.

Here it was worse, that fellow sitting on his backside in his comfortable Parochial House, eating, drinking, and smoking the best, a fat vampire on top of this incredibly miserable life that couldn't support itself, let alone the incubus their ignorance and superstition had planted on their shoulders.

The Monsignor's face came before him again, the sleek look, the smirk of self-satisfaction. This fellow hadn't a smirk; he was too cunning for that. Besides it wouldn't be so easy to keep up a smirk in the company of that girl. Queer to find her in such a house, a priest's niece with her mind stuffed with all the rubbish—confession, communion, transubstantiation—all the rest of that medieval trash that the modern world had flung aside.

He shook his head. It was hard to accept that picture of her. That glance of hers.

He shook his head again. What trash was this that was filling his brain—thoughts of purity. What was purity? Mere ignorance, another of the doses supplied by the dopers to keep women fooled. What could she be with her upbringing but another of those doped fools?

He gave his shoulders an angry shake. How could it matter what she thought? She was one of them, embedded in superstition, steeped in mummery, the vestments, the lights, the bell-ringing, the incense—all the tin-pot properties.

He had plenty to think about here between typhus and TB without bothering her. From the records, half the district must be rotten with TB, which meant that in these filthy airless hovels that every young person would have the germs racing through them, pullulating through the whole coming generation. Housing, food—everything was lacking, everything, and he couldn't supply them, couldn't even supply the dope the old doctor had manufactured for them—the beard, the top-hat, the omniscience, the bedside manner, the bottles, and all the other brand of voodoo that was the stock-in-trade of the old-time practitioner. They had been disappointed because he wouldn't give them the bottles, because he didn't play God Almighty. He had noted their glances at his worn clothes.

He groaned. Already on his first day he felt drained, morally and physically. The night in the filthy hovel, the heap of stinking rags on which the dying man was twisting and convulsing, the farce of the holy oils and the sacramental gabble over his body, the false humility of the priest, turning the other cheek to his insults. It had all got him down.

If only there had been somebody to share his struggle, somebody to come to, somebody who would supply her faith, her courage.

Her faith! He made a grimace. So, he was back to her again! All day he had been thinking of her, trying to fool himself with the pretense that she hadn't got [to] him. There was no sense pretending any longer. When he saw her that first day he had got a sense of eternity—he, Philip Ederney, a sense of eternity! With her beside him, he could do everything, perform miracles.

A bunch of barefoot children was coming along the road, their books under their arms. As they passed the house, they stared up at the new doctor.

His eyes softened. These were his hope. He walked softly towards them. They ran for all they were worth. At a safe distance, they turned and faced him giggling foolishly and calling out something he could not understand.

He must get sweets, have bagfuls of them the next day for them when they were coming home from school. If only he could get to them, he was sure he could win them.

The faces from Tom Flaherty's last night came before him, the ducking and bowing and welcoming smiles, the covert glances, the suspicions of the stranger mixed with the looks of hope and trust.

Trust—yes, it was the dawning of trust, a halfhearted sort of trust up to the time when he had cold-shouldered the young priest. From that moment, all had been bewilderment. The unfortunate gulls could not understand his lack of reverence for the sacred rites and the sacredness of the priest. They had been mannerly about it with that pitiful courtesy that was the only beauty in their lives, but they had been scared of him, scared and confused and ashamed like people who had witnessed an obscenity.

"God curse the blasted witch-doctors," he muttered angrily—then remembered there was no God.

He couldn't even blame the poor fellow in the soutane and stock, [although] he had made him feel small through the courtesy with which he had met his rudeness.

The ascetic eyes that denied the value of life had remained gentle. The fellow was glorying in being a Christian martyr. He was more dangerous than the plump satisfied ones, he was so sure of the value of his witchcraft, the holy oils and chrisms and unctions. Philip Ederney smiled grimly. If the reverend gentlemen was counting on his being taken in by his bogus saintliness, the turning of the other cheek stuff, he'd get a rude shock. He'd strip him of his sainthood before the eyes of those he was fooling. Next time he met him with his bag of oils and chrisms, he'd ask him before them all what he proposed to do to give the people the lives men ought to have for themselves and their children—the food, the houses, the decencies that were the right of humanity.

He'd like to hear his answer to that, some trash probably about the saving of immortal souls, the glory of suffering, camels going through the eyes of needles, the hogwash he and his sort had been ladling out to them while they rotted with typhus, TB, enteric.

He sniffed angrily. The children were still keeping at a safe distance. The sour stench from the rotting heads on the shore was deepening as the incoming tide shifted the piles of stinking fish and weed. It was everywhere—that stench of rotting life, decay, damnation.

The very rays they threw away because they had tails like the devils in hell were mocking him, waving their tails in derision in the flow of the incoming tide.

Chapter VI

On SUNDAY, LOCHNAMARA CHAPEL HAD TWO MASSES, AN EARLY ONE AT nine o'clock for Communicants and a later Mass at eleven for the main body of the parishioners. That late Sunday Mass was for the parish of Lochnamara the splendid event of the week, the family gathering of the community, a feast of spiritual nourishment and a gala event providing earthly as well as heavenly joys.

There the mountain men and women and the cabin dwellers of the barren shores and islands could rub shoulders with the splendour of the grandees, the doctor and his family, the priest's relations, the wives and daughters of the local shopkeepers, the schoolmasters and mistresses and even an occasional Local Government Engineer or National School Inspector or commercial traveller taking advantage of his job to get a little shooting or fishing in season.

On the Sunday after the new doctor's arrival, the little chapel was so packed that latecomers had to stand in the churchyard and get as much of the Mass as came to them through the church door.

All the morning crowds had been streaming down the boreens and along the east and west road, mountain women in their best black-hooded cloaks and scarlet petticoats, men in bright blue bawneens and their newest flannel drawers pulled on over their workaday ones, barefooted children in their father's or mother's cutdowns that made them look like rabbits in old sheepskins.

Besides the natives, all the notables of the parish were there, the shopkeepers in black clothes and hard hats, their wives and children in their Sunday glory of flowered hats and variegated skirts, the school masters and their ladies vying with them in their splendour, the shebeen men and women, a lesser breed but standing up bravely to the best on the profits of their illicit stills, and with them a flotsam and jetsam of gentry from the outside world—a Post Office inspector, the district nurse and a commercial who was a bit queer in the head and spent his Sundays in Lochnamara learning Irish when he could be having a rousing time in Roymore like all the other sensible commercials who were working the district.

Behind these notables in the pews, the bare flagged space that took up two-thirds of the chapel was so packed that there was no place to kneel. Never, except for the biggest funeral or wedding, had there been such a gathering in the Lochnamara chapel. The draw was the grand new English doctor with all the degrees and qualifications.

It wasn't only the sight of him the congregation were looking forward to, but the humiliation of Pat Culkin when the new man walked into the brand new doctor's pew Pat had presented to the Church, sure that Tony would occupy it.

That pew was a remarkable one, embodying Pat Culkin's ideas of grandeur, an eye-sore for eyes accustomed to the fine simple old pew that had once been filled with such dignity and piety by old Dr. Joe, his good lady and their grand haw-haw* family.

It wasn't that anybody had anything against Tony, the decent poor soak, but it would have been a sad come-down to see Pat Culkin's son in that holy of holies and there was much secret chuckling and winking when the devil put it into this new fellow's head to come to Lochnamara and keep Pat Culkin's breed where it belonged, in the back rows. Low and whispered the satisfaction had to be, for Pat Culkin had long ears and long claws and it would be a bold man or woman even amongst the clergy who would face a quarrel with him.

The satisfaction was even tastier for being so secret, and the school masters and the publican and shebeen men and their wives in the lesser pews smiled in secret communion with a most unholy joy on this day of days while they watched Pat's jaws as he chewed on his chagrin.

There was many a thing Pat was going to lose, and the devil in hell's cure to him when the new doctor took over, amongst them the calling out of the Rosary for the responses of the congregation before Mass. It was like his impudence to claim the right to call out the Rosary in Tony's place when Tony refused to do it. It had been an honour to answer old Dr. Joe's "Hail Marys," but to have to accept Pat Culkin as a leader of their prayers was a nasty pill for the God-fearing leaders of the Lochnamara Catholic community.

God knew that Pat's qualifications for presenting the parish to Him were far more the weight of drink and goods behind him than any special brand of piety. However, there it was, and it was a great satisfaction to sit waiting for the new doctor to take over the "Hail Marys" and put Pat in his place.

Pat Culkin's voice rose loud and coarse, putting an end to their hopes. The time had come to say the Rosary and the new man hadn't come. The coarse voice rang triumphantly round the chapel: "Hail Mary, full of grace . . ." They had to answer. Why had the new doctor allowed that to happen on his first [Sunday].

The Rosary was nearly over. Miss Nan in her place in the pew on the right was not responding as she always did. Nobody was responding properly today. The triumphant note in Pat Culkin's voice was grating on them, troubling them. He was acting as if it was he who had won the victory instead of being beaten to the dirt as he was.

The women were watching poor Miss Nan. It was hard on her that the new doctor had not taken his place. After the way the locum had used her while he was here, playing around with her and then leaving her like a pair of cast-off shoes. The whole parish knew she'd be watching and waiting for the new fellow to make up for the humiliation before the eyes of the congregation. After Mass, he'd surely be waiting in the chapel yard to pay his respects to the priest's niece. That was the least he could do and there would be a grand view of him then. But, before that they'd have a glimpse as he made his way through the black-hooded women kneeling on the chapel floor, then up the passage between the pews to his solitary splendour, so that the whole congregation, even those pushed to the back of the chapel under the choir gallery would have some sort of view of his arrival.

The second bell went and there was still no sign of him. The tension in the chapel was terrific. In the pews the young people couldn't help screwing their heads around. The women in the hooded cloaks, telling their beads in loud whispers, weren't paying much attention to their prayers. You could see that from the way their hoods wobbled every time there was a movement behind them.

The altar boys filed out of the sacristy in their white surplices, Fr. Ned following in his Mass vestments. A deep breath came up from the body of the chapel. The men standing at the back made a stamping sound as they pushed and jostled to get a place for their knees. The hooded women burst into a louder wave of prayers. The tension was becoming almost unbearable.

Even if the new doctor was from England, it couldn't be that he would be guilty of such disedification as to miss Mass before all the people on his very first Sunday. He must be in now, any minute, but the Mass was moving on and, if once the Book was removed, the doctor would be late.

Fr. Ned was slowing his pace, giving him time to come. Everyone could see that. He had always dwelt lovingly on the Confiteor and the Introit, but the time he was now taking over them was beyond all memory.

The Introit was ending, the Mass-server going up the steps, lifting the Book, moving it to the other side of the altar. Either the new doctor was not coming to Mass or, if he was, he'd be late.

A deep breath rose from the body of the chapel. Something must have happened, some sick call so urgent that the doctor had to risk losing Mass for it. Perhaps he had got the curate's eleven o'clock Mass at Cornboy after a call up the mountain where it was nearest to him. Anyway, it was almost certain he wasn't coming to Fr. Ned's Mass in Lochnamara.

In deep disappointment, the congregation settled down to their devotions.

Chapter VII

Fr. NED CHEWED HIS MOUTHFUL OF BACON AND CABBAGE. NEITHER needed chewing, for the bacon was the best mild-cured Limerick ham done to a "T" and the cabbage was the sweetest and ripest pair of white heads in the Presbytery garden.

Many a time Fr. Ned feared that his enjoyment of bacon and cabbage from Kate's marvellous hands bordered on the sinful, but today it was not their potentialities for sin that worried him. They had lost their flavour.

Against all wisdom, he had been hoping that the new doctor would turn up at Mass, that he would ask him to his four o'clock dinner with Nan and Fr. James as he had always asked Michael. In that kindly gathering, he felt that the doctor's heart must melt, that he could bring him into their happy little group, let things sort themselves out with God's help and this unexpected wise charity with which He had inspired the young priest.

He glanced across at James. He had expected nothing but trouble between him and the new man. James's childish bull-headedness and lack of understanding of any faith less ardent than his own was bound to make the other fellow's obstinate atheism flame up to meet it. He would have two rams on his hands instead of one, but, by the grace of God, James had been full of understanding, loud in his praise of the new man's zeal and skill and not a word about his lack of faith or the boorish way he had treated him at Tom Flaherty's. If Martin Mickle John hadn't told him, he'd never have known that the two men hadn't hit it off like the best of friends. Surely, the hand of God was in that.

He considered James thoughtfully. He wasn't eating, only toying with his bacon and cabbage, almost as bad as Nan who was not making much of a hand of her pretense of eating. There was some subtle change in James, had been for the past three months since Michael Leland came, though of course, that must be a coincidence. Leland and he hadn't a thing in common. James had never warmed to him, though after the first few weeks had been at some pains to hide his dislike.

Behind Fr. James the evening sun was lighting up the full tide that hid the raw bleak shore. Of an autumn evening when the tide was in and the sun sliding down over the sea, Lochnamara took on a glory that made the parish priest feel happy, very satisfied with his lot. Until that Dublin jackeen* had come, Nan had been a part of that joy, a flowing tide of life under a sunny light that never clouded.

In another way, James had been a sunlight of his own, with his ecstasy of zeal, his tirelessness in his quest for God, his loving service of the poor souls and bodies that were in their care. It reminded him of his own first years on the mission, his feeling that God was guiding him; though, even in those glowing years, he had never burned with the ardour that lit up James's face when he talked of the Holy Sacrifice or went out to the dying with the consecrated oil, the viaticum* that would send them prepared for the last journey.

Fr. Ned suppressed a sigh. There was enough misery at the table already without his adding to it with his groans. This new doctor was going to be a handful. Already he had James in a misery. There could be no other explanation of his gloom, which reminded him that he must talk this new trouble over with Nan and James, try to plan a story that would mitigate the horror of the new man's flouting the Holy Sacrifice openly. Something must be arranged, some explanation that would enable him and James to be friendly with Ederney, give him a chance of gradually coming back into the fold without the disedification and dismay that would grip the flock if they saw their spiritual shepherds making friends with so gross and deliberate a sinner.

"The new man wasn't at your mass at Cornboy by any chance, James?"

Fr. James lifted his head.

"What! Oh, the new doctor. No, Fr. Ned, he wasn't."

"They'll think he was until they hear he wasn't."

Fr. James stared at the parish priest with anguished eyes.

"Poor James, what a saint he is," the P.P. thought. "He's in a regular agony about it. . . ."

"Well James, we've had warning. It isn't as if we didn't know it was going to happen. Fr. Carmody believes it was the grace of God that sent him to us out of the atmosphere of atheism that surrounded him in England. I've more or less promised that we'll cooperate. We'll have to be friendly, meet him as often as we can, get him to look on us as friends, lead him on bit by bit."

"Nothing I can do will be left undone, Fr. Ned—nothing."

His voice was trembling with eagerness.

"I feel too that it's God's mercy that sent him here for the good of the people as well as his own good. He's a splendid doctor, I hear, a most single-hearted man, his whole mind and heart in the healing."

Fr. Ned nodded. This was going to be much easier than he could have hoped, so easy, as far as James was concerned, that he could hardly believe there wasn't a snag in it somewhere. James was a saint, but up to now he hadn't been the saint who turned the other cheek, rather the crusader type, like Ederney himself, as that cub Leland had observed, only on God's side of the fence.

"I'm very glad indeed, James, that we see eye to eye about Ederney. The trouble is that the people will be horrified if we make friends with a bad Catholic, treat him as if he was a good one."

"I'm willing to risk that, make an Act of the bad name they'll give us at the start."

Fr. Ned watched him shrewdly. James was letting a cat out of the bag, but what cat?

"He's making a penance of the whole affair for some sin he has committed," he thought, "but what sin could James commit? Some bit of scrupulosity, of course, the sort of thing young nuns worry themselves to death about. I wish there wasn't so much of the young nun in James."

He glanced at Nan. It couldn't have anything to do with her. She wasn't even listening to their conversation, only staring through the window past James's head as if he weren't there.

His eyes came back to James's face. It was strained, wild, full of tension. Nan's was no worse, not even as bad, but each was so bad that neither he nor she was conscious of the other's suffering.

He looked up helplessly at St. Francis blessing them from the opposite wall. There was nothing that he or even St. Francis could do about it. He rang the bell. Kate appeared, cleared the table, glancing reproachfully at Nan's plate and from it to Fr. James's. She was going to complain. Fr. Ned's eye caught hers. She pressed her lips together, shook her head again, and carried out the plates.

Every Sunday since Michael Leland had come, Nan had made the pastry herself. Fr. Ned, dividing it, felt that it was of a different consistency today. James was staring at it, as if he too was reading it.

Fr. Ned passed Nan her plate.

"Of course, James, there's more to be considered in this Ederney business than the bad name you or I might get from seeming to condone it. There's the effect of our condonation on the people. We can't explain to the parish that it's a conversion case, especially if Ederney shows no signs of being converted. If he was a Protestant, of course, the difficulty wouldn't exist. Nobody would expect him to go to Church or Chapel. We could be as friendly with him as we liked—but a bad Catholic—"

Fr. James stared at him blankly.

"A bad Catholic," he mumbled, then woke up.

"But God will change his heart. It's Our Lord's Holy Will for him to come to us."

His voice was shaking with excitement.

"Chosen us," he repeated, eagerly, anxiously.

He stared at the parish priest as if his whole life was hanging on his agreement.

Fr. Ned watched over him covertly. "Was it just one of James's lunatic visions that God had chosen him of all men to save this splendid erring soul? Somehow there seemed to be more in it than that. . . ."

He sighed and turned to Nan.

"You have no plan to suggest, Nan?"

"I? a plan? for what?"

"I mean, any way of being decent to Ederney without giving dis-edification to the parish. We'll never get as good a man if we lose him."

"He won't stay. A good man wouldn't stay. His heart would be broken by it. He'd have to go in the end." [Nan replied].

The words came rushing as if Ederney's case was a microcosm of all life in Lochnamara.

Fr. Ned put a spoonful of apple into his mouth.

It was pitiful, the way people took life, pushing aside the real things, the good things, hankering after the shoddy. Here was to-day's dinner, a joy; for even if Kate's hand in pastry was a bit heavy, the rest was delicious, the ham that melted in the mouth, the cabbage never so good with anything else in the world as with a real bit of Irish bacon done by somebody who knew how to do it as Kate certainly did. Even the pastry, if a bit on the heavy side, was good solid food. The apples in their sweet juice were a treat after the bacon and cabbage. The sun was shining outside; the day was calm and sweet as heart could wish, without any of the stress and strain of town, and surrounding it all that Catholic faith that made prayer an easy ascent of the mind to God, an ascent of the body, almost, so that every act moved toward God's ends. Yet, here was Nan with all her life before her making her day a misery over a shallow fellow she'd have forgotten in a few years' time; and over there, in the doctor's house, there was another to whom God had given so many gifts, but who seemed determined to make the world as difficult for himself and everybody else as the world could be made, when all the time religion could become as natural as breathing if he would only let himself go with God.

Fr. Ned sighed. Divine Providence was inscrutable, bestowing those gifts on Ederney and then slipping into the bag that ignorant pride that made him think he was a better judge of the greatest mysteries than the Church that had drawn on the best brains of humanity for nearly twenty centuries.

Chapter VIII

NAN CLOONEY WALKED ALONG THE COAST ROAD WITH A RESOLUTE FACE. She had let Michael prevent her going to Killeevan when the fever broke out there. She had wanted to throw herself into the work by his side. That, rather than pity for the poor creatures, had made her eager to nurse them. He had forbidden it. She hadn't been trained to do such work or to protect herself against infection. The District Nurse could deal with all the cases. He had been emphatic, and she had let him protect her, guard her. She had felt herself his possession, not her own.

Well, all that was over. Michael had gone, leaving the possession behind, leaving the typhus behind spreading rapidly from house to house with the unfortunate District Nurse worn off her feet trying to cope with it. Michael had gone out of it all, with his cool grey eyes that could caress so sweetly, while they didn't give a damn for the poor. The grey eyes were caressing more fortunate faces now, the fine Dublin patients who paid good money, the Dublin girl with the dough who could throw the bridge-parties and the race-parties, get the places on the grandstands of life that would bring in still more dough.

Killeevan hove in sight round its squat tower. Even in that miserable district, it was a plague-spot, the slum of a rural slum.

Philip Ederney coming out of a pestilent cabin after his night's toil marvelled at the homing hunger that brought migrants who had found homes in happier land back to this filthy hole to die.

He stood on the road drawing deep breaths of fresh mountain air. There was only one thing to be done with the village of Killee-van—burn it to the ground, scatter the ashes over the sea, and forbid any human beings to go near the place for years.

A woman came round the corner of the road. He waved her back. She came on. It was the priest's niece.

He hurried toward her still waving violently.

"Go back! Go back!" he cried. "The place is isolated."[6]

She still came on. He hurried toward her.

"You can't come any nearer. The place is isolated," he cried.

"I don't know of any authority that has the power to isolate it," she said quietly.

"I have. I have given instructions that nobody is to go from here to Lochnamara or any of the other neighbouring villages even for food. I'm arranging to have it sent to them. The whole place is raging with typhus."

Nan looked calmly into his hot, weary eyes.

"That is why I am coming," she said. "The District Nurse can't possibly cope with the work. She will die of the strain, if not of the typhus. With even one assistant, she may pull through."

"But you have no training, no knowledge of any sort, not even of how to protect yourself. Have you taken any measure of protection?"

"Not yet. That also she can teach me. You look all in, Doctor. You had better go home and get some sleep."

She made a move to pass, but he blocked her way.

"You realise that I have the responsibility for the health of the district, Miss Clooney," he said quietly.

"To some extent, Doctor, but I don't agree that either your powers or your responsibilities stretch as far as would make you competent to prevent the priest's niece from nursing her uncle's congregation."

"Has your uncle then sent you to undo the effects of my pernicious ministrations?"

She smiled pityingly.

"Poor man! You thinks our minds are pre-occupied with your childish show-off atheism. It happens we have a great deal more to think of. When my uncle does think of you, his thoughts come more from a fount of Christian charity, of the existence of which you seem to be unaware. He does not know that I have come to nurse these unfortunate people and I assure you that, when I decided that it was my duty to do it, the thought of you or your isms never entered my mind. Now will you be so good as to let me pass?"

His face softened, but he still blocked the way.

"I have to apologize, Miss Clooney. I have been stupid and rude when I should be grateful for the help you want to give us and the courage and kindness you have shown. Will you not forgive me?"

She put out her hand.

"Will you forgive me, Doctor? While I have been sleeping in my comfortable bed, you have been spending your nights tending these poor people. If you don't feel irritated by the smugness of an amateur like me, coming along fresh in the morning, giving myself airs—"

He pressed her hand.

"Miss Clooney, it's absurd. You're the very soul of sincerity. It's shining from your eyes, your voice, every movement of your body. I've never met anyone with less smugness and fewer airs. I'd be delighted to have your help. There's nobody I'd trust more, even though we have met only twice. If you can spare us any of your time, it will be most [appreciated]. What you say about the District Nurse is true. She's worn out. A Miss Culkin has been doing her best to help her—"

"Mary Culkin?"

"Yes, Miss Mary Culkin. Her father, I believe is the owner of the local pub, a gentleman who squeezes the poor mercilessly, but she seems a decent, helpful girl. . . ."

"Mary Culkin has been nursing all this time and she never said a word about it! Dr. Michael Leland allowed her?"

Yes, you see, the District Nurse asked him. She guaranteed to train her, to show her how to protect herself. They were friends and—"

"And Dr. Leland didn't believe I'd fill the job."

"I don't think it was that, Miss Clooney. It was simply that the District Nurse asked for her [because] they were old friends. It's possible also that Dr. Leland couldn't see you in the middle of this filth and horror."

"Yes," she said bitterly. "He thought me too precious to be of any use."

"It was not that, Miss Clooney," he began [and then] stopped awkwardly.

"From what you've said, you, at any rate will be willing to let me help you and the Nurse and Miss Culkin, Doctor."

"Nothing will make me happier if you will let me talk the matter over with you first, tell you what has to be done, and the precautions you have to take—all that. If you wouldn't mind walking back with me—"

He stopped [and] stared at her.

"Perhaps it wouldn't be the thing here," he said.

"Thing or no thing here, Doctor, I'm walking back with you. The sooner I learn all about what [I have to] do, the better, and the sooner you get to bed, the better. If you tell me while we walk back, we'll kill two birds with the one stone."

"And a third one, too," she thought wryly, "perhaps a fourth."

The air was sickening, a smell of disinfectant mixed with hen's droppings, pig dung, the mousy smell of typhus and the stench from the green pool of manure rotting in front of the door.

Nan had difficulty to keep from retching, but the nurse and Mary Culkin had done their best for her. Because she was new to the job, they had given her the best house in the village, one with a room besides the kitchen and loft.

She fought down nausea. Bridget Mullin's temperature was rising above 104. She had to be sponged to get it down if she was going to live.

When she got her cooled to below 103, she would have to give the enema. She carried the basin of water to the heap of foul straw covered with sacking that served as a bed.

"Now Bridget, Acushla,'" she whispered as she lifted up the poor emaciated body.

The patient was a young woman, but her dusky, sunken face [and] skeleton body might be that of an aged crone.

Her fixed eyes stared unseeing. Her hands were plucking at the bedclothes. She muttered incoherently, but she had passed the violent stage and made no resistance as Nan turned her body.

From the other end of the village, shouts were coming. They were waking Martin Folen who had died that morning. At times there would be lull in the merriment while the old women raised their keening wail that had come down thousands of years from the days of the old heathen rites. When the barbaric wail ceased, the roaring of the men began again in wild defiance of their world of misery.[7]

All the money Martin's brother had sent home from England was being spent to give Martin the wake that would bring honour on him and the family. They could live on that money for months if they saved it, but that would be to the dishonour of the dead, while the gallons of drink they had bought with it. . . . would be a boast in their mouths for years.

"God help them dancing over a grave," Nan thought miserably. "What can we do with them or for them?"

Bridget was lying deaf and unnoticing. Her husband, Paddy, was working in England in a coal mine. The bit of money they had got from him last week was put aside . . . for Bridget's funeral. Paddy himself would have expected that, would have thought it wrong to spend it on the food they needed so badly. Bridgie must have her wake.

A fierce desire seized her to save Bridget. She had become not only a patient but a symbol. The thought of that hard-earned money being spent on gallons of poison that would send men roaring around the filthy village, until they dropped on some midden,* was burning her. This new doctor was right. The problem was not to save their souls, but to rescue them from the squalor and hunger and misery that made them seize any opportunity for escaping into this pitiful dream of family dignity and pride.

She went into the kitchen to get the warm water for the enema. A couple of pigs lying on the straw in the corner cocked their heads. Hens roosting in a heap of turf mould began to cackle. An old woman got up from the sacking that lay along the outer wall opposite the dresser and began to pull a skirt over her head.

"Let me blow the greeshach* into a blaze for you, Miss Nan, Alannah,'" she cried.

At the sound of her voice the pigs began to grunt. Her getting up made them think they ought to get their breakfast.

"Down, you divils," she cried to them.

She began to blow on the embers. A dog lying in the outer ashes looked at her and at the pigs. Then, seeing no signal to discipline them, lay down again, put his head on his front paws and watched the women. From the lower village the shouts were getting louder. The old woman stopped her blowing on the embers.

"It's a great wake their givin' Martin Folen, surely," she said "every respect, and he deserved it. Seven gallons, no less, I hear. I hope the boys will be able to resist takin' too much and such lashins round them."

The satisfaction in her voice told Nan that she was thinking of the bit of money Paddy had sent home, the money that would make sure Bridget would have the wake he wanted her to have.

"Himself is at the wake," she said. "I hope he won't have too much inside him with all the lashins and lavins that's goin' on at the corpse-house."*

She crouched by the fire blowing the embers. Then she lowered the crook of the hanger [and] hung a kettle on it.

"It'll be a sore day for Paddy whin he hears that Bridget is gone. If the poor boyo could even come home and lead the wake, it wouldn't be so bad for him, but shure he couldn't afford to lose his job and he knows that she'll have a wake that'll bring honour to him and her, Glory be to God."

She took the kettle off the hook, poured the water into a wooden tub [and] added some cold while Nan kept feeling the temperature with her fingers. When the water was the right temperature, [the old woman] stooped over the tub [and] tried to lift it. Nan moved her gently aside.

"One handle for each of us, Mrs. Mullins, will make it easier," she said.

"Ah, then God bless you, Miss. God bless you and add to you every day for all you're doin' for us."

She caught Nan's hand and covered it with kisses.

Nan looked down at the bowed head, the old lined face streaming with tears.

"My God," she thought, "and there I was with all this around me, calling out to me day and night, and I deaf to it all, crying my eyes out because I couldn't get the love I wanted!"

The dawn was climbing the sky over the hills behind Killeevan when Nan left the Mullins' house. In the village the women were bringing their staggering, shouting men home from the wake. In the cabins, men were singing and howling, [and] women and children crying at them, pigs squealing, [and] hens clucking in angry protest. Drunken groups touched their hats to her and called God's blessings on her and Fr. Ned.

She went down the street towards the sea. A feeling of despair seized her. They were so gentle, so tamed even in their wild drunkenness that it was a misery to watch their pitiful attempts to escape by the only road that was left to them outside of their religion. Drink and Hope of Heaven—[what a] strange, crazy combination. . . .

At the end of the street there was a little pier . . . built more to give work than for use, since the villagers had nothing but curraghs* which they beached bottom upward on the shore above the tide mark. She made her way to the end of this jetty. The sea was surging around it, in heavy slow masses, washing into the little harbour, breaking with a dull roar on the beach, oozing through the heaps of rotting seaweed, rays, [and] dog fish.

As the [swells] surged past . . . Nan watched them with brooding eyes. They had come across the wide wastes of water to end in this filth. Her own life spread before her as it would be, the mornings to her uncle's house, seeing that Kate had the bacon and eggs ready for his breakfast, the empty days, week following week, meaninglessly—if the typhus spared her.

Steps were coming along the jetty. She turned. It was the doctor.

"They told me you had come down here," he said. "This sea air is sweet after a night in those hovels."

"What a full life you have, doctor," she said unexpectedly.

He gave her a sharp glance.

"Here in Lochnamara, life can't help being full, Miss Clooney."

"Yes," she agreed, "very full indeed, doctor, if you have a mission, as you have."

"And you, Miss Clooney. I feel that you too have the missionary zeal. May I walk back with you? There are some cases I'd be very glad to discuss with you."

"And I'll be very happy to talk them over with you, Doctor. Not that I can be of any help except for whatever nursing I can do. There are dozens of questions I want to ask you about the treatment of patients. My ignorance, I find, is abysmal."

Chapter IX

Pat culkin, his thumbs in the armholes of his waistcoat, surveyed the landscape with a benevolent smile. A bloody smart piece she was. He'd certainly hand that out to her. There were damned few girls who could fool him the way she had done, codded* everybody by her tactics. A damn smart clip, she was, all right, all gaiety, songs and music, laughing and play-acting with that Dublin pup, and as for love, soused in it up to the eyes. Divil a wan she hadn't codded, not a man nor woman nor child that ever suspected that it was hunting a good match she was all the time. Soused in love up to the neck. That's what everybody was saying.

Love, my eye! She had just codded them all, codded himself and the countryside. Here she was now turning the heat on the new man in exactly the opposite way—the way that'ud catch the likes of him. No more laughing and singing and musical nights. Oh no, but the stuff that would go down with this gomeral,˙ the loving care of the poor, nursing and visiting and cleaning up the stinking holes she'd never go next or near, if there weren't a boyo to be hooked that'ud take her out of all this misery.

Pat had no doubt now, none at all, about what her game was. She had missed her first spring. The second one she wasn't going to miss, and this time it wouldn't be at being a doctor's wife in Dublin, which wasn't anywhere, after all, compared to the big cities of the world.

No; this time the jump, if she could make it, would carry her somewhere—to London or Liverpool or Manchester or Birmingham—one of the big English cities that'ud be delighted to have the doctor back when she had the foolishness knocked out of him, as she damn well would, when she had him hooked good and proper.

A real smart clip she was and, when the time came to give her a helping hand, Pat Culkin wouldn't grudge it to her. It would be easy enough to do it by then with the doctor making such a cod of himself in the face of the countryside, not going to Mass or to his duties, speaking against the priests and the Church and all the other idiocy he was carrying on with.

Up to now the people were standing it, watching the priests and wondering why they were taking the thing so quiet. Damn good reason Fr. Ned had for keeping quiet and keeping that poor gob of a curate as quiet as himself. All the same, people were getting uneasy.

Never before in the whole memory of Lochnamara was there a man or a woman didn't go to Mass and to their duties, barring an odd "natural eejit" that couldn't be expected to know what he was doing. The idea that the doctor, who was almost one of the clergy, could do such a thing couldn't get into people's minds. Even now, when the fellow was doing it in front of their eyes, they couldn't get themselves to believe it.

A Protestant they could understand, or a black heathen like them they heard of from the returned Yanks, but a Catholic who reneged his faith! The thing was impossible, incredible, and, when it got right down into their minds, they wouldn't stand it.

Well, everything in God's good time, not too soon, either, until Miss Nan had hooked her man. Meanwhile the thing would be cooking nicely. Already the schoolmasters and school mistresses

were beginning to talk, particularly the young school mistresses
who had an eye out for the young doctor and were hoppin' mad
over Nan's gaffin'" him.

Pat Culkin rubbed his hands. With a little help from himself,
when the time was ripe, an odd whisper in the ears of the chaps
drinking in the pub, an odd flick of the tongue, a hint at Fr. Ned's
wish to get Nan off his hands, he could manage to stir the people
up, get them to make things so uncomfortable for the new fellow,
uncomfortable enough to help Nan shift him to Dublin or London
or wherever the blazes she fancied.

Well, good luck to them. Nobody was going to grudge it to them.
Life in a big place like London was a fancy thing if you were grand
enough to get the cream of it. If you were only a chucker-out in a
low joint on the back streets, there wasn't so much cream to be
lapped up, not like in Lochnamara where there was a decent fine
fat living for them that knew the ropes and the ways to pull them.

A tall thin figure rounded the corner, O'Roarty, the schoolmaster, who had tried to take over the saying of the Rosary before Mass
when Dr. Joe left.

A slow smile spread over Pat Culkin's broad face as he watched
him humping it toward him. He was another o' thim, about as big
a gomeral as this world had ever produced and that was saying
some. Still, he had enough sense to learn his lesson since that first
day he had tried to edge in that people should take the lead in turn
in calling out the Hail Marys, not leave it to the wan man. . . . All
the poor galoot wanted was to get a chance of edging Irish into the
saying of the decades.[8] He was a "Gael," one of those poor goodges'
who thought that earth would be turned into Paradise if only the
Irish language was brought back and English driven out of Ireland.

Pat watched the thin bluish face float toward him. A queer face
it was. The face of a ghost.

An Englishman who was staying at Pat's pub once for the fishing
had confessed to him that of all the faces in the world, he hated
that sort of floating "Celtic" face worst.

"Dangerous fools," he growled, "not enough flesh and blood in
them to make them alive to the good things of the world, nor the
dangers of the world. . . . I'd sooner have a thousand of the snouty,
tusky, pushing sort than one of these bloodless ghosts that hasn't
even a life to lose."

He [had been] looking at Pat's jowl as he spoke. It was a compliment, no doubt, even if it was put in the unmannerly English way,
and God he knew, that what he had said about O'Roarty and his
breed was only God's truth. They were no good to man nor bashte,'

no good to anyone but the school inspector who wanted to boast to the Department how grand Irish was doing in his district. They didn't drink and they didn't smoke. They didn't do one damn thing a decent human being would do except breed like rabbits, for the glory of God and the honour of Ireland, and shove Irish down the throats of children that hated the living sound of it. A racket it was, a bloody racket, a part of the political card trick the government boyos were playing up in Dublin, making out that Ireland was the center of civilization and Irish, the heart of the grand Gaelic culture that was goin' to save the world.

"The mission of Gaelic Ireland is to bring back Christianity and civilisation to Europe as the Irish missionaries did twelve hundred years ago—aye, to the whole world."

The first time he heard Liam O'Roarty give out that rubbish, he was sure 'twas codding he was, preparing to go into politics, where, the worse the blather, the more votes you got, but Liam was too big a gomeral for that, far too big a gomeral for any politics.[9] The poor fellow meant it! It made him happy and high in himself without any harm done to anybody, except the unfortunate childher that had to take the knock to get credit for him and the school inspector.

"Gu manny a jay ghuit," he greeted.*

Pat Culkin shook his head.

"You always have me with the grand Irish, Mr. O'Roarty, and to think I could have had lashins* of it from my mother and father, if only I had had sinse."

"You could learn it even now, Mr. Culkin. It would be a grand example indeed to the whole countryside."

Pat shook his head mournfully.

"If I thried wance, I thried a dozen times, Mr. O'Roarty, but it was like catching a sand-eel. Wan moment I thought I had it an' the next, it was through me fingers. No, no, I'm too ould a hand now to take part in the great revival. It's the young wans you'll have to shape in the way they should go and it's finely you're doin' it, be all accounts. Fr. James says that the Inspector has reported that in the next gineration there won't be a word of English heard in the parish. Glory be to God, what a grand change that'll be an' a protection for our people against the atheism and the immorality that's floodin' the world from the English language."

The schoolmaster looked doubting at him.

"I was wondering, Mr. Culkin—you see, there's a matter of grave trouble—I mean, I wonder if I might talk to you. The priests, of course, would be the proper people, but, with Fr. Ned's niece going on the way she is with the new doctor, and Fr. James—I don't know what's come over Fr. James at all—"

He hesitated, afraid he might have gone too far criticising a priest.

Pat Culkin's emphatic nod took away his fears. He went on gratefully—

"Fr. James used to be such a tower of strength for the language and our holy religion, I thought he'd be the first to face this new danger, but I don't know what's got into him—"

"Come in, Mr. O'Roarty. There isn't a man in Lochnamara, nor the road aisht or wesht of it that has the good of the people as much to heart as you have, nor the good of our Holy Faith and our grand ancient mother tongue, not even Fr. James himself, God bless him. It isn't often you honour this house with a visit, but, every time you do, I feel as if a breath of our grand Gaelic culcher is blowin' through it. Come in, and let Mary make a cup of tay for you, seein' as how you don't take anything stronger."

He took the schoolmaster's arm affectionately.

"And how is Mrs. O'Roarty after the hard time she's been through? It isn't aisy being a woman, Mr. O'Roarty—not half as aisy as it is being a man, barrin' in the countries where they do have conscription."

O'Roarty's face darkened.

"That's what I wanted to talk to you about, Mr. Culkin. A woman's way is the hard way, I know; but there's our Holy Faith that says it's her bounden duty before God to bear it, not flinch away from the duties the Sacrament of Matrimony has placed on her."

Pat Culkin nodded emphatically.

That's only the plain word of the docthrine," he said, "nothing but the plain honest word, an' I must say, Mr. O'Roarty, that you and the Missus have been a model to the parish in that respect, a dozen children, no less, never a year without its holy fruit since you came to Lochnamara."

He drew him along a dirty passage filled with porter barrels into the private snug' he kept for favoured customers. On the wall a picture of St. Patrick helping the snakes out of Ireland with his boot added an air of sanctity to the room. One school inspector had hinted that St. Patrick didn't wear boots and that in any case he wouldn't have needed them, his prayers and commands were so potent, but the picture of the rolling wriggling snakes being booted out gave Pat Culkin a thrill of pleasure and he refused to change the picture. Besides, if he did, what could he put up in its place and it was a good Chicago picture guaranteed correct by the artist.

"I couldn't tempt you with a glass of something, could I? We have the finest old Jameson and the best old Port this side of Lisbon."

Pat Culkin dusted one of the worn horsehair chairs. Liam O'Roarty sat down, took off his hat and put it on the table. With the hat off, his head looked longer and narrower, the pale blue eyes, more otherworld[ly].

"No, thank you, Mr. Culkin," he said. "Since I was a child I've been wearing the Sacred Heart badge and never during all that time have I been unfaithful to it through one drop of drink passin' me lips."[10]

"Well then the tay it'll have to be, Mr. O'Roarty."

He opened the door and went out. A wave of smells came on the air—stale plug, stale porter, turf smoke, bacon and cabbage boiling.

From the kitchen his roaring voice came to O'Roarty.

"Mary, like a good gerrel, will you get a cup of rale tay for Mr. O'Roarty. 'Tisn't often he honours us with a visit, so make tay that'll make it impossible for him to even pass our door without coming to give us God's blessing."

Pat Culkin came back and sat down facing O'Roarty.

"Faix and it's right throubled he is," he thought, "or he'd have done the customary protestations against goin' to the throuble o' makin' the tay for him."

"It's good news anyway, Mr. O'Roarty that the Missus is doin' so fine now. There was wan night when I hear it was touch and go with her."

O'Roarty turned his wraith-like face to him.

"That's the trouble, Mr. Culkin. The doctor says if we do it again, she'll never come out of it."

He mopped his forehead.

"It's against the teaching of our Holy Church, against God's law what he says," he cried wildly.

"You don't mean to say, Mr. O'Roarty—"

Pat Culkin paused delicately.

O'Roarty's eyes flashed with a light that transformed the ghost face.

"I do, Mr. Culkin. Mairead's head is turned by the nonsense he's after been pourin' into it. She says her life is more important than my pleasures, that a dozen children ought to be enough for any dacent man even if three of them are dead."

"You went to Fr. James about it?"

"Yes. I went to Fr. James, sure I'd get every help and sympathy from him."

"You don't tell me now that he's failed you. He was always hot on the track of tampering with the holy sacrament. Surely, he wouldn't let this docthor interfere with the duties a woman owes to her husband and God."

O'Roarty's eyes were glittering with fanatical light.

"He's gone over to the enemy," he whispered. "Do you know what he told me? That the doctor was right in a way, that the Church had acknowledged that there were cases where a man ought to consider his wife's health; not birth-control. Oh, no."

O'Roarty gave a hoarse laugh.

"Nothing like birth-control, of course. That was against the law of God, a heinous mortal sin, but there were ways a woman could be saved without sin and without the restriction of a man's natural needs that might drive him to sin with other women. Do you know what they are, Mr. Culkin, those other ways a man could avoid sin?"

Pat Culkin shook his head. This was getting more and more interesting, the spiciest bit he'd heard in a long time.

"And you say the Church itself has discovered other ways," he said. "Blood-in-ouns,˙ that's the sort o' thing ought to be in all the papers."

O'Roarty laughed bitterly.

"Aye, Mr. Culkin, but wait till you hear the ways our Holy Church has discovered. Just wait till you hear them. You feel a man's natural needs, the needs the holy Sacrament of Matrimony was created to fulfill, and what do you do? Do you fulfill them? Not you! You sit down and begin to count the days from you know when and then the days to you know when and you find a day you can do it without harm to her. Then you sit down and wait for that day, just keeping the natural hunger of your flesh under lock and key like a man dying of thirst with the water all around him, but he mustn't drink it, not he—"

He sprang up, upsetting one of four spittoons.

"God! What do they take me for! I'm a man with all a man's needs. It isn't as if I were the sort of fellow who could get away from his human needs [through] drink, or feed them full with lust and fornication and debauchery like some of the others," he shouted.

Pat Culkin turned the spittoon right side up and caught [O'Roarty's] arm.

"Aisy now, Mr. O'Roarty. Shure an' all, it's only advice, foolish advice from a man who knows nothin' about women or a man's needs. It's that Nan Clooney [who] has been putting notions into his head about how wimmen are thrated be min an' how things ought to be made right for thim. An' that gerell' is full iv the most ridiclus notions and Fr. James is only a child, so he is."

O'Roarty dragged his arm from him.

"Decadence, that's what they want!

> Woe to the land to hastening ills a prey
> Where wealth accumulates and men decay[11]

"But that's what they want, us with our dwindlin' population to go down into decay like the decadent countries around us—England, France, with their birth control, slidin' down the slippery slope into hell till they're eaten us by the Bolshies, the yellow men, the Indians, the blacks—all the fellows tat breedin' like rabbits."[12]

Pat Culkin drew him down gently into the armchair.

"Shure, you can do what you like. 'Tisn't as if the docthor's talk was the word of the doctrine. How is he to know what happens between yourself and Mairead? Anyway, he won't be here long. As you've noticed yourself, that Clooney gerrel is hot on his track."

O'Roarty looked bewildered.

"All the parish is talking of it, Mr. Culkin, and a good deal of scandal it's givin'. I must say, the priest's niece to be so thick with a pagan that doesn't go to Mass or his duties and is talkin' day in day out against God and our holy religion and the duties a woman owes to God and her husband and Ireland under the Holy Sacrament of Matrimony. . . . but I'm afraid I don't follow you, Mr. Culkin."

"What's comin' into my mind, Mr. O'Roarty, is that it's the grace o'God, mebbe, that's workin' through her. With a girl like that for his wife, 'tisn't long he'd be able to keep the haythen tricks. She'll soon put sinse into him an' if she can't do that, 'tisn't here she'll lave him to be the mock and the scandal of the parish, a danger to herself and to her uncle. No, Faith! that gintleman'll ayther conform to the ways of our Holy Church, or it's out of this parish he'll go on the top of his head before this year is ended."

O'Roarty looked at him dolefully.

"Till the end of the year is a long time to wait, Mr. Culkin."

Pat clapped him again on the shoulder.

"It won't be till the ind of the year, not the ind of the quarter, even, I'll guarantee, with that clip so hot on the trail. She has him damn well hooked already and when she's caught him, I can tell you, 'tisn't here she'll leave him an' . . . all his degrees and certificates. Divil a, Mr. O'Roarty, it'll be London for her or some [other] grand English city, and if she needs a bit of help to shift him when the time comes," he winked confidentially at the schoolmaster, "I'm thinkin' it isn't yourself or meself or any of the other devoted sons of our Holy Church in Lochnamara that'll be grudgin' her that helpin' hand, God bless and save her, the honest crathur."

Chapter X

IN THE PARLOUR ON THE FIRST FLOOR OVER PAT CULKIN'S SNUG, MARY Culkin and the District Nurse were having the cup of tea they always had together on Nurse's afternoon off. Usually the talk was of the difficult births or the overshort pregnancies; occasionally the details of some dramatic deathbed [scene]. Today, it covered neither births nor deaths, though it hinted darkly at the former if things that were going on were allowed to take their course.

"What Fr. Ned can be thinking of I can't imagine," the Nurse was saying. "You take my word for it, dear, if he doesn't look out, he'll find his good niece carrying more than he or she has bargained for."

"Nan is too good a girl for that," Mary protested mildly. "I'm sure she wouldn't let any man touch her outside the bonds of holy Matrimony."

The Nurse laughed a thin, queer mocking laugh that sounded all the stranger coming from the thick lips hanging over the heavy jutting chin.

She gave Mary a pitying look.

"How good you are, dear," she said and stirred her tea, slowly and methodically.

"Do you know, I don't think the sugar we're getting these last few years is half as sweet as it used to be before that. They say it's the beet that's making the difference. The sugar we used to get was from sugar cane."

She settled herself back against the antimacassar on the red armchair. The small eyes set firmly over the fire were saying plainly that she wasn't going to waste any more time talking about Nan Clooney.

Mary Culkin looked despairingly at her. She shouldn't have said that about Nan's purity. If she had only let well alone she would have got the whole bag of gossip, but praising Nan to Eily Bruton was like waving a red flag in front of a bull.

Her only chance now was to get back to it in a round about way.

"Are you finding the new doctor any better of late, Eily?"

The same thin mocking laugh greeted her question.

"Him!" said the Nurse, "Him! If only you could know, dear, what I've been going through with that man!"

She sat up in the chair and began to talk pompously with what she thought was an English accent.

" 'The brain is, I must tell you, Miss Bruton, a relatively late excrescence of the central nervous system. In dealing with mental cases, one has to watch as closely the more archaic structures, the mid-brain, the spinal cord, the glands of internal secretion, the guts. Medicine has as yet relatively little knowledge as to the causes of the state of mental or even physical well-being. . . .' "

The sharp, thin laugh rang round the room.

"When I told him about Dr. Joe, the confidence he inspired, the love the whole countryside had for him, my dear, he was just hopping with rage, frothing at the mouth about the old fox ambushing the rabbits behind his beard, his bottles, his frock coat, his Latin gibberish, his exorcisms—exorcisms, mind you! 'You're sure he didn't kill a kid on the altar and pour out libations,' he sneered. Well, my dear, that's the sort of gentleman I have to deal with now, God help me!"

She took a chunk of cake, threw herself back in the chair, and began to chew it while she looked up at the picture of St. Teresa over the mantelpiece.

"It's a poor lookout for Nan Clooney if she hooks him," Mary Culkin ventured.

The little reddened eyes came round to her.

"Did you ever see her with him, her head drooping forward so that the golden curls will swing on each side of her face?"

She paused with a mocking smile.

"You didn't, I can see. What an innocent you are, my dear—a poor, pious innocent."

"I wish you wouldn't always be jabbing at me about my innocence, Eily," said Mary irritably. "I'm not as big a fool as all that."

The Nurse selected a jam tart from the plate.

"No offense intended, dear, no offense at all. You know that, I'm sure; but dear, just open your eyes and see what that good lady is trying to pull off with our grand atheist doctor."

Mary looked at the fierce out-thrust of the big bust, the square face that seemed to be oozing venom.

"Or am I only imagining it?" she thought, "because I'm jealous of Nan, hoping Eily is jealous too, God forgive me."

"It's queer the way some people get away with it, queer and strange," the thin sharp voice was saying, "I confess to you, dear, that when I see her at it, my skin wrinkles up with disgust [at] her tricks—and yet these men—what fools men are when a 'little Annie darling' like her starts on them."

The small blue eyes swung round slowly to Mary's face.

Even your good Fr. James—but, there now, I won't hurt your feelings, dear. I know how fond you are of him."

"If you mean that Fr. James cares for her—" Mary began hotly, but the mocking little eyes silenced her.

"If it was her immortal soul he cared for, he wouldn't be letting her go on the way she's going, not even if he had to refuse her absolution to stop her scandalising the parish, but I'm afraid he's too much in dread of losing her good graces to interfere with her goings-on. Yes, dear, that's what I am afraid is happening to your good, holy friend, Fr. James Clogher, and it isn't me alone that's thinking that, but every man and woman with an eye in their heads in this parish. Now if there was anyone friendly enough to warn him, I'd say 'twould be the greatest charity, for the poor man is making a show of himself with his devotion to that piece of goods before the eyes of the parish—"

Mary Culkin's eyes filled with hope.

"If you think I could be any help, Eily—" she began eagerly.

The nurse leaned forward so that her bust stuck out aggressively over her knees, but Mary Culkin didn't see the bust this time. It was a long time, a long, long time since she had had an excuse for going to talk to Fr. James, except in the confession box, and of late he had given her no chance there, cut her short when she tried to spread her confession into a good talk, shut the sliding lid in her face as soon as he had given her absolution and penance. It was starvation of the soul to be cut off from him, worse still to hear the way people were beginning to talk about his craze on Nan Clooney.

If only she could get to him now, strip Nan Clooney of her pretenses, not in envy or malice, but in charity and the Christian spirit that would save both him and her. What a blessing that would be, a great blessing and happiness for everyone, and that was what Nurse was saying, giving expression to her very own thoughts.

"If there's one person in Lochnamara who can save Fr. James from becoming the talk of the parish, it's you, dear. The poor man has to be saved from himself and when are we ever going to have as good an opening to do that as now when that little gold-digger is showing her hand, running shamelessly after one doctor after another and not stopping, mind you, because the new fellow is a black pagan—not she. What does she care what he believes as long as she hooks him? Now is your chance, dear. If you neglect it—ah well."

She nodded at the swan painted on the mirror-screen that hid the fireplace, poured herself another cup of tea, put in a good serving of cream and sugar, selected a tomato sandwich and sat back with her eyes on Mary's face.

"What grand sandwiches you make, dear. Many a sandwich I've tasted in many a place, but never one equal to yours, even at Dr. Joe's, and you know how good Mrs. Doctor Joe was at getting sandwiches neat and sweet. All the same, dear, they weren't a patch on yours and as for your hand in making a cup of tea—"

She waved her sandwich up at St. Teresa.

" 'Tis she herself would have enjoyed a tea in this room, dear. A grand sweet tooth she had too for the good things of this world and there's one thing I'll say for her, she didn't let liars and frauds get away with it—not she. If they crossed *her* path, they got it good and proper.[13] Now, let's have a look at your photograph album, darling."

Chapter XI

Mrs. GLOIN MOVED HER HAND OVER THE IRONING BOARD. LITTLE IRONing she had to do for poor Fr. James who never wore a cotton shirt, let alone a linen one, nothing but coarse woolens. Even at night he wouldn't wear pyjamas, but a nightdress like her father, God rest him, used to do a half a century ago, and all for mortification, a penance for his sinful love of all the bright and lovely things—bright colours, pictures, dainty cups, dainty clothes.

Poor Fr. James. Since she came as a young bride to this land of bog and shore she had been keeping the curates. It had added a bit to the money her husband made as a weaver and it had given her and Tim the company they couldn't have got from the poor ignorant natives around them, but never before had they [known] anybody who mortified himself like Fr. James in penance for his love of lovely things.

A decent kindly lot of boys the others had been, all that long line of curates, some of them now in their graves, some parish priests, or even monsignors, a decent lot of boys, rough and "country" in their ways compared to the priests in the eastern diocese from which she and Tim had come to set up his loom by this dreary shore, but decent and kind and hearty, and, from the first day she was able to toddle, Mary Culkin had been round their feet worshipping and adoring them.

Poor Mary. It was queer that crackedness some girls had on priests. Put a soutane on a man and it seemed to change him for them into something different, something holy and pure, to be worshipped [and] adored. With the exception of one or two so rough that even Mary couldn't make idols of them, she had been at the feet of them all; but never till Fr. James Clogher came, had the poor girl made a proper show of herself.

Pure, he surely was, poor Fr. James, as holy and pure as God ever made them. His craze on Nan Clooney must be a thorn in the flesh for him. Farther than that it would never go—never. Mrs. Gloin was as sure of that as she was of the truths of religion, but breathe a word against Nan and the man bridled up in a way that made you pity him. Now Mary Culkin was going to do it—poor cownshuch.˙ What would happen between Fr. James and Mary when those fool words came out of her mouth Mrs. Gloin didn't care to imagine.

It was no wonder that with such a father as Pat Culkin, poor Mary took refuge in priests, anything that was far from that low cunning brute.

All the same, there were bounds to everything and the way she had been pestering Fr. James of late under a pretense of bringing him all her sins and scrupulosities was getting to be a scandal. Now at last she was going to put her foot in it properly, coming with the sins of Nan Clooney. It was that ruffian of a nurse for certain that had put her up to it. Even Mary would hardly be such a gomeral as to commit such a piece of incredible folly off her own bat, but Nurse Bruton was capable of anything and she'd be killing two birds or three with the one stone. She'd be rubbing salt into poor Fr. James's love wounds, getting Mary Culkin danced on and perhaps even getting one in on Nan. For all the curate's love for her he might be open to suspicions that would gall the soul in him.

He seemed to be making an Act of her goings-on with the new man, lacerating himself with the whips of a mad jealousy that he must feel, for all his urge to crucify himself. Well, she could do nothing about it. The days when she had been in love with the young lad who became her husband rose up before her—mad, glorious days when the world was transformed and transfigured, and life seemed a vision of eternal glory.

Mrs. Gloin shook her head. The glory soon faded out. The miseries of the coming child had brought reality back with a bang. That first childbirth had been very painful. Now the children were all flown, Tim was dead, and her life, ended. Had it been worth it? What else would have been any better? These were the things one could never tell about life. Better perhaps live in the dream [and] never let it come to reality. But then dreams were unsatisfying for a flesh and blood woman and probably faded like everything else. Well, God be good to people who kept their dreams. She hoped Mary would not lose hers through her foolishness today. Curse that Bruton woman! A lot of silk handkerchiefs it would take to put today right for Mary.

She cocked her ears. The door was opening above, somebody stumbling down the stairs. Through the kitchen door she got a glimpse of a face slobbered in tears. Then the front door shut very quietly, Mary Culkin had 'taken the count' as her husband, God rest his soul, used to say in the good old days when John L. Sullivan was the joy and the pride of every true-born Irishman.[14]

Yes, Mary had 'taken the count' she was asking for, poor creature. Fr. James would go on loving Nan in spite of her, making it an act of suffering. Fr. Ned would go on playing his own game, whatever it was, and the people of Lochnamara would go on wondering at the strange things that were happening [to] their pastors and their religion before their eyes.

Fr. Ned Clooney walked up and down the gravel path in front of his house with bowed head. He had finished his Office for the day. Nan had made a grand cup of tea and an omelette for supper. The stars were shining brilliantly over the sea; the lights in the village below him and the scattered cabins that dotted the mountainside all spoke of the toil of the day—peace, repose, and rest.

At this time of the evening in the autumn days, Fr. Ned's soul was usually at peace, but not tonight. . . .

At supper Nan had finally placed the decision on his shoulders.

"I do not love him, Uncle. I have no hope that I can ever love him. There are times when I feel that he is nothing but a sickening lump of self-glorification; that, if I married him, my act will shut me into a prison out of which I'll never escape. . . . But if it's part of your plan for saving the man's soul, well, then, I'll marry him.

My life is wrecked in any case. It's just possible that marriage may turn out a work of salvage for me as well as for him. I can't tell. In my present mood the future is so dark that anything is better than the mere emptiness of life without meaning. Love has become a filthy business that concerns me no longer. What else is there for a woman like me? If I were one who could go from one orgy of love to another, start on the same round after each failure, life would be a much simpler business, but I'm too much of a fool to do that. The goose in me is infinite, so what do you say to my marrying the man, Uncle dear, cutting the Gordian Knot and tying another one?"

The priest sighed. This was just the sort of responsibility he hated. If he could know for certain that it was God's plan to use Nan, everything would be clear, but nothing was clear, for he had no conviction that this infatuation of the doctor for her was God's doing. If Nan loved him, instead of nursing her infatuation for Michael, things would be simple enough, though the man's atheism was a stumbling block. . . . The fact that she didn't give a rap for him made things very difficult. What in Heaven was he to advise?

"I'll have to think all that over, Nan," he said. "I'll go out and think it over. It isn't the sort of thing one can decide straight off."

He paced up and down, then stood on the gravel path staring at the invisible sea, hidden behind its veil of mist. With a moaning sound it lifted its waters and flung them onto the beach. As they raced back, the stones lamented with the long wail that had been his companion for over twenty years, before Nan came with her burdens.

He turned away; resumed pacing. If he had a curate with whom he could talk things over, a man with his feet firmly on the ground, he would not feel so much alone, but poor James was a child, a dreaming child, sure that God had selected him and Nan for a great conversion. As well go for counsel to Shawn Sara, the idiot boy. James would burble over with blather about love that comes to those who share a high and holy mission, the rescue of the poor [and] the diseased.

There was a time when James had wanted to go off and devote himself to the service of the lepers—to Fr. Damien. But he had got him out of that notion, but he was still hanging on to the "No greater love hath man than that he lay down his life for his friends" stuff. Nan's life would be great "stuff" for James's notions. No, there was no comfort of security to be got from James.

The curate who had preceded him had a habit of grunting when he was bothered. He had hated that grunting noise, wished the man in Jericho many a time, but he wished to Heaven he was back with him now, for the fellow was the rock of sense with his two flat feet firmly planted on the ground.

Well, wishing was a hopeless way to solve problems. He'd have to put the thing off till guidance came from God. There was nothing he could do but pray for inspiration and offer up the Holy Sacrifice for guidance. If God had meant Nan to save the man's soul, He could not refuse him the light . . . a priest must have if he was to guide his community the way they should go.

"I'm always running under God's coat," he thought ruefully. . . .

Chapter XII

LOCHNAMARA HAD NEVER SEEN SUCH CROWDS SINCE THE SOUPERS HAD been driven out of the parish in the days of the famine, their Bibles kicked into the sea, their soup vans sent reeling after them, their sermons drowned with tin-cans. That was so many years ago that even the oldest people had no memory of it, but the tradition of that great victory had been handed down.[15]

Since the new doctor had come to Lochnamara the people had been troubled in their minds. Never before had there been any man or woman, let alone a doctor, in Lochnamara who didn't go to Mass or to his duties. In Lochnamara a doctor almost counted as a priest, but Sunday after Sunday this doctor was missing at Mass—not being late, merely, or missing it because of a sick call, but missing it altogether and, worse still, saying things about the holy oil and the Sacraments that no Christian ears should hear.

Now, Glory Be To God, all that was changed. Here at last was the doctor reneging the devil, making his marriage vows with bowed head in the holy sacrament of matrimony with the priest's own niece and the blessing of our Holy Church.

All the morning the people had been pouring in for the wedding feast to which Fr. Ned had invited the country-side. Mountain men were there on their shaggy little ponies, their women in black hoods, riding bareback behind them, their daughters in crates and carts in their communion dresses kept for the biggest occasions. The island men in their blue flannels made a brighter display than even the shebeen men on their side cars in morning coats and

boiled shirts or the teachers in their new Ford cars. Brightest of all
were the girls back from service in London or Liverpool with skirts
that made even the teachers' wives feel dowdy.

As the wedding pair knelt in front of the altar during the Nuptial
Mass, the congregation strained their necks to see the bride's
clothes and listen to the responses. In the body of the chapel the
fifth and sixth class school girls were waiting in a row to offer the
bride posies of mountain flowers.

In the midst of all their rejoicing, Philip Ederney knelt in an
angry maze. The candles on the altar, the sing-song of the Latin,
the faces of the congregation, the vestments, the surplices of the
Mass servers were bringing back to him floods of association. The
maddening thing was that these associations were waking old feelings he thought were long dead.

He glanced at the woman kneeling by his side, her lips moving in
prayer. The same look was on her face that had been on his mother's when [she] had prayed beside [him]. The smell of fresh linen
came, mixed with the smells of sweaty clothes, sweaty shoes [and]
heavy breath. He had been brought back to this by the shape of a
woman's face, the lights in her hair [and] eyes, mere surface things,
colours and forms that would fade, leaving him tied to a wife with
whom he would not have one single thing in common. In the end
she would turn into an old Lochnamara gossip while he [burned]
with scientific hungers.

He turned his face away from her profile. It was no use thinking
of these things, thinking he could turn back now. Even if he could
turn back, would he? He knew he wouldn't, couldn't. His love for
her was an illusion, a trick of nature to lure him into conformity
with nature's purposes, but he could not master it. It possessed
him. Without her he could not live. Whether he could live with her
would have to be left to the future.

Calling it a trick, [or] an illusion, didn't help. Illusion was the law
of life, the taking of appearances for reality, giving up life for them.
The mummery in which he was taking part was a recognition of
this, the exploiting of the illusions of these primitives.

Outside a seagull screamed. The pounding of the waves filled the
chapel, drowning the voice of the priest. The day was calm, but out
to sea there must have been a storm, for the Atlantic was swinging
huge masses of water onto the strand. Pound, pound, pound, it
went, like the pounding of his heart. He seemed to be in a tunnel
in utter darkness. Never before had he felt like an animal caught in
a trap.

She had not set the trap for him. It was he . . . who had trapped himself. The blue scarf round her throat caught his eye. She had come to him only after repeated refusals. Whatever tricks her uncle and others might be playing, she had been completely sincere with him. There had been no traps, no lies, none of the subterfuges women and clerics dealt in. He had snatched at her. When, worn down by his importunity, she had agreed to marry him, she had laid down her conditions clearly. The marriage must take place in a Catholic Church. The children, if there were any, must be brought up as Catholics. He must never try to tamper with her faith or theirs.

In his infatuation he had handed everything over to her—his future [and] the future of his children. She had told him that she still loved Leland [and] could not promise him that she would ever cease to love him. He had accepted that also. He had sold himself for the mess of lentil pottage without even getting the pottage in return—but no, he had not become her property, not that. He had sold his unborn children to her, but not himself. He was his own man still.

The Mass was over. He was walking down by her side through throngs of congregating people. He felt a muzziness in his head, the sort of thing he had seen on the faces of men on the way to drunkenness. She was smiling, laughing—rather, pretending to laugh. She had wanted to precipitate the end of her former life, have done with all that once and for all. He had come in useful, but her feelings were not going to be dealt with so easily as all that.

Fr. Ned sat at the top table between Nan and Philip Ederney. On either side of them the priests of the neighboring parishes were waxing merry over glasses of steaming punch. The legs of mountain mutton and sirloins of beef and piles of chicken and hams were melting away before their hearty onslaught. At the tables that ran down the room on each side, the fun was waxing fast and furious, joke flashing after joke, story chasing story, loud hearty guffaws drowning the roar of the talk.

No feast could be more hearty or satisfactory to the man who had spent all the little money he had [and] run heavily into debt to provide Nan with a send-off that would do honour to a queen, but Fr. Ned was eating slowly, drinking little. He had no illusions about what Ederney was thinking of such carousing.

If he could have avoided all this display [and] let the young couple slip away quietly after their marriage, it would have been a better start to their married life. Ederney would not have been galled. Even Nan would have preferred it, but he could not have done it without disappointing the parish—rich and poor—and none more

bitterly than the poorest, who had been looking forward for weeks
to the great day he would be providing for them. He gave a side
glance in the direction of the bridegroom. There was no understanding that face. He knew that his thoughts were bitter, stupid
thoughts about the shamefulness of this extravagance, the fat
priests gulping down the champagne that had been wrung from the
blood and sweat of the poor.

Out in the yard and the outhouses, the tables were laid for those
poor—planks and boards and barn doors on barrel creaking and
groaning under such things the parish priest knew his people liked
best—smoked flitches of bacon running over with juice, heaps and
heaps of white cabbage and floury potatoes and onions, and barrels
of porter foaming and frothing in the jugs and bowls and tin-cans;
but this alien mind was seeing nothing but the barren soil, the outcrops of rock, the boglands over which they had sweated to provide
these guzzlings.

Worst of all, do what he would, the priest could not banish the
same thoughts from his own mind. [The guests] were in full enjoyment of the things they had been dreaming of all their lives; but
how could that be a justification? Who was paying for it all but
themselves out of the misery of their days? The bitter Gaelic prov-
erb came to him, "An alms out of his own share to the fool." What
was it but a sop to the dog, a dirty escape from the need to supply
these people with decent houses [and] decent lives? He was seeing
himself through the doctor's eyes, a fat spider who had sat there
doing nothing but battening on his people.

Fr. Ned groaned in spirit. On his left, Nan was talking gaily to Fr.
Pat Cloonran, but her voice had a hollow ring. It gave him the feeling that she was trying to lift the tombstone he had placed over her.

He had made a grievous mistake in allowing this marriage, [in
fact], encouraging it. In his blindness he had thought of Nan as
God's special agent sent to Lochnamara to save this erring soul.

He knew better now. During the nuptial Mass the bridegroom's
face had been an open book, page after page of disgust, humiliation,
[and] rage. The anger and frustration in that face had been frightening. How could he or she escape from the horror of that too close
propinquity.

He started. Ederney was leaning towards him, whispering in his
ear. He was sorry he would have to leave the wedding dinner, [but]
there was a most urgent case up at Cornboy. He could not leave the
woman unattended any longer. Would Fr. Ned explain to the bride
[and] to the guests?

Without waiting for an answer, he was getting up, hurrying down between rows of jolly faces crowding the tables. The buzz of talk and laughter stopped. Men and women went silent, staring at the hurrying figure with the crouched shoulders, the head flung forward.

"One can almost see his tail between his legs," the parish priest thought miserably.

When the door closed behind him the silence continued. The eyes were on the top table now, on the face of his bride [and] her uncle who was rising from his seat.

"Ladies and gentlemen, Dr. Ederney has asked me to make his most sincere apologies. He has three extremely urgent cases which he cannot leave unattended. You know what a doctor's life is. I know you will understand."

He sat down. Fr. Pat Cloonran got up from Nan's side.

"The doctor was speaking to me about those cases. They were on his mind," he said. "I think you are to be congratulated, ladies and gentlemen, for having such a conscientious medical man."

"Always he will have that way of escape open to him. He will be able to live in a country where she can't follow him. But what escape will she have from that intolerable propinquity?" her uncle thought miserably. "Yes, I have put a tombstone over my Nan."

The silence was hammering his temples, but Fr. Pat Cathery was coming to the rescue. The feud old Fr. Tim Cinncait had carried on for years with his late Lordship* had often been told, but it was one that never failed to tickle the ears of the hearers. Fr. Pat was beginning to [retell] it now in his hearty, cheerful voice, sending it along with a swing. When the story came to an end with his Lordship's death and the old parish priest afraid to go out in the dark for fear he'd meet an episcopal ghost hunting for him with a crozier, "and a red-hot crozier, too," the roars of laughter that shook the room blew away the last shreds of the gloom the bridegroom's unnatural conduct had brought on the guests.

Outside the whine of the bagpipes showed that they were bothering little about the man's flight. In the house Fr. Pat had set the ball rolling and the tables were agog with stories about the antics of priests and bishops dead and gone many a day. The bagpipes were wailing out "The Waves of Tory," "The Walls of Limerick," [and] every jig and reel that was ever danced at a pattern or a wedding.

From the other room the roar of songs was drowning out even the yowling of the bagpipes. In response to a call for a song, Fr. Tim Loughran was giving "The Fair Hills of Holy Ireland." Tony Culkin followed with "Phil the Fluther's Ball." The punch was going around merrily giving a heart to the songs. From the yard the pipes kept screaming, setting the dogs barking and the geese screeching for miles around. The shadow of the alien spirit had lifted.

"God is good," Fr. Ned thought. "In the long life they have before them He will work His will. No disaster short of death is irreparable. Who knows what may happen today [or] tomorrow [or] what spark may set a fire ablaze?"

It was after midnight before the feast broke up. As the cars and carts rolled home the badgers and foxes stopped in their hunts, wondering what deviltry the men and women were up to with their howling and shouting. The seabirds started to scream and screech in anger at being wakened from their sleep along the rocks. The bogbirds answered with protesting cries. Foxes barked [and] mongrel dogs answered them. . . .

To some of the returning revelers it seemed that all nature that could give voice along the shores and the mountains of Lochnamara was protesting against the union of Nan Clooney [and] this alien creature who had intruded so unreasonably and unseasonably in their community.

※

Fr. Ned and Nan avoided each other's eyes. The cries of the guests were dying away. The ticking of the clock [and] the pounding of the waves against the shore were the only audible sounds. The look on her face reminded him of a spider simulating death when a man comes near. The memory of the days when she lay laughing on the heather [with . . . sunlight falling on her hair] came to him. He put his arm through hers [and] led her out of the house.

"I find it hard your not having a honeymoon like any other bride," he said.

She laughed.

"What a cunning old fox you are, Uncle, diverting my mind to a lack of a honeymoon. Imagine a honeymoon with Dr. Philip! Can you imagine it, my darling old goose or fox? Which are you tonight, Uncle—Daddy—Mammy—fox—or goose?"

"Your husband is too conscientious, I know, Nan, to leave the Black Shore in the hands of a substitute while the typhus is still hanging on. Don't think I don't understand him."

"And who was ever a-saying you didn't understand him, darling Brer Fox? Knowing our Philip, you surely don't think I was even dreaming of a honeymoon with the man."

"I'm not apologising for him, Nan. The man is as honest and open as daylight. The eyes that look out of his face have an innocent frankness. No thought of his will ever be hidden from you. God has sent him to us, Nan. It's all the will of God."

"And stranger even than the ways of men must be the ways of God, Uncle."

"She's in despair," he thought. This whimsical talk is the worst symptom and I'm responsible for it. Why in Heaven didn't I prevent her from sacrificing herself [and] stop that fool James from egging her on?"

"It's a grand destiny, Uncle," she said. "What more beautiful destiny than to be a scapegoat for the sins of men? I wish I could transfer it to Fr. James though. He'd glory in being a scapegoat."

"You won't be a scapegoat, Nan. Don't think such wild things. You were chosen to carry out God's holy purposes. Believe me, it was not an accident that Our Lord inspired Philip Ederney to come to Lochnamara; and you will not be alone. Every day Fr. James and [I] will remember you in the Holy Sacrifice."

"I know—I know. One long vigil in this vale of tears and then the eternal joy only the martyrs understand. Sleep through the worst of it. Sleep is absence. Have no need of the food of human presence. Live horse and get grass in Heaven tomorrow. Yes, but tonight I've got to go to the home of that man—" She took his arm—"tonight."

"Every pure young woman feels like that, Nan, on her marriage night."

"God bless your old grey head, Uncle. What bags and bags of comfort you've stored in it for the poor people you've had to deal with. Did you ever think you'd have to be handing me something out of those bags? Now, did you ever guess it, old goosey-goosey? Of course it will be all right. Every pure young woman and the rest of it."

"She's carrying it off bravely," he uncle thought, "but all the while she's like a hare with her ears pricked. Yes, a hare. My poor Nan."

"You have got the better man, he said softly. "In a month's time you will know how true and good your man is, and he loves you. It isn't riches or respectability he's after, but love and goodness."

She swung around [and] faced him.

"Do you know what I've been realising of late, Uncle? That never during all those years have I planned my road. I've drifted into this marriage as I've drifted into everything else. Fr. James has certainly planned for me; but when I look back, I can see no springs of motive in myself. I wanted Michael, it's true; but I wanted him because I had to want him. There was no sense of direction, just drift, a downward slow descent—"

"Nan, Nan—my child."

She smiled deprecatingly.

"That downward descent is a grand phrase, but there's no need to pity me, Uncle. I'll come through. My power of dramatising my situations is remarkable, most helpful. You can't down a person who dramatises. This blather about the downward descent is part of these dramatics. Why a descent? The man is far too good for me. I've no doubt I'll work the stuff on him easily enough. Those high-brow men are easy to handle, not like the doughboys of the Leland breed. I could never have done anything with Michael. He could make rings around me, but this high-head—yes, he'll be easy to handle."

"Don't be contemptuous of him, Nan. He's a first class fellow. He has taped˙ that I am a coward, a moral coward and he despises me for it. Even if there wasn't a poor man or woman in the parish who wasn't welcome to the feast, what right had I to flaunt our plenty in the face of their misery?"

She put her arms round him and gave him a hug.

"Don't you start the dramatics, Uncle. They're my monopoly. You're as full of guile as a plover hiding in her nest. Full of guile, you are, darling old goosey, but there isn't a bit of use in your trying to get my thoughts away by pretending to turn the heat on yourself. There isn't a trick in your darling old bag that I haven't taped for years and years—"

"Well, well, we won't quarrel over it, Nan."

"Who's talking of quarreling, daddy-mummy? Is this just another one of your tricks?"

"They aren't tricks, Nan. In front of that man I feel conscious of negligence [and] slackness. Our Lord, Who looks into men's hearts [and] reads their deepest motives, will judge, and when he judges, I hope he will find my motives as pure as those of your husband."

"My pure husband! Why the man is having the time of his life. Other boys imagine themselves as G-men, colossal criminals, tremendous explorers . . . and the rest. My big boy is a long way above that. He is the world saviour, the antichristine Christ come to wipe out the abominations of the scarlet woman [and] save this enslaved people from witch-doctors—you—my hoary blood-sucking Uncle—[and] that villainous Fr. James. The man lives in the image of himself as a tremendous fellow. That's his way of helping himself liberally to a bit of the world."

"What a cynic you've become, Nan."

"I, a cynic? Not a bit of it. It's only one augur recognising an-other. It's my road of contact with him. The sublime splendour of the ordinary life is not for either of us. Poets may rant about it, but he and I know better. Ordinary life is as dull and flat as a pancake. What is it up against the splendours of an infinite frustration [and] his glories of a saviour-dom? Nothing, my dear old goose—just a noise from the drain-pipe, dirty smells, old clothes [and] stale cabbage."

Chapter XIII

A MAN APPEARED HURRYING TOWARD THEM.

"It is he coming for you, Nan," Fr. Ned whispered.

He didn't know why he whispered, some apprehension at the back of his mind perhaps. He was glad that Philip Ederney had not let her come alone to his house.

As the doctor came near he called out a greeting.

"Well timed, doctor. I was just bringing the bride home."

Ederney stood awkwardly in front of them looking timidly at Nan.

"I'm awfully sorry I had to leave you in the middle of our wedding, Nan, he said, "but there were two of those typhus cases that couldn't be left for the whole night."

"No need to excuse yourself; we've all been making explanations for you," she said.

Ederney turned toward the priest.

"It wasn't disrespect for you—Fr. Ned," he said awkwardly.

"The first time he ever called me 'Father.' " the priest thought. "What a sacrifice for the poor man."

"I know that, doctor," he said. "With you your duty comes first. I can't tell you how much I respect you for that. However, this is your wedding night, not a night for talking about my feelings towards you. You'll be wanting, I know, to take Nan home."

She clung to his arm.

"Won't you come along and have a cup of tea with us, Uncle? You'd like him to come, Philip."

"So, her brave words were hiding fright," the priest thought. "Poor Nan."

Ederney looked at the ground.

"Indeed I would," he said dully.

The priest drew his arm away.

"I couldn't take tea," he said softly, "not after all that eating and drinking; and a wedding night is a wedding night."

He put her hand into Ederney's.

"In the whole wide world I don't think there are two better people than you two, God bless you," he said softly.

He turned back and trudged along the road home. His body was a heavy as lead. That would pass. It was merely a reaction to the drink he had to take to keep in tune with his guests. If only that dread would not keep coming up in his mind.

"That will pass too," he thought. "After all, she will be beside me, with me, almost as much as ever. If only I could be sure of God's purposes."

He sighed heavily [and] stood looking out to sea. In the distance the lights of a ship glimmered faintly. He glanced back along the road. Nan and her husband had disappeared. In the bedroom window of the doctor's house a lamp was lit.

He turned away hastily and hurried home. As he opened the door, the grandfather clock in the hall struck twelve. From the rooms the voices of waiters and the clatter of crockery seemed to be mocking his dreams. They were gathering up their dishes and service-ware, hurrying to be ready with their crates for the morning bus [and] shake the dust of this hateful hole from their feet.

"I won't sleep if I go to bed," he thought. "What's the use of lying there tossing?"

The diningroom had been cleared, the tables removed. He wandered from there into the sitting-room. It had also been cleared and tidied up by those indefatigable hurrying men. They had even stoked up the dying fire for him; yet, the house seemed to be pushing him out.

"I could walk off this weary despair," he muttered and went out, but he could not get himself to leave the house. There might be a sickcall," he thought.

He went back into the house. If he could get absorbed in a book it would pass the time until his eyes grew heavy. He went to the book shelves. [His old friends] were all there—Dante, Shakespeare, *Don Quixote*, the lives of St. Augustine [and] St. Teresa. He took Dante off the shelf [and] turned the pages of the *Inferno*. It was no use. Augustine, Teresa, Don Quixote all seemed to turn their faces from him.

He found his Office. It was already another day. He could read the Office of the new day [and] begin [it] by submitting his will to the will of God.

The Latin words danced before his eyes so that he had to read some of the sentences twice, but he kept on reading. The deep sonorous rhythm was calming the soul.

Chapter XIV

THE DOCTOR'S RESIDENCE WAS AN IMPOSING BUILDING FOR LOCHNA-mara. Like the priest's house, it was two stories and was roofed with limestone slabs instead of the thatch that covered all the other houses in the parish. In a room on the second story, Nan lay on the bed she should [have been] sharing with her husband. In his shyness he had not dared to invade her privacy and she had accepted his sacrifice shamelessly. Some night she would invite him to share the room that was his by right, but not tonight, not on the bed Michael had slept in. She would change the bed, get a new one from Roymore that would not be tormented by memories.

Michael was a liar, a poor mean creature, who had run away from the typhus, the misery, the filth—all the evils Philip was facing with high courage.

She kept on repeating to herself that Michael was a liar [and] a thief. On the divan in the room opposite, a man was lying whose worth was a hundred times as great, a man who loved her deeply.

She tossed around [and] lay on her back staring up at the ceiling.

She got out of bed and began to pace the room. She should go now, at once, to the room in which her husband was lying.

She went to the door, caught the handle, and stopped.

"After all, does the man deserve any better, slinking out from our wedding with his tail between his legs as if he was ashamed of me?" she thought.

She went back to her room [and] bathed her eyes. In the corner there was a wireless her uncle had given her as one of her wedding presents. She went over to it [and] twiddled the knobs. The outside world was waiting there for her. . . . She went back to bed.

"Did any girl ever have such a wedding night?" she [wondered].

She was wakened by the sun shining on her eyes. For a few moments she lay gathering her wits. Then she remembered. She sat up, squatting with her chin on her knees.

"I'm a wife," she thought, "married and done for. Yes, that's the right phrase. Done for. My cloud-cuckoo land of dreams is finished. Was I a sleep-walker when I walked into this?"

She listened. There was no sound from the room opposite, but it was early yet, only eight o'clock by the little black-faced clock on the mantelpiece.

She began to dress slowly, stopping to listen for his movements, but there was no sound. Silence lay heavily on the house.

She went to the window [and] looked out at the sea. The sunlight that had wakened her [was clouding] over. She could see it still out to sea, but a grey mist was coming over it. There were no colours, no lights on the stones or the water.

She finished dressing [and stepped] out on the landing. The door of her husband's room was ajar. She tapped. There was no answer. The room was empty, the divan tidied up.

For a moment a wild thought came to her that he had gone, left her and Lochnamara and all the misery.

The front door opened cautiously. He was closing it carefully so as not to waken her.

"I'm up, Philip," she called to him. "I'll have the breakfast ready in a few minutes. You take rashers and eggs, don't you?"

He came to the foot of the stairs.

"I'll put the kettle on, Nan," he said and went to the kitchen. "I don't usually take breakfast, but this is a special morning. You needn't put down any rashers for me, though."

She ran down the stairs.

"You rest yourself, Philip," she said, "I'll have the breakfast ready in a jiff."

He was running the tap, lighting the gas, [and] smiling defensively at her. She went to the cupboard for the bacon [and] busied herself with the pan.

"He still feels himself guilty, an intruder," she thought. "He guesses I spent my night weeping for lost ecstasies."

"You go back to the sitting-room, Philip," she said. "I'll do the rest. Do you like toast with your coffee?"

"No toast—just plain bread, Nan. You see, I never take anything on ordinary days."

His face was happier now, almost gay. The open collar with the sun-tanned neck under the shabby coat seemed to bring him nearer.

"Poor fellow," she thought. "How badly he needs a human life beside him."

"You wouldn't mind if I stay in the kitchen and help you, Nan?"

"I'd love it. Is there anything you feel like doing?"

"I could make the coffee. I've the name for making good coffee."

"Then go ahead while I'm frying the bacon."

"There could be worse beginnings," she thought, "a little boy and girl playing house isn't a bad start. If we can keep this up we might emerge on some sort of decent adult life later on."

At breakfast she smiled at him.

"Funny that I don't know a scrap about your life, Philip—what your father and mother are like—"

His face darkened.

"And you know as little about my childhood," she went on. "Shall I begin first and loosen a shower of memories on you?"

"I've often wondered what your childhood was like," he said, happy again.

She began to tell him of her days in the French convent while her father and mother were in India, of her delight at the prospect of going out to them, the blackness that fell when the cable came to say they had been killed in a railway accident.

"They were only faint memories to me," she said. "Perhaps if I had met them I should have been disappointed. Fr. Ned took their place. Since their death he has been father and mother to me."

Again the darkness on his face.

Her heart fell.

"What an ass this man is," she thought. "It looks now as if there will be times when I will want to murder him. What hope in Heaven is there of my being able to force an entry into the thing's wax-works mind? Who is it that talks of the blind implacable race of simple souls? Whoever it was, must have suffered from somebody of the breed of this fool."

She went silent watching the man's face. "The curious thing is that behind the lunacy there's a hunted look. That will get me in the end. I will end up doing, thinking [and] saying what he wants out of sheer pity."

After breakfast, Nellie, the old woman who did for the doctor, came in [and] greeted Nan vociferously.

"It's late, I am today on account of the wedding. I couldn't get a wink of sleep at firsht, I was so merry with the dhrink, but indeed we had raison an' yourself comin' like sunlight to the docthor's house, Miss Nan, God bless you and give you increase."

Nan put her arm through her husband's.

"I'd love a breath of fresh air, Philip, if you aren't tired after your night."

What was the use of thinking about guarding herself against

him? Her life had been settled. Nothing now would change the total. Eternity would come in the end [and] dissolve the settlement. Until then she would have to make the most of it.

The pressure of his arm on hers was stopping her breathing.

"Night until the end of the world," she thought. "How was it Milton put it—'Dark, dark, dark, in the full blaze of noon! Irrecoverably dark, without all hope of day.'[16] Yet, can I be so bad when I can dramatise it in this way? From now on everything I do will have an absolute value. What a great piece of dramatics that is—absolute values, a soul to be plucked from the burning. Splendid. What better way of escape is there for me except through ridicule?"

They strolled along the sea-road. The mist had gone and a soft sunlight was making the Black Shore and the boglands things of beauty. He began to talk about his patients. His eyes lit as he described the symptoms [and] the remedies he was thinking out. The children were his worst trouble. Infantile cholera, gastric enteritis, TB—all the evils arising from malnutrition were playing havoc with them.

"He doesn't see the beauty that has come on the boglands," she thought. "He sees nothing, will never see anything beautiful; but his intentions are splendid, so there's no use in despairing. Besides I'll probably be able to handle him. I know what to say to men like him, men with ideals. Michael I could never have handled; but this man will be as easy as making pats of butter, if I keep my head. He'll never have the slightest idea of what's brewing in my mind, not like that thief who read me like an open book."

She took out her cigarette case, lit a cigarette [and] inhaled. He hated to see her inhaling. Smoking was bad, inhaling the worst of all. He had a way of repeating things that were maddening. But that was one of the things she wouldn't stop for him. There were probably plenty of others. All the time there would be these little wearing frictions.

A vision of the years in front of her came to her. As the days shortened, the rain would come—sheets of it. One day would melt into the other with the fretting sound of the sea behind them. He'd go on objecting and she, inhaling. When the whiteness he prophesied from her smoking came along, it would make her more fatal.

A picture of herself with white anemic lips and a deathly mask rose up before her. She made a grimace.

"Still playing a part," she thought, "always the grand little part. Why should it be anemia? I'll probably fall into flesh [and] become a stout comfortable woman, hunting for gossip. Small-boned women like me often get fat and heavy. I'm not doing my job now

[by] going on with all this playacting. I must listen to what the man is saying [and] get the habit of listening. My God, what a bore it will be, not the grand uplifting tragedy I've been pretending, but just a crashing, rotten bore."

"What an interesting case, Philip," she said. "Do you think the woman will recover?"

Chapter XV

THE DOCTOR'S RESIDENCE WITH ITS WHITE-WASHED WALLS STOOD OUT clean and sanitary against the huddle of the cabins below it and the brown boglands and the swarthy shore, but the inside of the house did not bear out the promise of white cleanliness.

Philip Ederney had been so insistent on the cleaning up of the cabins that Nan expected the house to be like a hospital or convent in its spotlessness. Bleak and unhomely it was as any convent or hospital, but when she went over the house, she found that, while Philip Ederney had been busying himself with the unsanitary conditions in which poor people were living, he had forgotten to look into the condition of his own home and that Nellie had taken advantage of his absent-mindedness to let things slide.

Besides, old Dr. Joe and his good spouse had troubled themselves little about the condition of a house they were leaving. The wallpaper was hanging off in places. The stair carpet was torn as well as filthy. Every corner was full of junk.

Nan got rid of old Nellie [and] set about training a young girl Mary Culkin had got for her. With the girl's help, she managed at last to get the house in decent condition.

With her husband, things were less easy.

"Round after round, he gets me down," she thought, "but round after round I'll get my breath back in my corner. I'll hold on. There will be scores of rounds to go, but I'll hold on. The job my uncle has given me I'll never be able to do, but there's no reason I shouldn't be able to do my own job as a wife. The man is dead lonely, his life a bleak white shell like the house. If he was the sort who took bacon and eggs for breakfast, went on a bend with other men, smoked, played golf, he mightn't be half so easy to handle. All this no drink, no smoke, no breakfast is part of the gull that isolates him from common life [and] makes him need me so badly. The one danger is that he may be too far away even for me to get at him."

But it wasn't easy to keep up this optimistic mood. His library was particularly depressing. She turned over the pages of the books and journals he had piled everywhere. There wasn't a single novel or book of poems or even of travel or biography amongst them, nothing but scientific work that assumed a world of empty purpose.

"This is the stuff in which he is drowning," she thought, "and I'll drown with him if I don't manage to replace this trash with the drama of life. But how can I get the drama of life to the man? How can one get blood into such a determined ghost? He glories in being a ghost. Well, I'll have to try in any case. The first thing to do is to get his surroundings warm and bright."

She changed the curtains for ones of warmer colour, put new covers on the chairs [and] sofa.

"Better not try to anticipate things, to deal with them as they arise. It isn't only the emptiness of his life I will be filling," she thought, "but the emptiness of my own, of this bleak house in which I am forced to live."

She lit a cigarette. The house was standing out against her. Before she came he had put his impress on it, but bit by bit it would change, cease to be a space enclosed by four whitewashed walls. Even now there were times when she could feel a new pulse beginning in it. When Philip came, the throb of life seemed to die away, but that was only imagination—could only be imagination. The man loved her [and] wanted to come to her. He would be bound to love the house she was creating. There were times when she asked him to come for a stroll in the evenings in the dusk, when she played and sang for him, or prepared a special dish for his dinner, a Creme de Volaille, Oeufs à la Nicoise, any of the scores of dainty dishes she had learned in the Domestic Economy Section of her Convent School in Paris. His delight was pitiful. It was also saddening, for it was as clear as the hard white light that seemed to come into the house with him that the sweetness of her singing voice, the pieces of Brahms or Bach or Handel meant nothing to him. She wondered if he even got the flavours of the dishes she went to so much trouble to prepare.

What delighted him was the joy of having her do these things for him, the sight of her hands moving over the piano, of her eyes when she looked up at him.

How long would these transports last? How could a woman hope to keep the love of a man whose contempt for her thoughts and beliefs were as deep as his must be for everything she cherished? Did thoughts and beliefs really matter in human lives? Beliefs, perhaps. Yes, beliefs might matter a great deal.

She looked round the sitting room. It was here she would have to shape him, draw him to her in the coming winter when one day would melt into another and the solidly falling rain would draw them together as they sat warm and close by the peat fire, listening to the howling of the Atlantic winds.

She had done the walls in warm cream. In the lamplight they were restful and comforting. Already they were drawing him to her. In the evenings after supper he would love to sit here beside her talking about his cases. She encouraged him to tell her the details [and] questioned him about Pat Flaherty's duodenal ulcer, Breed Kelly's colitis, little Shawn Sara's hydrocephalus, but as the days shortened it was harder and harder to keep the effort up. When she was deadly tired and wanted to lead the talk round to the things she cared for—music, ballet, books, travel—he listened politely [and] tried to show some interest, but when she finished, he was back again after a decent interval to his talk about his patients.

It spoiled the symphony she had composed [and] drove her back to older dreams. Faces from the past came to her—cinema stars she had adored as a girl—and Michael's face, the cinema star of life.

As the night winds wailed around the house and the shadows flickered on the walls, she found it more and more difficult to pretend to share his interests. It was not for talk of colitis and hydrocephalus that she had put the creamy distemper on the walls [and] gathered the colours and shapes of pictures and furniture that would give ease and rest; but she could not get him to let her have any other.

As the winter days drew in, the old dreams gathered strength. She began to realise that it was for those dreams she had created the room. She laughed miserably. Had she really hopes to mould Philip to the image of that other who laughed and sang from morning to night, lilting the latest dance tunes, the gay Parisian songs, filling the Black Shore with a sunlight that outshone the sun—or, had she been fooling herself all along? Were the Italian prints, the bright curtains, the scarlet cushions [and] the Persian rugs on the floor not for Philip, but for that other?

"What a rotten type I am," she thought. "There is that man fighting a desperate battle against every form of disease in filthy hovels. Any decent woman would be by his side, cheering him, keeping his heart up [and] welcoming his talk of his difficult cases.

After all, he must talk to someone about them or burst, and here I am whining for pity because he can't see the scarlet cushions, the Italian prints [and] the Persian rugs, [or] sing the latest American songs. Oh, damn me, damn me, damn me, even now at the eleventh hour let me go and stand by him instead of dreaming about that lounge lizard."

But, when she suggested that she might help, he demurred. Now that the typhus was stamped out, the Nurse could deal easily with all the cases. She would certainly resent the intrusion of the doctor's wife. Already he had had to speak to her about her antiquated methods. She was sore and resentful and would jump at any excuse for trouble.

"I'd better ask her to tea, then. That'll help to smooth things over for you," she suggested, but again he demurred.

"I wouldn't, if I were you, Nan. She's a venomous [and] spiteful woman. You can't make a friend of her. Her dislike of me has become a regular fixation and she has joined you with me in that hatred."

"All the same, I'll ask her. She probably thinks we're looking down on her. A chat over tea can be a great healer, Philip."

"As you will, Nan, but she's dangerous, a viperous mind and a viper's tongue. If you do ask her, be careful what you say. It will be twisted and turned, if I know anything of that good lady."

Fr. Ned, however, was delighted with her intention to ask the Nurse.

"Your husband is right about her character, Nan. The woman is sore over Philip's loving you. She had hopes of him, you know. Her hopes have been getting more desolating for her. The poor woman is getting on and she never was a beauty, God knows, but what harm can an ask do? Your husband will have enough to face without the venom of her tongue added to it."

They were sitting at the fire in his sitting room, he on the corner armchair, she, on the sofa where she had so often sat with Michael.

She put her head back on the cushion Fr. Ned had insisted on placing behind her and shut her eyes. He never talked now of his mission to save the doctor. Her failure to get Philip Ederney to come to Mass with her must be troubling him, but she knew what his hopes were—that, when she became the mother of Philip Ederney's children, with even the first child, certainly with the others, her husband would be lured bit by bit back to God.

"But there are no children coming," she thought, "no house full of young voices in the future. Is it that my mind is refusing them? If I could bury my memories, would they come? If some day God would grant me the strength to forget Michael, would the children of this strange loving man come to us?"

She got up [and] looked down at the priest.

"There are no children coming," she said, "and the man knows it is my refusal. He sees my dreams of Michael depriving him of his children. He is suffering agonies of jealousy. All the symptoms I used to watch with callous amusement in the old days in others are in his face when he thinks I am not looking—the brooding eyes, the screwed up mouth—everything. God help him. The curious thing is that it seems to make him much bigger than when he's preaching about his mission. There are times when he looks like a lion caught in a trap and I feel a shameful joy in the greatness of the capture. Deep privacies seem to open up too from that heady draught; but you'll think me only a shameless hussy, Uncle, a hussy and a gabbler—"

"My dear Nan—" he began, but she cut him short.

"I hear you've got a new oil stove for the kitchen. Let's have a look at it. I'm thinking of getting a new one [to replace] that old thing Dr. Joe and his missus left us—"

Fr. Ned got up [and] took her arm.

"Those deep privacies you spoke of are the thing he needs. He's been lonely all his life without them; lonely to death, and no wonder, with no hope even of God's grace to light his way. You'll give him the depths as well as the company of life. Of all miseries, that rack of loneliness is the worst. Don't I know it, Nan?"

In the kitchen Kate was scrubbing the floor. She ran to Nan [and] squeezed both her hands.

"It's like sunlight to see you, Miss Nan, God bless you, and, like the sunlight, the oftener you come the more you'll be welcome. 'Twas a sad day for Fr. Ned the day the docthor tuk you from us."

Chapter XVI

It will help to bring homeliness to the house having people coming to tea," Nan thought. "It's a good thing these women are coming. Why should I feel this ridiculous fright? Even if the Nurse is coming to pry out my secrets—our secrets—what is there she can pry into that that little maid hasn't given to the countryside ages ago?"

She wandered restlessly from room to room, trying to see things as the Nurse and Mary Culkin would see them.

"Deadness," she thought. "Will they get the deadness, as I get it, the square flatness I can't get out of the house; or, is it my imagination?"

She came back to the sitting room. The tray with the cake and sweet biscuits gave the room a sort of warmth. From the kitchenette the smell of the little scones she was keeping hot on the stove was coming in comforting waves.

"Ridiculous that I should be afraid of them," she thought. "This foolishness of Philip's is getting me down."

She stiffened. The rat-tat on the door knocker was the danger signal. They were here.

The District Nurse came in first. Her black coat and heavy black hat held Nan's eye for a minute. Then her hand was being squeezed in a firm grip that said—

"Don't think you can get away from me, my good woman. In this parish of Lochnamara there's no place where you can hide from me."

The stony eyes were repeating it. Behind them the timid embarrassed face of Mary Culkin was apologising, soothing.

"Won't you take your coat off, Nurse? It was awfully good of you to come this afternoon when you're so busy."

"I'm not as busy as all that, not now, Mrs. Ederney."

Somewhere in the words there was mockery, in the thin voice, perhaps, that came out of the heavy square face.

"I'm going a bit potty," Nan thought. "I must be to be imagining all this rubbish."

The Nurse had settled herself solidly on the sofa as if she intended to remain there always. She stared around the room.

"My word, what a change you've made in this room, Mrs. Ederney, compared to Dr. Joe's time—so grand and modern you've got it. Lucky Mrs. Joe can't see it as it is now. She'd get a fit."

"Every generation has its own taste, don't you think, Nurse?"

This was going to be more difficult than she thought. If only Mary would come into the talk [and] help her a bit.

"Aye, Mrs. Ederney, I suppose so."

The thin sharpness of the voice, so strange [coming] from the heavy build, was unsettling. Everything about her was unsettling.

The little maid came in with the teapot [and] lit the oil lamp under the kettle. As Nan made the tea, she thought, "I shouldn't have asked her. Why on earth couldn't I have accepted her hostility [and] let her do her worst instead of bringing her in here to spy and sneer? I was sure Mary Culkin would help to bridge the gap, but there she is, sitting there like a dumb goat."

Mary, as if she felt the complaint, began to talk—

"What pretty teacups you have, Nan. I never saw these ones before."

"They were a present, Mary."

The Nurse, her knees firmly apart, accepted one of them from Nan.

"Whoever gave them had an eye for a bit of colour," she said slowly. "I'd bet now it was Fr. James. Never have I met a man as mad on colours as he is, and such colours—almost garish, you might say."

Mary Culkin's face flushed scarlet. She gave Nan one quick jealous glance. He had never given her a present, hardly even thanked her for the silk scarves and handkerchiefs [and] fur-lined gloves she showered on him.

Nan passed the cake to Mary.

"There's honey here too, Mary, if you'd care for it."

"A pity to spoil cake with honey, don't you think, Mrs. Ederney?"

"O God," Nan thought, "why did I ask this devil? If she'd even concentrate on me [and] let that poor girl alone."

"There's cake honey adds a good deal, too, Nurse," she said, "the lighter, fluffier stuff like this."

The Nurse laughed, a thin, uncalled-for laugh.

"There isn't a thing you aren't wise to, Mrs. Ederney, not a thing. Fancy even having thought out the sort of cake honey goes with. A grand home you'll be making for the doctor, a real home, especially when the children are beginning to come. That's what my poor mother, God rest her soul, used to say. 'The home begins when the children start coming.' "

Mary Culkin began to talk hurriedly.

"You haven't lost the knack of making scones, Nan. These little scones of yours are as nice as you've ever made."

A Jack Yeats picture on the wall caught her eye.[17] She jumped up, spilling her tea over the saucer.

"O dear, what an awkward creature I am, Nan, but that picture. . . . I've never seen one like it. What a lovely bit of colour, Nan. It makes the room shine."

"I'll bet 'twas Fr. James gave you that too. There isn't another eye in Lochnamara that would pick out such a scream of blues and reds as that—is there now, Mr. Ederney?"

Mary Culkin's body sagged as if the knife-like voice had gone through it.

"Would you like to see some of my new clothes, Mary?"

The words had hardly left Nan's lips when she realised her mistake. There was nothing that hateful woman wanted to see more than the intimate things of Nan's private life, the evidence of her own eyes for whatever venom she wanted to brew and spew; but it was too late now to save the situation.

"The one thing above all things we were looking forward to seeing, Mrs. Ederney."

The woman was up already, her squat body leading the way to the door, Mary's face behind her, drawn and strained.

The Nurse looked around the bedroom, at the silk stockings where Nan had thrown them in her hurried dressing, at the yellow silk knickers she had flung on the chair, the lipstick, the nail polish, the bottles on the dressing table.

She went over to the bed [and] fingered the lace on the green pyjama jacket, then swung slowly round and examined the rest of the room with a meditative look—the bright red sandals, the slippers with the golden rosettes.

"What does it matter what she thinks?" Nan thought despairingly, but already [Nurse Bruton] was staring with hostile eyes at the red sandals, the rosettes, the lipstick. Even the envelopes on her writing desk looked silly and the lilac note paper.

The District Nurse began to giggle. The other two looked at her.

"You'll excuse me, Mrs. Ederney, but the funniest thought struck me—the queerest and the funniest. Fr. James couldn't have given you a present of all this stuff, surely, but do you know, you'd almost think he was at the selecting of them, they're so bright, almost flaunting-like."

Mary Culkin flared up. "Fr. James does not go in for flaunting things."

The Nurse wagged a chiding finger at her.

"Darling, I'm afraid you're hardly an unprejudiced observer where poor Fr. James is concerned," she said pityingly.

"She always calls me 'darling' when she is going to give me the worst stab," Mary Culkin thought; but the Nurse had higher game than her. She was looking around again at the frocks [and] the underwear. Following her eyes, Nan saw them as something garish [and] 'flaunting.'

"But they aren't; they aren't," she thought fiercely. "It isn't true; they go with me [and] with one another."

"Who'd ever think Dr. Ederney would be fond of such nice things, him that's so grave?" said Mary Culkin.

The Nurse nodded to her.

"It just shows what I've often said to you, dear. You never really get to know a man until you live with him."

She turned to Nan.

"I'm sure as a married woman you'll forgive me for the bit of coarseness, Mrs. Ederney. I'm afraid we—District Nurses—don't keep as refined as we ought to be, but then, as you know, it's the dirty end of the stick for us morning, noon, and night, the dirtiest end of all a nurse's job and that's saying something. 'Tisn't like young ladies like yourself, God bless you, brought up in the refinement and protection of good nuns all your lives, sheltered from everything. When you're married, of course, well, you know what I mean, but by that time the refinement has got so deep into you that you never lose it, I expect, not like some of us who were thrown flat down on the world to fight our way from the time we were kids. Well goodbye, Mrs. Ederney, and thanks for a lovely evening. Don't trouble to come down with us."

Her feet clumped down the stairs. Nan stayed on in the room. It was discourteous, but she could not get herself to accompany them.

From outside the voices of the men cutting seaweed on the shore, the baying of an ass in the distance, the lowing of the cows being driven home to be milked—all the confused rumble of the life of the Black Shore was coming to her as part of the Nurse's words, making her room a silly excrescence of life.

"My one stronghold. My one nest of peace," she thought bitterly. "Now she has ruined it, the harpy! Nothing is my own any longer, not even my clothes!"

The silent thoughts rang false.

"I must see things as they really are," she muttered, "as they really are, as they really are."

With the words came the picture of Philip in his shabby coat [and] old battered hat. It was a favorite phrase of his that one must see things as they truly were. A smile crept over her face.

"My precious schoolboy," she whispered.

With the thought of him a sense of triumph came to her. She had won, though she hadn't wanted the man. Nurse Bruton had lost. What she was doing was according to the laws of nature. They were just two women taking their chances against each other. The woman who had lost was trying to get some of her own back and small blame to her. In such [a] struggle, Nurse's chances would be nil. She was handicapped from birth. Why shouldn't she hit back, poor devil? Even the way she put her hand over that gash of a mouth was pitiful [and] her trick of feeling her bulbous purple nose.

The door slammed below. It was only now Nurse was leaving.

"Trying to pump the little maid," Nan thought, but her bitterness was gone.

Chapter XVII

IN THE SNUG UNDER THE PICTURE OF ST. PATRICK AND THE SNAKES, PAT Culkin stood with his legs apart looking down at the District Nurse. In the armchair with her squat body, her thrust-out bust, her legs apart, she made even Pat Culkin look ethereal.

"God," he thought, "what ugly divils womens can be whin they're rale sinful ugly like the wan in front o' me. If she even hadn't rigged herself out in that quare get-up, a mixture of hin and parrot, but there—"

The District Nurse, before taking a glass of whiskey he had put on the table beside her, was looking round at the door.

"There, there, ye needn't have a haporth˙ o' fear, Nurse. Sorra person 'ill come next or near this snug till I give the word. I've given ordhers about that, an', as I'm thinkin' you know be now, ordhers I give in this house are obeyed."

"Well, Mr. Culkin, here's health and prosperity."

She sipped the whiskey daintily [and] out the glass on the table. Pat Culkin stretched his hand for the whiskey bottle. She put hers on his.

"Not now, Mr. Culkin. One glass they say is health, two, the beginning of the slippery slope."

She let her hand rest on his. With the chance of the doctor gone, Pat would be a good match—not the sort every woman would pick, of course, but, for a woman who would be a match for him, a good proposition if only he could be got to see that a wife who knew her way about could be a great deal of help, even to him.

Pat drew his hand gently away from the caressing fingers. It was very little evidence a sthrap˙ on the lookout like her would need before she'd begin thinking of an action for breach of promise.

" 'Tis what I'd have expected from you, Nurse, though God

knows I'd like to show you the hospitality you diserve and that's sayin' some. For the greatest of good sinse an' dacency an' modheration you're a model to this parish and I wish to God you could put some of the same grand qualities into that poor docthor you have the misforthune to be working with. I hear from Mary he's a great thrial to you entirely with his foolishness an' figaries an' all his new fangled nonsense about disinfectants and sanitation an' divil knows what. Disinfectants and sanitation in Lochnamara! The world know 'twould take the Atlantic Ocean itself, an' it all disinfectants, to wash the durt an' the girms out of Killeavy alone, not to sphake of the mountain side an' the shtinks and cess-pools that's shorin' up every cabin on it."

The District Nurse's lips had snapped together when Pat Culkin withdrew his hand. If he thought he was going to soft-soap her with his blather, this bog-trotter who had made his pile in a Chicago slum would find that it wasn't with bog-trotters like himself he was dealing.

She stared up at the picture of Saint Patrick.

"Thinking I'm using it to dhraw custom to the pub—that's what she's thinkin', the bitch of a divil," Pat Culkin thought. "Aye, faix, that's what she's thinkin' an' worse."

The menacing thrust of the big bust, the stance of the knees wide apart, like a wrestler watching for a grip of the enemy, the waggle of the gaudy feather that topped the hat, left him no doubt that he had made the worst of mistakes.

"Begob, it's meself has put me foot in it. If 'twas ugly she was before, it's ten times as ugly th' ould divil is now with that wickedness on her mug,'" he thought. "It's palavered she'll have to be, soothed and soft-soaped before I can get anywhere with her."

Aloud he said soothingly, "It's meself that's been sore disappointed in the man, sore disappointed, thinkin' he'd be sinsible enough to see the sunlight in front o' him and ask a dacent woman to marry him, a woman with weight an' sinse an' dacency, not a thrickie' whose wan idea would be to get him out of the parish to some fancy place, Dublin or London or wan o' them big cities where she could flaunt round in all her glory with others like her, but the poor man didn't even have that much sinse, God help him."

The Nurse closed her lips with a snap.

"I wouldn't be so sure of that, Mr. Culkin, not so sure at all."

Pat stared at her.

"Begob, there's me foot in it agin," he thought, "me two feet, up to the belly and beyant, a dale beyant. But who'd iver ha' thought the ould sthrap 'id have the neck to purtend the docthor 'id took

the side o' the road she was walkin' on, if there wasn't wan other
female in the woruld."

He nodded his head in delight.

"D'ye know now, Miss Bruton, that raises me opinion o' the man
lagues and lagues, changes it altogether. How I iver thought he'd
have the eejicy not to see the prize that was in front o' him put
sthraight in front o' him by God himself, as you might say, I can't
make out now, whin I come to think ow it. 'Tis the man's quare
notions in other ways, God help him, but shure he isn't all blind,
not all blind in every way. He couldn't be, an' it's glad I am to hear
he had the sinse to see a prize an' it right in fornint him, even if
'twas out o' the poor man's rache."

"It takes two to make a bargain, Mr. Culkin, and with *me*, my
holy religion comes first, first and foremost all the time, Mr. Culkin.
There's many a man that came begging me to marry him, Protestants and freethinkers' up in Dublin when I was in training, men
of education and standing, but, if a man isn't sound on faith, I
wouldn't touch him with a forty-foot pole."

She looked up at the picture of the Sacred Heart.[18]

"I must say, Mr. Culkin, that there's few things have given me
such pleasure and edification for many a long day as the sight of
the holy picture placed by your own hands where it says plain and
clear that, even in the midst of the joys of life, the mind of man
ought never to forget his Saviour and the need of ensuring eternal
salvation."

Pat shook his head deprecatingly.

"I do me best, Miss Bruton. The lashte I might do for our holy
religion is to keep meself and other poor sinners reminded that in
the midst of the joys of life, as you say, we are in the shadda o'
death, and grieved and sorrowful I am to hear from your own lips
that you couldn't see your way to save the docthor's soul. A sad day
'twas for Lochnamara whin, instead of you, 'twas that poor thrickie
he had to take as a sekend besht."

Nurse Bruton waggled her finger at him.

"Nothing against her now, Mr. Culkin. In her own way she's as
good a girl as is goin' and I'm sure she's doin' her best with the
doctor. Fr. Ned's niece couldn't not do her best to save the man's
soul."

"Ah, but the quality o' the besht she's able to do, Miss Bruton—
isn't it that that's failin' us an' the docthor an' every livin' soul in
Lochnamara?"

"Still she's doing her best, Mr. Culkin. What more could the poor
girl do?"

"I'm afeard then 'tisn't much headway she's makin' with that besht of hers, Miss Bruton. Whin they were married, we were all waitin' anxiously on the next Sunday to see her ladin' the man into the chapel. Did he come? For tin minnits I held the Rosary back meself to give her the full chance to bring 'im. Did she succeed?"

"I've no doubt in the world she tried hard, Mr. Culkin. It isn't the poor girl's fault that she hasn't got the weight to move a man like Dr. Ederney."

Pat Culkin stared down at the heavy squat figure [and] the protuberances almost bursting the clothes back and front.

"Weight! Begob, that's the word, the wan right word. 'Tis how ye tuk it out o' me mouth, Miss Bruton. 'Tis weight that does it. In all the whole wide woruld is there anything that weighs like weight? 'Tis often and often I heard Fr. Ned say that 'twas in the Holy Book itself that weight can move mountains and that's why I'm thinkin' 'twas a sorrowful day for Docthor Ederney, aye, and for Lochnamara, the day you turned the man down and left his salvation and ours in the hands o' that poor thrickie that hasn't a thing in her head, but her dhresses and her shifts, and her petticoats. 'Tis ashamed an' grieved I was whin Mary told me about the gaudy lot of thricks she had to show you up in that bedroom o' hers."

Nurse Bruton shook her finger chidingly at him.

"Now, now, Mr. Culkin. How could a man of your weight and experience judge a poor girl like her, understand the joys the likes of her gets out of clothes? 'Tisn't only that they're all their joy, their delight, but 'tis the most natural thing in the world too, considering that most of them haven't a thing else in their heads, not a thing else to fill their lives, but dresses and sandals and paints and powders and underclothes and dances and such childish things. 'Tisn't every woman can plumb the experiences of life like you and me, Mr. Culkin."

Pat Culkin wagged his head in violent affirmation.

"Little children most of them are, an', like little children, cravin' for gewgaws an' fa-lalas."

Nurse Bruton's eyes softened as they rested on Pat's.

" 'Tisn't their fault, God help them, and this much I'll say for Nan Clooney, Mr. Culkin, even if her mind is empty, she was always a pure pious Catholic girl. 'Tisn't her fault if a burden is thrust on her that she can't carry. That much I'll say for her and I feel it's only due from me to the poor girl, considering that in a sense it was my own refusal of the burden—but what's the use of talking? Since Mary and [I] paid her that visit, I confess to you, I'm all unnerved and uneasy. 'Tisn't the room—though it was full of such gaudy

trash that 'twould sicken an honest man. No, it's the foolish innocence of the girl going on with her gewgaws and her frippery, without an idea in her head how much is at stake for herself and her
husband and the whole parish. If our pastors weren't looking on so
foolishly without stirring a hand, 'tis to them I'd have gone, but, as
for poor Fr. James, you know how he is about that girl, God help
him, and what could you expect of Fr. Ned, a weak kind-hearted
slop always, if ever there was one, and now having good family reasons for turning a blind eye; though, mind you, Mr. Culkin, I'm
sure 'twould pay him better in the end to face the music."

The corners of her mouth went back in a clench. She looked up
[again] at the picture of the Sacred Heart over Pat Culkin's head.

"It's leadership that's lacking in this crisis. It's leadership we'll
have to have, Mr. Culkin, and in all of Lochnamara where's the
man who can give that leadership but yourself?"

She caught Pat's hand [and] squeezed it. This time he left it in
her grasp.

"Breach or no breach, I'll have to let her paw me if I'm to get any
good out o' her," he thought.

"The man who put that picture on the walls of his own most private, intimate room, Mr. Culkin, who carries his devotion to Saint
Patrick into his daily life and his business affairs. . . . who else have
we who can save this parish from the risks and the scandal that
unfortunate pair are bringing on it and on themselves? Save them
from themselves must be our motto, Mr. Culkin, no matter what
means may be found necessary, and 'tis only strength and weight
and devotion can do that, the strength and weight and devotion
only yourself can supply."

She wrung his hand with a grip that made him wince.

" 'Tis soft and sloppy I must be gettin' with this aisy life," he
thought ruefully, "whin the likes o' her can bring a grin to me face
with her grip."

"I'm afeard, much afeard, 'tis only the bare thruth o' the word
you're sayin', Miss Bruton," he murmured sorrowfully. "If only you
knew the nights Mary and me has spent sayin' the Sorrowful Decades an' the Joyous Decades and the Glorious Decades for the souls
o' thim two, the length o' days, day after day, Mary has lit candle
after candle in front of St. Francis, you'd have some notion o' what
a grievous thing it is to hear that all thim Decades and candles have
gone wesht in the face o' the legions and legions of divils from hell
that's thryin' to invade our parish undher cover of that poor eejit's
skin; but from what you tell me, Miss Bruton, gone wesht they are,
an' now it's up to us, up to you and me to give battle in a way they'll

undershtand, with the help o' God an' His Blessed Mother an' all the saints and angels and the flag of Ireland and the Holy Ghosht flyin' over our heads an' our hearts for the glory o' God and the honour of Erin."[19]

Chapter XVIII

A FEW DAYS AFTER NURSE BRUTON'S VISIT TO THE SNUG, MASTER O'roarty sat in the same chair she had graced. In shape and spirit, he was so different that Pat Culkin, looking down on his wraith-like face, could not help making comparisons.

"Begob, I wronged her," he thought, "wronged her all out. 'Tis quare how different ugliness can be. 'Twas that led me asthray altogether for 'tis he takes the cake. If it's ugliness you'd have to name on her mug, afther all 'tis the ugliness of life, but this divil in front o' me, this bloody ghosht, 'tis the horrors o' death he'd put into a livin' craythur."

O'Roarty glared at him as if he read his thoughts, a glare so venomous that Pat Culkin turned instinctively, went to the window, and stood staring out at the sea.

"Begob, 'tis the evil eye he's thryin' to put on me," he thought, "as if the likes of a poor craythur like him could iver put the evil eye on Pat Culkin."

Master O'Roarty kept up his glare at the heavy rounded back.

> Like little wanton boys that swim on bladders
> This many Summers on a sea of glory
> But far beyond their depth.[20]

he quoted softly.

"Aye faith, that fellow Shakespeare knew a thing or two, all right," he gloated in a loud whisper to the unresponsive back.

Pat Culkin swung round.

"Wor you talkin', Mr. O'Roarty?"

O'Roarty cleared his throat noisily. He had a bad cold on the chest. Treats of sweet cake and chocolates and honey were his form of self-indulgence.

"Even a man doesn't drink or smoke that doesn't mean he oughtn't to have some little comfort in his life" was a favorite aphorism of his; but unfortunately his stomach was weak and had a way of turning the sweets and cake and honey into sourness and the sourness into phlegm that choked his nasal and bronchial pipes and brought on headaches and stomach-blocks. When he was plagued this way, like many other men in similar conditions, he tended to look on his fellow creatures with jaundiced eyes.

His upward gaze at Pat Culkin was full of malice.

"Quoting Shakespeare I was, Mr. Culkin," he said softly, "just quoting Shakespeare about people that swim on bladders when crack goes the wind out of the bladders and down the boyos pop, down into the depths and dumps. Faith, that fellow Shakespeare knew a thing or two, even if he was a Sassenach.'"

He coughed heavily, aimed at the nearest spittoon [and] missed.

Pat Culkin went ostentatiously to the scene of the mess and polished it off with his heavy boot.

"Sorry, Mr. Culkin, very sorry indeed I am," O'Roarty said in a voice that said he'd do it again and again if he felt that way.

"Begob, 'tis a row he's afther, a bad, wicked row. Seething and chawing for a row, he is," Pat Culkin mused, "an' lather on, he'll get it, an' plinty; but not now. I couldn't afford it now, not whin I'm needin' him an' th'other masthers in this sthruggle that's facin' me."

"If I could only pershuade you to take a good shtamin' glass o' punch, 'twould kill the cowld in no time, Mr. O' Roarty," he said amicably. "Couldn't you let me pershuade you to take it jusht this wance as midicine? Shure there's nothin' a man can't take when 'tis midicine."

O'Roarty looked up at the picture of Saint Patrick [and] from it to the Sacred Heart button on the lapel of his coat.

"When I pinned the Sacred Heart button on my chest, it wasn't with the intention of getting excuses to evade it, medicine or no medicine," he said truculently.

Pat Culkin gazed blandly at him.

" 'Tis how he hates me very guts," he thought. "It can't be all becos I took the rosary out of his mouth and said it in English. 'Tis just plain hate, pure plain hate, same as I always felt meself for him and the likes iv him."

"Well then, the tay it'll have to be, Mr. O'Roarty," he said heartily, "the tay as always, an' a grand dhrink it is, surely, no betther, for thim that has the vartue an' the conshtancy to shtand up to the hunger for dhrink an' masther it."

He went to the door.

"Mary," he called out, "Mary, a rale good cup o' tay for Mr. O'Roarty—tay with heart to it. He's kilt with cowld an' he's so resolute
in his piety, he won't take a glass o' punch even as midicine, so
make the tay as good as the punch with a kick an' a half to it."

Master O'Roarty looked down at the table, a piece of grand ma-
hogany got at an auction in Liscarna House.[21] The prospect of the
tea should have mollified him, but the stale smells of porter and
tobacco smoke that came through the door were giving him a feeling of nausea, and the added smell of bacon and cabbage and stale
onions was stirring the nausea to venom.

"Begob, 'tis shniffin' the very shmells he is an' addin' the porther
shtains an' the whiskey shtains on the table to thim an' puttin' it all
to my account," Pat Culkin thought. "The very divil himsel' must
ha' got into him this time."

O'Roarty looked up.

"You might remember a talk we had some time ago, Mr. Culkin,
about the doctor and his goings-on."

" 'Deed an' I do, Mr. O'Roarty, 'deed an' I do, an' it's 'mea culpa,
mea magisima culpa'[22] with mesell all the time iv late about the way
I misled you and mesell with that same talk. Shwimmin' on bladdhers, I was, as you said so thruly, shwimmin' on the bladdhers
of good sinse and intintions of Mrs. Ederney, an' the divil a more
burshtin' pig's bladdher any man or boyo iver wint floatin' on; for
the woman, be all accounts, isn't showin' as much sinse or dacency
as 'ud cover a pigshtye. If she'd an ounce of ayther wan or th'other,
it's half way to London she'd ha' got that poor nacheral weeks ago
from dhrivin' the people diminted the way he is with his blather
and his impiosity. Instead o' that, what's the gerrel doin' but toyin'
with fa-lalas, lace shifts and gold shlippers and the divil knows
what? So, at any rate, the ladies tell me that they saw her at it. Lace
shifts and gold shlippers here in Lochnamara!"

O'Roarty watched him grimly.

"I'm glad you're apprised so exactly of the situation, Mr. Culkin,"
he said pompously, "for all the information at my disposal, and 'tis
a fair amount, points to a similar diagnosis. Meantime, I'm being
denied my rights, a very fundamental deprivation, Mr. Culkin, very
fundamental, even worse, if I may say so, than your good son's deprivation of the dispensary job you and Dr. Joe had been keeping so
warm for him till he'd get qualified."

He licked his lips. That was one in the eye for the dirty dog, sure
he was codding everyone with his blather about God and holy Ireland. Much he cared about God and holy Ireland, shouting out the

"Hail Marys" in English in front of the whole congregation; but he'd have to be used, dirty hound against dirty hound, Greek against Greek. He'd fix the doctor, all right. When it came to dealing with his enemies it wasn't the way of the Cross or the Sorrowful Mysteries for Mr. Patrick Culkin any more than when it came to squeezing the sweat and blood of the poor. He'd rosary the doctor. See if he wouldn't. When Pat was done with him, Dr. Philip Ederney would have other things to think of besides depriving husbands of their rights, and the devil mend him, the dirty renegade, the man that turned his back on the Holy Faith and the Gaelic League and the Gaelic civilisation that was our greatest heritage outside the Holy Faith. It wasn't as if he didn't know any better. When he was a kid in England, the Finn McCool Branch of the League had taken him in hand, taught him Irish and his duty as an Irishman. He had turned the back of his hand on all that as well as on the faith of his fathers that was rooted in it. Yes, the devil mend him too and let him get everything that was coming to him when the other scoundrel turned his own bag of dirty tricks on him."[23]

"Indeed an' indeed I'm thinkin' it's up to you and me, Mr. O'Roarty, to guard an' difind our Holy Faith and the morals of our people against the foul invader. Birth control an' divil's docthrines about the stopping of childher before they even get as far as the womb can't be tolerated any longer in this God-fearin' townland. If our pastors, God forgive 'em, have diserted their flock, it's up to you an' me to save the sheep an' the lambs an' ewes that's left diserted. Thruly an' piously an' in all Christian humility, Mr. O'Roarty, with the Holy Ghosht flyin' over us, as I'm shure he'll be, an' the green flag of Erin alongside o' him, it's you an' me will have to rescue the eternal salvations of the flock that's left sthrayin' and blatin' for protection in this holy Gaelic parish of Lochnamara."

In spite of himself, O'Roarty felt a warm glow of piety and patriotism flowing through him. He began to wave his arms.

"The hungry sheep look up and are not fed," he chanted
"But filled with wind and the dank mist they draw."

He closed his eyes and wrinkled his forehead.
"There's a line there I can't remember," he groaned.
"It doesn't matther, Mr. O'Roarty, shure, what do a line of pothery more or less matther," Pat Culkin encouraged.
O'Roarty began to sway his shoulders.

While the grim wolf with privy maw
Daily devours space and nothing said[24]

He chanted as if he was singing "The Old Gaelic Strain."

Pat Culkin watched him with meditative eyes.

"Crazy, begob, clane crazy the craythur is with broodin' on the loss of his marital rights," he thought. " 'Tis aisin' down he wants."

"That sounds like more grand pothery you're sayin', Mr. O'Roarty," he said soothingly, "grand pothery altogether."

O'Roarty opened his eyes.

"Poetry it is," he said, " a poem that was made hundreds of years ago by one of the greatest blackguards an' scoundrels that ever hated our Holy Faith and our Gaelic culture, a friend and a henchman of that scoundrel, Oliver Cromwell."

"Do you tell me now? 'Tisn't the likes o' him I'd iver think you'd be quotin', Mr. O'Roarty."

O'Roarty swung around fiercely on him.

"And what else did the Sassenach scoundrels leave us to quote when they didn't leave a single line from an Irish poet in the schoolbooks they put on the programmes to ruin our Holy Faith and our Gaelic nationality?"

> God bless the Queen an' make of me
> A happy English child.[25]

"That was the sort of blaggardly stuff they had in them same books. You must remember it yourself, Mr. Culkin."

Pat Culkin scratched his head.

"I ought to, thin, Mr. O'Roarty; shure, I ought to, but sorra wan o' me rimimbers wan thing they put in me head at school. In wan ear and out th' other it wint, like wather off a duck's back. 'Tis mesell was the poor scholar intirely."

"Well, you didn't lose much. It wasn't like it is today when we have our own grand Gaelic in the schools. However, that isn't what concerns you and me at the moment. Our business is to start

> That two-handed engine at the door
> Stands ready to smite once and smite no more.[26]

Pat Culkin nodded his agreement fervently.

"What you're sayin' about Injuns is right, Mr. O'Roarty, but I'm much afeard we won't be able to get thim in time for what we want. Whin I was beyant the wather, I never had any dalins with thim, though I did hear how they were grand at scalpin'. However, I'm afeard 'twould be too long a wait to sind for thim. It's ourselve'll have to do the scalpin' an' whin we've done it, I'm thinkin' an' hopin' an' prayin',' for wan should always pray, hopin' and prayin' I am that the docthor will rue in sorrow and grief the hour he first hears the aisht shore shoutin' to the wesht shore an' the shtone roarin' against the two of them on the bare black shtrands of the seven villages of Lochnamara."

Mary Culkin came in with the tea. The gentle eyes in the rough reddened face looked appealingly at O'Roarty.

"I hope it's to your likin', Mr. O'Roarty. I've brought a jug of boiling water in case it's too strong, but I know how you like a good cup of tea, and that's the fresh top o' the cream."

She glanced from one face to the other. There was something spicy going on, something about Nan Clooney and the doctor that she'd have loved to hear, but the men were being confidential and wanted to get rid of her.

"You'll pour out yourself. You'll know how much milk and sugar."

She wondered if O'Roarty mightn't ask her to stay. He and she had always got on well together.

"Thanks, Miss Culkin."

He didn't get up as he always did. A question about Mrs. O'Roarty might help, and indeed ought to be asked in common politeness, but there was something in the air that made her hold it back. She went out, shutting the door softly behind her.

Pat Culkin nodded after Mary's back.

"Sad and grieved she was to give me the evil news, Mr. O'Roarty. Twice a day since that unhappy marriage, Mary has been puttin' up a votheen* candle for Nan and that unfortunate man o' hers before the image of Saint Francis. Every night, she and me, and Tony, when he's here, have rimimbered thim at the night rosary. No wan can say we haven't exaushted the deeps o' prayer before we allowed oursel' to be forshed into other mishures. Well, Mr. O'Roarty, our prayers weren't heard and I'm thinkin' I may say with confidence and with faith that, if they weren't, it was because God and His Blissed Son and the Holy Ghosht, afther puttin' their head together, decided there was only wan way to clean up the dungheap that fellow is makin' of Lochnamara, and that way is to clean him out hoofs an' horns and all with a bang that'll be heard from here to the gates o' hell itself."

O'Roarty poured himself a cup of tea, put in four spoonfuls of sugar and half the jug of cream. He lifted the cup in a gesture of consecration.

"And here's to that sentiment, Mr. Culkin; here's to clean living and high thinking and the Gaelic culture and our Holy Faith and down with all atheists and shoneens* and West Britons that dare to lift their heads between the holy shores of Ireland."

Chapter XIX

PHILIP EDERNEY WAS TIRED. ALL DAY HE HAD BEEN GOING FROM CABIN to cabin over bog-holes and swamps, across the pools of slimy dung that lay in front of the hovels where the sick people lay on filthy sacks and all day, in return for his services, he had been receiving only sour looks [and] averted [glances]. He could not understand it. It was as if some unnatural malignity had suddenly been turned loose on him in return for all his self-sacrifice and loving service.

As he passed a huddle of cabins . . . a boy flung a clod at him.

"Atheish!" he shouted. "Divil!"

His face darkened. It had been on this generation that he had been pinning his hopes.

> Here's a health to Hannigan's aunt
> An' I'll tell you the raison why—
> She ates becos she's hungry
> A' she dhrinks becos she's dhry.

Tony Culkin's hand was on his shoulder.

"If only you'd take Hannigan's aunt as your model, Ederney— just take that plain, practical woman for a model, what a blessing it would be to the parish, to the world, to all the people who want to help you. Yes, you'd come as a boon and a blessing to men like 'the Pickwick, the Owl, and the Waverley pen.' "[27]

Ederney crouched away from the hand.

"There you go again. I'm the one friend you have in this parish, Ederney, and that's the way you feel about me. It's as impossible to help you as to help a suicide; for a suicide you are, coming to Lochnamara of all places in the world with your atheism and your advice to restrict families and the rest of the rubbish."

The words were insulting, but the man's face [showed] friendliness.

"Atheish! Divil!"

Stones were coming through the air. A group of children was closing in on them.

Tony Culkin ran at them.

"Who the hell do you think you can pelt—you bog-rats?"

The children scattered [and] stood silent at a safe distance.

Pelting Pat Culkin's son wasn't as safe as making a cockshy* of the English doctor.

Tony Culkin came back.

"God damn that booze," he said, 'here I am out of puff already, me that used to be a champion runner. However, to come back to you, Ederney, if you aren't too tired—God knows you look all in—but still, we're one of a profession, you and me, and, if you can stand it, I'd like to give you a few words of fatherly advice."

Ederney made no answer, but Tony, ignoring his silence, swung into step behind him.

"You'd never guess now, Ederney, why these kids are acting in such a blackguardly fashion toward the doctor who has come here to raise them up out of the abyss," he said softly.

"I have no interest in the intrigues of priests against me," Ederney said loftily.

"The priests! Dammit, man, they're getting it in the neck even more than you from your jig-actin'. If you think it's the priests who are raising these kids and their daddies and mammies against you, you're a bigger fool even than I thought, and that's sayin' some."

"Somebody has started something very nasty and underhand[ed] within the last few days," Philip retorted.

Tony surveyed him with mocking eyes.

"And of course, it must be the priests—never anybody but the priests," he chuckled. "You'd never guess, Ederney, not in a thousand years, would you, that you're suffering from diabolic possession."

"So that's their Reverences' game, is it?"

"No, it isn't their Reverences' game. The poor devils of Reverences are not the authorities for diabolic possession in your case, Dr. Philip. I'm not at liberty to say who the aforesaid authorities are, as the lawyers would put it, but the word has gone forth that the poor Englishman is cracked and crazy with the legions and legions of devils who have got into him with one deadly purpose—the ruining of the souls of the people of this parish of Lochnamara. According to the same high authorities, there's one way and one way only to get these devils out of Dr. Ederney's skin, and that is to boycott him and them, and keep shouting at him and them, until it's borne in on their infernal brains that the parish knows they're there and the game is up. There's a rumour out that for every shout of "devil," there'll be an indulgence of a hundred days for the shouter, but that, as the newspapers might say, lacks confirmation.[28] What doesn't lack confirmation is that whenever Dr. Philip Ederney goes near a house or a village, every pig in the place is to be watched with the greatest care by their owners, because once a time the farmers of a parish in Israel lost their whole stock of hogs when devils in a certain man in that parish decided that the game was up and went home on board the pigs by the sea route. The fate that fell on those pigs has stuck in the country minds more than all the sermons, as indeed you might expect, Ederney, if you knew a damn things about us. The pig is the crock o'gold to the small people of the Black Shore and the ladies and gentlemen, who constitute, what I might by stretching a point, call the Reception Committee, know that the best of all ways to keep the people from calling you in except under the direst of necessity is to warn them about the danger to those pigs."[29]

Tony chuckled.

"You haven't noticed them driving the pigs away from your shadow? You wouldn't, of course."

"I'm very tired, Dr. Culkin. I've had a long day and I'm all in."

"And you think I'm drunk and worrying you perhaps because I'm burstin' with jealousy."

Ederney gave him a side glance.

"No, I don't see any sign of drunkenness, neither do I read much envy of my job in your face, Dr. Culkin."

"Thanks for that much discernment. As a matter of fact I'm no end thankful to you, Ederney. You've saved me from a lifelong grave in this hell-hole and that's why I'm telling you what's being put round about you and why I'd like to give you advice that might put you wise to the only way you can circumvent the parties that are plotting against you. Will you listen if I repeat you a little sermon, Ederney?"

"What is your sermon," Ederney said wearily.

"It isn't mine and it's not from the Gospel, so you needn't be afraid of it. It's from the mouth of a history professor we had when I was at college, an old fellow with a dirty grey beard and a dirty long overcoat he never got out of. Half the week he boozed the head off himself and in the other half he taught us more than the whole bunch of dry sensible ones 'ud do in a year. Now, of all things in the world, rhythm was his hobby, body rhythm, brain rhythm, but above and beyond all, what he called community rhythm. 'Every society, gentlemen,' he used to bellow, 'every society has its own

special rhythm and if a man or woman wants to shape that society
he must work within its rhythm, inside it, in the flow of the stream.
Amongst you there are many who will be clergymen, doctors, ad-
ministrators here and abroad. I pray you, when you are dealing with
a society, do not violate its rhythms'—and so on. We thought the
whole thing a cod of a course, went around asking one another dirty
questions about our rhythms, then forgot them. I thought myself I
had forgotten his sermon long ago, but, queerly enough, Ederney,
it must have been lying somewhere in the bottom of my brain all
the time, for now, when I see you going round, prancing like a
bloody fool against the whole tune of these poor devils' lives, it
comes bobbing up, and I can see there was a hell of a lot in old
Timmy Cloran's preaching about rhythms."

"It's very kind of you to pass Mr. Cloran's wisdom on to me, Dr.
Culkin, but I'm afraid—"

Tony Culkin cut him short.

"Oh, come off it, Ederney; doing the drawing room stuff on me
is only throwing pearls to swine. There are only two things bitching
you, and bitch you they will, if you don't drop them. One is your
tripe about the need to have small families; the other is your tripe
about religion. If you want to do your work here, I mean your
proper real work as a doctor, you'll have to drop them both."

"I see," said Philip dryly.

"The trouble is you *don't* see. You're as blind as a bat in daylight.
You don't see that in trying to keep families small in this cursed
hole, you're . . . depriving the poor of the one and only sport of their
miserable lives, and [smashing] the only industry of the place, the
one industry that brings in sterling and dollars, supplies, labour,
and exports."

Philip glanced sharply at him. The fellow seemed to be on to
something.

"You might elaborate that," he said.

"I might, but I think I'll leave the sport side out. To try to get it
into your head that a man needs a bit of sport to keep his life warm,
and that, not even barrin' drink, procreation is the noblest, most
ancient sport in the world, would be like trying to get a mackerel to
understand the pure joy of having a game of croquet with the rector's wife on the rector's lawn—so we'll leave that point and come
to the industrial side of the argument. For every child born into a
house here, the Eire Government, between children's grants and
Gaeltacht* grants, pays at least ten quid* a year up to the age of fourteen. Every boy or girl that's exportable to England or the USA a
few years later sends home on an average at least twenty quid a

year. Got that, Doctor? It's just a plain multiplication sum. I expect
you know enough about multiplication to grasp that the smaller the
multiplier, the less the income. So, up with the babies. There are
families in this parish . . . drawing a good hundred quid a year from
these swarming families alone—got that, doctor?

"Then why in heaven's name are they so poverty-stricken?"

"Ah, now we're coming to it. Did you ever hear of a plutocracy,
doctor—the evils of a vile plutocracy? Well, an all-seeing Providence has taken sure and safe steps to prevent its growth in the
town of Lochnamara and these sure, safe steps consist in the creation of my dad and his grand credit system. Talk of the credit system of Alberta![30] . . . The credit system of Lochnamara embraces
every man, woman, and child in the parish at one hundred percent,
two hundred percent, God alone knows what hundred percent,
since only God knows how deep any man, woman, or child is in
debt to the dad. . . . When the pounds come in or the dollars, the
dad knows it. He has the Post Office and the Post Office knows everything. Long before the pounds or dollars come, they're owed to
him, and to him they go, or as much of them as he wants to take.
For mind you, dad isn't a shark. He doesn't believe in eating up the
parish in one swallow. He's a moderate cannibal feeder, is the dad,
taking only what won't kill them—three quarters of the pounds or
dollars, the services of the boys and girls, half or three quarters of
the profits on the kelp, all they can spare of the crop and the mackerel or herrings when there's a good catch. So, the proletariat is
kept pure, the dangers of a plutocracy warded off—"

Philip Ederney stopped [and] faced the other.

"You hate the whole horror, Dr. Culkin. Why don't you stop it?"

Tony chuckled.

"Me stop it! Me, that's depending on it for the booze that makes
my life bearable—ah now, doctor, we aren't all heroes like Dr.
Philip Ederney—and that's what I'm comin' by the long way round,
doctor dear, just this secret word in your secret ear. Those that
cross the dad's path get hit bad, if they give him a chance to get in
a wallop. Now, there isn't a grander opening for a punch to the belly
of a doctor in Lochnamara than the name of being an atheist and
the name of being an advocate of birth-control—no two grander
openings for a good, hearty foul below the belt—and don't you think
the dad is the man who would draw back from a foul against a man
that has done the dirty on his son by robbing him of the dispensary
his daddy was keeping warm for him from the time he first went to
college."

They had reached the doctor's house.

"Won't you come in, Dr. Culkin? I'm exceedingly obliged to you for the decent way you've warned me. I think you know my wife and I'm sure she'd be glad to welcome you."

"Thank you—thank you, doctor. Yes, Mrs. Ederney knows me well, too well to have any respect for me. I'm a wastrel, a boozer, a good-for-nothing. I expect you've heard all the glad story already. I'm a bloody coward too. If I wasn't, I'd come in, in the face of the public, and make a common cause with you, but I'm not going to do it. A couple of days ago, a couple of the pious God-fearing men of Lochnamara laid their plans to put a halt on your gallop and get you out of the parish by as wicked a boycott as ever struck a rack-renting landlord.[31] I'm warning you now. Further than that I'm not going to go. I'll not take your cases, but I'm not going to side with you either. I'm too dependent on the booze that makes life tolerable; but if you take my advice, you'll either get out of here or, if you stay, you'll join the tribal rites [and] go to your duties like a good decent Catholic."

He gave Ederney a shrewd glance.

"You call yourself a scientist," he said, "well, a good scientist knows that he has got to put something in the place of what he's taking away. What are you going to give them here instead of the glory of eternal joy, if I may ask?"

"A decent life here on earth."

"Aye, faith and a hell of a long time they'll be waiting for that in this hell-hole, a very big hell of a waiting. But what's the use of talking to you about rhythm, doctor? You know as much about [these people] as you know about God or the saints. You've got a saint besides, a girl that's fit to be an angel without ever having to put on wings. They'll maybe not get you, doc, when you try to smash through their rhythm, for you're as deaf and blind as a lobster inside his shell, but she's not deaf, doctor, and she's not blind, and she's in the middle of the rhythm. Worse still, she has an unfortunate uncle who is the parish priest of this hell-hole [and] who is the conductor of the whole orchestra. They'll get him through her and she won't be able to bear that. However, there she [is] at the window looking out for you. Good-bye, doc, good-bye and don't prance in on top of our tribal dances any more than you can help, for God's sake and hers and all the sakes that ever were or will be."

He waved his hand to Nan and was gone.

Philip Ederney went slowly up the path [and] hung his coat and hat on the rack with measured movements. Tony Culkin's nonsense about rhythms left him unmoved, but if he told Nan about his warnings, she might be deeply troubled. She might start to worry about him, beg him to take Tony's advice [and] leave Lochna-mara, or conform to [the] superstitions she believed in. He loved her deeply, deeper than his own life, than anything in the whole world, but there was one thing he could not do for her. He could not betray his principles a second time [or] take part in the tribal dances and the rest of the mummery of the clerics who were keep-ing the people in a state of darkness and ignorance that gave the filthy usurer his chance to batten on them.

Rhythm, indeed! There certainly was rhythm—the rhythm of the hoodoo men and their victims. If the witch-doctors fell out amongst themselves because of her being his wife, there might be a chance of breaking that tom-tom dance, splitting the tyranny that was squeezing the heart's blood of the people into the witch-doctor's fleshpots.

If only that could be made to happen here, other parishes would soon follow. There would be the beginning of a wave of liberation that might sweep the country.

When he sat down opposite Nan for the supper all he said was, "Pity Tony Culkin's such a soak. He seems a decent chap, plenty of brains, too."

"Decent he is," Nan agreed heartily, "as decent as they make them, and as brainy as he's decent, but he's given himself up as a lost soul. Tony is finished, I'm afraid, dead and done for. He tried to swallow Pat Culkin's filth and he's died of the dose."

"He's not dead yet," said her husband softly.

Nan gave him a pitying look across the table.

"He thinks he can save him," she thought. "He's sure that he can save everybody: what a mad conceit there is bubbling at the back of the man's mind."

"There's one person Pat Culkin loves better than himself, better than all [others] in the world," she said softly, "his son, Tony. Mary means little to him [and] all the rest of mankind are creatures to be fleeced."

Philip looked up with a hopeful glance.

"You think he'd cooperate, if I tried to reform Tony?" he asked eagerly.

"Pat Culkin cooperate with you? Pat is killing Tony as surely as if he took a knife or hatchet to him, but do you think he has any idea of that? Try to save Tony and you must first rescue him from Pat [and that] will make Pat feel you're a double thief, a robber who must be destroyed. No—no, Tony can't be rescued, so leave bad alone; leave bad alone or it may become worse."

Chapter XX

IT WAS RAINING, THE COLD RAIN THAT HAD BEEN GOING ON FOR DAYS. Out to sea the waves were curling into white caps before they hurled themselves viciously against the east strand.

The drumming of the rain and the tumbling of the breakers followed by the melancholy dragging back of the water over the tormented stones was filling the air, filling the world.

Nan stood at the window watching the rain sweep the road, the white-crested rollers driving up the beach. As they drew back over the stones, they snarled resentfully.

"Yes, it's one of my down days," she muttered. "Up and down I go like a Jack-in-the-box, one day full of confidence, the next, down in the mud. Is it possible to be always up in the air unless you're a Philip Ederney? Does even Philip Ederney always live on the heights? Can it be that there aren't moments when he realises that he's making a thorough mess of everything, that he's as ignorant as a tinker's ass, without any more idea of what people are thinking here than he has about music, literature, painting, or the ballet, that there might be worlds of joy and vision outside his ken? Can the man be as big a fool as all that, never to get a glimpse of his own blindness [and] incompetence? But how can I criticise him—I, who was imbecile enough to bring Bach [and] Beethoven into his house, [or] the piano I bought in my early days when everything was springtime. An idiot's dream [and I] the worst imbecile of all.

"To live on with him here, part of me must die," she thought.

Her notion of Philip and herself coming together in the cosy firelight, the soft lamplight, seemed today such lunacy that she could only laugh bitterly at it.

"Or is it this devilish weather that's getting me down?" she thought.

She turned and looked slowly round the room, at the divan where he was accustomed to sit, his pale tense face looking drained against the coloured cushions. He too was being drained of life. The hollows growing under his eyes, the loose hanging of the hands as if they were letting go their grip, his growing silence about his work, the lack of zest when she tried to make up to him by questions about his cases, all were telling the same story. The part of him that mattered was dying.

"I am to blame for that," she thought. "It isn't Pat Culkin who is getting him down, nor the ingratitude of the people. They couldn't get him down if he felt I was beside him; but I can't be beside him. I made this nest for us, warm and cosy, and the cosier I make it, the more out of place he looks. I can do nothing with him. He is far away, beyond my reach, a wild, hopeless creature, untouchable [and] untamable."

Untamable—yes, that was the word. He was a wild isolated creature who could understand nobody, [or] enter into any sympathetic comradeship. Her mind went back to the evening she had told him of a letter her uncle had got from the Bishop enclosing an anonymous scrawl accusing him and Fr. James of aiding and abetting an atheist [who was egging] on the Catholic women of Lochnamara to practice birth-control.

He had been discreet enough to make no comment, but she could see from the look in his eyes that he had been glad of the news, delighted that he was embroiling the ecclesiastics with one another.

How could she ever come close to a man like that by any way she knew—warm firelight, softly coloured cushions, warm intimacy? Do what she would, the sense of savage ignorance in the man had come between them for days after that episode. The estrangement had drained him and there had been worse to come—the evening when, in the false intimacy of the firelight, she had been fool enough to make another attempt to get him to see the point of view of a fervent priest.

She had begun to tell him about James's ecstatic devotion. He had listened with rapt attention. In her delight over that deep attention, she had gone on and on with the details of the young priest's piety.

"At last," she thought, "at last his mind is beginning to understand the mind of a man like James vowed to God. After all, it isn't so different from his own dedication of himself to the poor."

When she finished, he had sat silent for a while. Then he said, "I had been wondering if the diagnosis was right. It was. He is a most interesting case—epilepsy in its early stages."

"Epilepsy!"

"Yes, concealed epilepsy. It often shows in that way. It's the stuff so-called saints are made on. There can be no doubt that Paul was a hidden epileptic. His epistles are the case history of one. Even—"[32]

The look on her face had stopped him. If he had gone on to say that Our Lord was an epileptic, she could hardly have refrained from throwing the book she had been reading at him. He did not say it, perhaps had not been going to say it.

He had poured out apologies [and] pleas for forgiveness.

"I had no intention of saying what I said, Nan. You know how I look at everything from a medical angle. It came before I was aware of what I was saying. Won't you forgive me?"

"There is nothing to forgive. It's quite possible. I've often thought that some saints suffered from hysteria."

The words were comforting enough, but the voice was so cold that he realised that he had been near disaster.

"How in heaven can I ever follow her into that country she lives in," he thought, "and if I can't get there. . . ."

He watched her timidly with sidelong glances. Then he realised that she too was watching him from beneath her lashes.

"There are times when he's like a little boy doing obscene figures on a wall," she thought. "What a squalid need."

She got up, went to the window [and] stood looking out at the swarthy shore. He slipped out, but she couldn't hear his steps on the stairs. What was he waiting for? She walked restlessly around the room, an empty, silly space that meant nothing. Her impress was not on it. Neither was his. He could leave no impress on anything—house or space or person. He was a ghost, a phantom. He must be standing outside the door unless he had gone down the stairs so carefully that she couldn't hear him. It was a house in which you heard everything, a house of noisy echoes. It would be like him to slink down the stairs like a guilty thing. He hated the noises of the house as much as she did, but unlike her, he never complained. It was his way not to complain.

She stood with her elbow on the mantelpiece, staring into the fire. The days of their old estrangement were back again and there was nothing she could do about it. The moment she came near him he said something outrageous that drove her away.

The night she had invited him to share her room came back to her—the sudden light in his eyes. It had not lasted. Very soon she could see in the eyes the recurrence of the old dread. He had hoped for everything from that night and there had been nothing—a mere contact of bodies.

His footsteps were sounding on the stairs now. He had been waiting outside on the landing, hoping she would call him back. His dread of being flung into the desert of loneliness was with her night and day, but she could do nothing about it. He himself was the obstacle between himself and the community.

A face was looking at her from the turfflames, Michael's face— the man with no ideals, no trustworthiness, nothing but the warmth, the happiness, the comfort of life.

She had hoped that, with her, he would fade out of her life, but she had never needed him more.

Her body, her mind, her whole life were crying out for him.

She began to pace up and down between the window and the door. The rain lashing against the windowpanes was a symbol of what her life had come to.

Even if she could get her husband to leave Lochnamara, it would be no relief for her. Fr. Ned and Fr. James she might save from further misery, but escape from Lochnamara would be no escape for her. It was from herself that she had to escape and there was nobody to escape to.

Talking to her uncle or Fr. James about her troubles was useless [and] irksome. They answered with encouraging words about the omnipotence of prayer, words that had lost their meaning. God alone knew how she had prayed, tried to storm the citadel of Heaven with passionate entreaty. Nothing had come of those stormy prayers, nothing but the rebellion of despair which made her sometimes wonder if there could be a God.

She shivered. It was damnable to be so clear-sighted. She almost wished she could get back to those days of self-deceit when she was able to delude herself with the notion that it was possible to get him to realise the feelings of the people [and] their sense of outrage over his lunacies. Now the absurdity of the notion was so patent that she couldn't understand how she had ever entertained it. Sympathy, understanding with any other except herself seemed to be beyond him. Even this boycott was beyond him. He could not understand that to the people of Lochnamara [the boycott] was a mere act of defense against a robber who was trying to steal their one inestimable treasure, the vision of Everlasting Glory that made up for all their earthly misery, [or] that all Pat Culkin and the others were supplying was the leadership the priests had refused to give.

Her mind went to Fr. Ned and Fr. James.

Pat Culkin was getting at them through her and her through them. Pat knew every move in the game. After the first week of the boycott he had recognised that anything the inhabitants of Lochnamara did or said or refrained from doing or saying could have no more effect on the doctor than the buzzing of flies, that to him they were nothing but the colour of their urine, the nodules on their joints, [or] the sourish smell of their sweating bodies.

Besides, there were rebels who did not agree with the boycott— men like Owney Foran, the saint of the parish, who kept reminding the people of all the doctor had done for them. There were others whose wives, children [and] husbands the doctor had saved, [and] who were speaking openly against the boycott [and] saluting her and Philip respectfully when they crossed their path. It was a small opposition, but, if time went on, it might grow and Pat Culkin never took chances. He would try to finish off the doctor with the greatest possible speed and for that purpose, she was the person to be attacked, the Achilles heel of Philip Ederney.

If life could be made unbearable for her through the recoil of the attack on Fr. Ned, Pat Culkin calculated that the doctor would have to go.

So, the full force of the boycott had been turned on her. The women particularly had been got at, their superstitious fears worked on by Pat's agents. They hurried past with heads hidden under their black hoods if she met them on the road. If she spoke to children, they were called hurriedly away [and] the sign of the cross put on their foreheads against the evil eye. The very beggars shrank from her when she offered alms.

[She poked the fire and dropped into the armchair wearily.] They wouldn't get her that way. If her trouble had been as external as all that, things would have been easier. Her trouble was in memories of golden days [and] evenings that died in a blaze of light over the sea.

The plain that had been a silver shield now lashed over the road, covering it with torn weed and the masses of stinking debris and dogfish that had been lying on the shore. In the village the miserable cabins with their thatch held down by stones, their barred windows [and] their doors stuffed with rags and old sacking, crouched away from the howling waters.

Those women with their red petticoats thrown over their head who scurried down the road were frightened beasts.

Mary Culkin was no better, a beaten thing, bowed to acceptance. The wives of the teacher, the shebeen men? She felt like murdering the beaten dogs.

Her mood changed. Tears were running down her cheeks. Her temper had sunk into a despair that had no violence. She seemed to be listening to the death rattle of the world of her childhood [and] youth.

There was a knock at the door. She got up [and] stood at the bookcase so that Ellie would not see her face. She knew why Ellie had remained in spite of the boycott. She had been told to stay by Pat Culkin. Her share of the war he was waging against them was to supply a daily report of every word they spoke [and] every act of their lives.

"Come in," she called out, stooping to handle the books.

The door opened.

"Well, what is it, Ellie?" she asked.

"I—Nan—I thought I'd call."

It was Fr. James.

She turned. No use trying to wipe away her tears even if she wanted to.

"Nan—Nan—"

He ran over to her instinctively.

"James! she cried, "Oh James!"

She threw her arms round his neck [and] dropped her head on his shoulder.

He was trembling violently, a blind impulse shaking him.

Then his arms were round her and he was raining kisses on her hair [and] face.

For a few moments he pressed her to him. Then with a strangled cry he threw her from him and ran wildly out of the room.

Nan picked up his hat [and] went to the door.

"Fr. James," she called. "Fr. James."

The front door banged. He was gone.

She went back to the drawing room [and] shut the door quietly. As she stood . . . looking at the hat, a smile lit her face.

One of Philip's theories that had seemed the most idiotic to her was that people saved themselves by turning their backs on memories. He had never been able to explain how [one] did it. [One] just did. All his imbecile cocksureness was in those words, but today she began to see that there might be ways of doing it. Michael had made a tangled skein of her life. Now, for the first time, she felt a slight unravelling of it. It was not that she was in love with James. There wasn't a chance of that, yet the waves that swept up the beach had lost their deathliness.

"What a curious beast I am," she thought. "I can bring myself back to look at the world with the eyes of a hopeful child because James has made a fool of himself over me. I thought I was dead to everything, but here is my zeal for the hunt as fresh as it was in the days before Michael, my heart ready to start on the same old round. James is poor game, but he has become a saviour, a liberator. True, he's in anguish [and] overwhelmed by the consciousness of sin. He is a goose, a mere nuisance to anybody like Fr. Ned who has to use him, but he has been of use to me—this dear goose—and, after all, if he is a goose, so am I, for he has liberated me."

Her mind drifted to the first conquest she had made. She was a girl of fifteen and walking in a tail.˙ The tail of a boys' school was passing. They had been playing cricket and were in white ducks˙

Suddenly one of them had stopped, his eyes fixed on her face. The remembered sensation of joy was back again. [She] couldn't repeat with James the details of that hunt—the letters in the hole of the wall, the sighs, the tenderness—until she grew tired of the boy.

"No, that won't do with James," she thought. "I'll have to be a mother to him, my angel goose."

She smiled a whimsical smile. The picture of an angel ending up as a goose was an amusing one. Everything had become amusing.

"A mother I'll have to be to him," she whispered to herself. . . .

She held up the soft black hat [and] pressed it to her cheek.

Chapter XXI

THROUGH THE DARKNESS FAINT LIGHTS GLIMMERED. OVER JAMES Clogher's head ragged clouds scurried across the sky hiding and revealing the stars that stared at him. The stray lights [from] the scattered cabins were staring at him. From below, the thunder of the billows came up followed by the long withdrawing roar of the sea.[33]

He stood in the darkness listening to the pounding and whining of the waves. God had not accepted his atonement. He had given up everything [and] handed her over to that man, but God had not been appeased. God's grace, which he prayed for [and] toiled for had not come. Since the night he had first discovered his love, he had gone to the Holy Sacrifice in such dread, his hands trembling so at the Elevation of the Host that he had feared he would let It fall. Every morning Christ's wounds bled new for him, the wounds he himself was inflicting by his sin. Now he had crucified the Saviour afresh.

He felt himself shivering in the cold wind. The rain had stopped, but his clothes were soaked through. His mind kept going over the years of his life that had led to this—the sinful pride that he had taken in his brains, his fervour, his contempt for his comrades in the diocesan "batch."

They had been too far below him to be envious when he headed all the dioceses in every branch of theology year after year, finishing up on the Dunboyne Post-Graduate course when they, poor fellows, were glad to scrape through the final exams [and] escape from Maynooth to the country curacies where the poor peasants would look up to them.[34]

His course had been mapped out for him by the Bishop. After the Dunboyne, he was to come as professor to the Diocesan College. From there a good parish would have been his rightful prize; but only long enough to give him parish experience. After that it would be a Secretaryship in the Bishop's Palace, a training in the duties he would undertake when he too would be called to the espiscopate or the professorship at Maynooth. . . .

In his arrogance he had refused all that [and] begged the Bishop to let him serve in the poorest, most miserable curacy of the diocese, a curacy of filth and fever, of sick calls in hovels, a post all others were glad to avoid.

"A Saint," they had whispered. He could see it in their faces. He had fooled them as he had fooled himself, but he had not fooled God. God had looked into his heart and seen the arrogance, the devil's pride that had been the source of his "saintliness." God had withdrawn His grace [and] left him at the mercy of the Evil One.

He knelt down on the sodden bog and bowed his head.

"O God," he prayed, "forgive me, a worm, a proud, shameless worm that has dared to resist Thy will to substitute my own miserable pride."

For hours he stayed kneeling in the sodden earth. It was the least he might do to suffer this small misery in atonement. He was shivering with cold, but, when he rose from his knees, he felt comforted. The wild ecstasy mixed with the agony was no longer tearing his heart.

✳

The storms were gone. Morning after morning the winter sun came over Knocnagullich flooding Lochnamara and its sea with a silvery light. In the garden of the doctor's residence leaves that should have fallen weeks before still glistened like jewels.

Nan, walking along the gravel path, felt that summer had come again, the long weeks of sunshine that seemed to be smudged out forever. She could think of Michael Leland without bitterness now. Philip had often told her of the freshness people feel after an operation that has freed them of some internal oppression. She was feeling like that, revelling in the sunlight. The Black Shore had not changed. It was as it had been, savage, desolate, a place of bog and grey crags, but the sun was transforming it and its stormy sea. A measure at least of peace and brightness had come back to the earth.

Michael had become an incident, a summer episode. The summer was gone. An autumn glow had taken its place, the red of ferns and of autumn heather, the thought of Fr. James Clogher's love.

From the garden she could see him pacing the road in front of the curate's house reading his breviary. She had no doubt that he had regained peace. He had "made an Act" of his love for her, transformed it into a punishment for his sins. She had feared that he would have wanted to fly from Lochnamara, that when he had confessed his sin to Fr. Ned, her uncle would get his Lordship to transfer him at once as far from her as the limits of the diocese would allow.

For days she had gone in fear that Fr. Ned would tell her that James was leaving them, but the days passed and Fr. Ned gave no sign. James must have decided not to let Fr. Ned know anything about the scene between them, [and gone] to the big town to make his confession. He was going about his duties now with more fervour than ever. When they met, he saluted her calmly as if he had forgotten what happened.

She had no intention of questioning him or her uncle.

"What a rotter I am," she thought. "No decent woman would feel as I do because a priest had fallen for her, but I have some excuse, perhaps. I wanted a child. James is the answer to my prayer and I am not going to give him up. He has said nothing to Uncle Ned. He must have gone to Roymore [and] got absolution there from one of the Order priests.[35] He can't bear the thought of leaving me. What a grand excuse it would be for him if he wants to stay with me, to decide to battle against his love, transmute it into a passion for my soul, for all the souls under his care. 'Suffering is such a purifier,' he can say to himself. By staying and suffering instead of running away and trying to forget, he will become a more understanding shepherd of souls than the cocksure scholar who came to us from Maynooth as an act of charity. Yes, surely James has decided to fool himself, and perhaps it isn't all foolishness."

Starlings were chattering over her head. The first thrush she had seen since early spring flew across the garden. No thrush mated in Lochnamara. When the first touch of spring came over Knocnagullich, they left the Black Shore [and] went inland for their love time. Now, when love and family broodings were over, they were coming back to the barren shoreland to sing their winter song as if the escape from the love urge should be celebrated by an outburst of joy for the barrenness of a dead land.

※

Fr. Ned sat staring into the turf fire. There was a lull in the storm that had been blowing up in his parish. Nan seemed to have settled down at last after those earlier weeks of discontent. He did not understand her new happiness. She and Philip seemed no closer than before and there was no one else in Lochnamara who could light up the young woman's face. That drunken wastrel Tony Culkin could not do it . . . whatever feelings he might arouse in the hearts of mountain girls. His thoughts turned to Fr. James. He shook his head. There was nothing in that. When James came at first he had been delighted, but his delight had been short-lived. James had turned out to be seven different sorts of fool. Still, he wasn't that particular sort. Drink or women weren't the pitfalls into which he was likely to tumble. His missionary zeal was the trouble with James. The conversion of the doctor would be his great triumph, the substitute for the missions to the lepers, [or] to the slums of London [or] Manchester. . . .

Fr. Ned's mind went to Pat Culkin. He, not the parish priest, was the ruler of Lochnamara. No peasant's family in all the parish but was in his clutches. When he had settled down in their midst [and] married the daughter of the only shop in the place, he had taken over a web of credit that had already enmeshed the poor of the parish. He had extended that sinister web until its ramifications made him master of every family in the seven villages of the Black Shore.

The sons and daughters of his victims were at his disposal for any service he needed in his shop, [on] his land, [or] his boats. If they left the place [and] went to Roymore or Dublin or England, they still paid him a tribute, since most of the savings they sent home were seized by him to pay off the debts of their families—debts of which no family knew the amount that piled up so monstrously year after year.

A horrible octopus the fellow was with his tentacles gripping the countryside in a grip that could not be loosed. The Gardai˙ were afraid of his influence, if [they were] not under his control. His command of votes made him a big man of the area from the Government point of view. Even the Police Superintendent and the District Justice had to be wary of crossing swords with him, and it was all done with such a soft touch that nobody could point to any single act of aggression.

Fr. Ned shook his head despairingly. To plumb the power and the deadliness of Pat Culkin's murder-machine was beyond anybody in Lochnamara. In a district where all were savage children, Pat towered over the land in his man-of-the-world knowledge. He never quarrelled, never bullied. It was the silkiest of gloves over the hardest, most murderous of hands; but when he struck the blow would go home.

The priest got up [and] paced the room. If Culkin [could get rid of] the doctor through the boycott, that might be a solution of the trouble—a painful surgical operation, but still a solution. [There was, however,] no sign of his succeeding. Philip Ederney was not the man to be moved by a boycott and Nan was standing fast. Pat could never get Philip Ederney, but it wouldn't be Pat's way to leave it at that. Already he was planning another move. What it was the parish priest could not guess, but every instinct told him to beware.

The door opened violently. It was Fr. James, his eyes flaming.

"God help me, he's on the rampage agin," [he] thought.

"Yes, James, what's the trouble now?" he asked.

"Maggie Mickle John is going to have a baby. Tony Culkin is the father. We can't let this sort of thing happen in our parish."

The curate's voice was trembling with passion.

"How do you know Tony is the father?"

"Maggie says he is."

"I'm afraid Maggie's word is hardly good enough for us to go on, James. Hanging it on Tony would give it the touch of respectability it wouldn't have if she confessed that some mountainy man was the father. It's possible, of course, that she's telling the truth, but it's poor evidence. Apart from the question of respectability, Pat Culkin can be touched for the money to send her to England to avoid the scandal. No mountainy man can afford [that]."

The curate's eyes narrowed [and] grew cunning. He knew Fr. Ned's weakness, the craze to hush things up, let sleeping dogs lie rather than raise a stink in the parish. Well, he'd be no partner in that sort of game.

"I'm afraid I'll feel it my duty to speak about Tony Culkin from the altar, Fr. Ned," he said quietly. I haven't the slightest doubt that it was Tony. Maggie Mickle John isn't the first girl he has ruined. I'm determined she'll be the last."

Fr. Ned frowned. James was going to be difficult. He himself didn't believe it was Tony. Maggie Mickle John was a strap, if ever there was one, over-sexed and unbalanced. The mountain boys knew where to look for a willing victim, a welcoming victim.

"The girl has never had a particularly good name, James. I feel that, if you denounce Tony for her sake, you may be walking into it very badly. If I were you, I'd make a little more investigation before I took such a drastic step."

"What sort of investigation? You don't think the people will turn informer on Tony, Fr. Ned? There isn't a hope of their doing it. Pat Culkin has them in his pocket."

"True enough, James, but, if you act precipitately, Pat is just the man who would take an action for slander against you for ruining his son's chances as a professional man, and what hope would you have in winning such an action? My idea is that before you do anything drastic, one of us might see Pat [and] put it to him that there is this rumour about Tony."

The scorn on the curate's face was withering, but he said quietly enough, "I cannot see what good a talk with Pat Culkin can do."

"At least it will show that we didn't act precipitately if you [decide to] speak against Tony Culkin from the altar later on."

"I can't for the life of me see what good it can do, but have it your own way, Fr. Ned. If you think you can do something by talking to Pat Culkin, I'm willing to wait, but I'm not going to let Tony Culkin off unless you make a bargain with Pat that Tony leaves Lochnamara for good and Pat pays a good indemnity to the girl. That is, of course, unless you forbid me officially to deal with this scandal."

The parish priest sighed. James was right. He was at his old game of putting things on the long finger and Pat wasn't the sort for whom it paid to put things on the long finger. He was sapping his influence with the parishioners already, telling them that the P.P. had sold their immortal welfare for a good marriage for his niece. He looked up at the curate.

"I'll do what I can, James. As you say, it's hard to see what one can do with Pat Culkin, but it's my duty to try not to seem vindictive for his attacks on me."

Fr. James smiled knowingly.

"I'll be praying for your success, Fr. Ned," he said with an unusual touch of sarcasm.

As he went out he was still smiling sarcastically.

"If I weren't a priest, what a joy it would be to help him to a [kick in the pants]," Fr. Ned thought.

His mind went back to Pat Culkin. The flood of poisonous stuff Pat was pouring into the Bishop's house would have done him infinite damage if his Lordship hadn't had the deepest trust in him. He had shown the Bishop Fr. Carmody's letter about Philip Ederney's excellent qualities, and the Bishop had accepted it as a sufficient reason for forbearance. He was lucky indeed in his Bishop's wide humanity. But how long could even his charity and humanity last under the flood of poisonous stories that was being poured into the Bishop's House week after week under Pat Culkin's guiding hand?

"I don't bother his Lordship with most of them," Fr. Lander's, the Bishop's secretary, had told him. "He's relying on you, Fr. Ned, to make sure that this unfortunate man in his headstrong zeal does not force us to step in to safeguard the faith and the morals of your flock. If only you could report any progress in his conversion, it would help his Lordship immensely in dealing with the attacks that are being made on him and you."

Fr. Ned [poked the fire and threw himself into the chair]. That was the curse of it. He hadn't one atom of progress to report. Nan, who had been his great hope, had made no headway. There were times, even when it seemed to him that her own faith was not what it had been.

He put down the poker [and] crouched forward in the chair staring at the fire. Could it be that Culkin was right? That he had betrayed the parish [and] handed Nan and the others over to an agent of evil sent under the guise of a worker for the poor? The devil had many disguises, many ambushes. He knew the weak spots of every heart [and Fr. Ned's] own weakness—that craving to avoid trouble [and] struggle, to take the line of least resistance [and hope] for the best.

Chapter XXII

In MARY CULKIN'S PARLOUR, PAT CULKIN LOOKED ACROSS THE HEARTH AT Fr. Ned with a beaming face.

"You say it's about a matter of throuble you've come, Fr. Ned, but throuble or no throuble, I can say this, with God's truth, there isn't a man in Ireland or out of it gives me more pleasure to see sittin' forninst me than yoursell, an' I can tell you why, though you know it yoursell already. You're made up o' wisdom and plain honest sinse without any coddin' or foolishness. I wisht to God others in this parish had a tinth of your Riverince's undershtandin' of things as God made them, not as thim fools think they ought to be. Now, before we shtart thalkin'—"

He lifted his glass, got up [and] made a sort of bow to Fr. Ned. Fr.

Ned nodded [and] took up his own glass. Even if he had to make
trouble, he didn't believe it was made any better by mixing it with
bitterness. The soft beginning of a talk was often half the battle if
the other man was the sort that could listen to what you were saying, not merely be listening to his own answer without taking in a
word of your talk. Pat would listen, watch and listen. There was no
doubt about that.

The priest put down his half empty glass [and] smacked his lips.

"You certainly keep good stuff, Pat. I don't believe that even up
in Mitchell's or Morgan's in Dublin you could get the likes o' that.
However, to get down to business. I'm glad to hear you say you
think me considerate. God knows, I do my best to see every point
of view. There are people who think that I am perhaps too much
given that way, but there are times—well, you know yourself, Pat,
that there are times when it doesn't help much, and, God's truth, I
don't know how we're going to get out of this trouble I'm coming to
you about. You haven't heard, by any chance, that Maggie Mickle
John is going to have a baby?"

Pat Culkin nodded.

"I heard that lash night. It's very hard on poor Mickle John, a
dacent hard-working man if there iver was wan; but the girl is a
sthrap, always was. When she'd come into the shop here, it used to
make me feel ashamed the way she'd look at the min—any man
this side o' seventy. Aye, faith, I often said she'd bring their grey
hairs to sorrow and indeed, what's makin' me believe in the grace
o' God was that He resthrained her so long, for she was rarin' and
tarin' at the bit, wansht she was fourteen."

Fr. Ned twiddled his glass between his fingers.

"You heard who she's namin' for it, Pat?"

"No, troth, I didn't. Some gintleman I'll be bound, a school
masther or a thraveller or a garda.* It won't be the bog throtter that
threw her down, anyway."

Fr. Ned looked into the fire.

"I'm afraid your guess is nearly right, Pat. It's Tony she's naming,
Dr. Tony."

Pat Culkin slapped his knee.

"I knew it, though I forgot Tony, the highesht wan o' the lot. Who
else 'id she go for but the highesht? If your grand new Docthor was
here long enough, it's him she'd have named, the bitch, but you
can't blame thim. To claim to be the docthor's woman even for wan
few minutes in the dark, there's few o' them wouldn't think it a
greater honour than to be married to the pick o' the poor divils
they'll have to marry in the end. Well now, Tony will be amused

whin he hears it. That's wan grand thing about the boy. He niver bears malice. 'An' who else would she pick on an' me there for the pickin'?' That's what he'll say between the fits o' laughin', but it's a bad biziness all the same, a very bad biziness for the poor father and mother that's disgraced before the counthryside."

Fr. Ned sighed heavily.

"I'm afraid, Pat, that Mickle John believes her story. He says Tony was all around the place about the time the thing must have happened."

Pat Culkin gave a hoarse laugh.

'An' what else would you expec' the poor man to say, Father? He has to cover up the disgrace, God help him, and the fac' that Tony boozes a bit give him a grand chance. I'll bet now he said he was ravin' mad with potheen whin he done it. That 'ud be the right shkin to put on the shtory. Another dhrop o' the stuff, Father?"

The priest shook his head.

"It's great stuff, Pat, but a little of it goes a long way. Yes, he said Tony was meddling with the potheen. The neighbors have the same story. He was seen with Maggie—"

"O' course they'd ha' seen him with Maggie. They're a dacent, kind lot an' they'd swear thimselves black in the face to help a frind. They know how soft-hearted I am to any wan in throuble and there isn't anythin' they wouldn't say to get a handful o' money for Mickle John to aise the poor man's throuble. Aye faith, Father, 'tis meself knows thim well, an' yoursell, too, 'tisn't how you're ignorant ayther o' what they'd do to help a poor man that's down. Shure, we're all like that, we Irish, God help us; but it's a good way, a very good way to be, an' it'll be the bad day for the counthry whin we lose it. It was that shouldher-to-shouldher made us win agin the landlords, agin the English, agin all the forces of evil that was crushin' us—"

He made to pour whiskey into the priest's glass, but Fr. Ned warded off the bottle [and] got up.

"I'm afraid things are going to be bad this time, Pat. I don't know myself what I was hoping for when I came to you, but whatever it was, it hasn't happened and now things are going to be bad, very bad indeed. Fr. James, I'm afraid, is going to talk about it from the altar—"

Pat Culkin lifted his bulk slowly from the armchair.

"An' thin," he said softly, "so Fr. James is the man who's goin' to talk about it, is he now?"

He fixed the parish priest with his eye.

"I've been shparin' Fr. James this many a day," he said in the same soft purring voice.

The priest's heart sank. [Culkin was] a beast of prey. But what on earth could it be? James, for all his folly, was a saint, not the sort of man who would give Pat Culkin a grip on him.

"Sparing Fr. James! I'm afraid I don't get you, Mr. Culkin."

The parish priest tried to make his voice hard and stern, but Pat Culkin was only giving him a grin.

"Well, perhaps 'twas your Riverence I was shparin', for, as I said whin you came in, 'tis yoursell has always shown yoursell the dacent kind-hearted man with no ear for lies agin your parishioners— none o' the foolishness o' poor Fr. James, the crathur who'd swally anything. Hosomever, if Fr. James forces me, I'll have to show him up in his thrue colours even if your Riverence takes part o' the knock an', God knows, I'd wish to shpare you that same part, for it'll be a knock in your wakesht shpot, Fr. Ned. I know well how you love her."

Black spots were floating in front of the priest's eyes. He groped for a chair [and] steadied himself. His instinctive dread had been right. This ruffian had something up his sleeve, some piece of folly of James's that he could twist and twist into a scandal.

"Hadn't we betther sit down and talk it over like the two sinsible min we are, Fr. Ned? There's no harm done yet an' there's no need for any harm to be done, thanks be to God, no need at all. All that's wanted is a bit o' confidence an' the plain shtrait word, sinse you an' me doesn't lack sinse, whatever them other craythurs might do."

The priest sank into the chair. His mind was working again. He would have to do a bargain. Whatever folly James had committed, there was no question that he had done something that had put him in Pat Culkin's power. That purring voice was full of confidence.

"Have another dhrop, Father? This sort o' thing is thurrible on a man."

The priest waved the bottle away, but Pat Culkin poured out a stiff glassful for him.

"It's quare the lives o' sinsible, honest min like you an' me to be upset by the giddy-goats that hasn't as much sinse in their noodles as you an' me have in our little fingers, Fr. Ned, but so it is, but the ways of God are beyant human undershtandin'. All we poor sinners can do is accipt thim humbly, make an act of our misfortunes and thry to mend the tares the foolish wans we love do be makin' in our lives. There's Tony now. He's the dead shpit of his poor mother, God rest her, and, that God has rested her, I know. She's lookin' down at us this minit thankin' God it's you an' me has to dale with the throuble, not dunderheads that'd make everythin' worse—"

The priest turned his head slowly with an effort.

"What do you have to tell me against Fr. James?" he asked in a low voice he could not keep from trembling.

Pat Culkin pushed the glass of whiskey towards him.

"If you take a glug of it, Fr. Ned, 'twould aise you," he said gently.

The priest got up.

"I don't want easing," he said. "If you've got any charges to make, make them."

Pat Culkin lifted himself lazily from the chair.

"Me? Sorra charge I want to make agin anywan. It's how I was always hatin' to say the durty word, an', well, you know it, Fr. Ned. If there's to be durt to be shturred up now, it isn't me'll do the shturrin'."

"You've flung insinuations in my face about Fr. Clogher. I have no inkling what you mean by your aspersions. I demand you make your charges here and now—"

Pat Culkin put his hand on [the priest's] arm.

"Aisy now, Fr. Ned. It's no wondher your flusthered, knowin' as you do that I wouldn't be afther sayin' the few things I said if I hadn't the God's proof they're thrue, an' indeed it was Mary privinted me talkin' to your Riverince whin fursht I heard about the throuble. 'Don't worry his Riverince,' she said. 'The throuble will pass. Nan is a good gerrel, a rale good gerrel an' Fr. James is the besht o' preeshts in shpite o' this wan little lapse he's fallen into.' That's what Mary said. A saint that gerrel is, if iver there was wan, an' she loves Miss Nan, always did since the first day she set eyes on her."

"Would you ask Miss Culkin to come here?'

"Now, now, Father, I'm thinkin' the two of us can carry this between us without dhraggin' in the wimmen—"

The priest made a movement towards the door.

"If you won't tell me, I shall have to ask Miss Culkin—"

Pat Culkin caught his arm.

"Listen, Father. Mary won't make no charges anymore than I'd do mesell agin any wan that's kith and kin to you. Our tongues wouldn't let us, we bare such friendliness to you and Miss Nan and Fr. James. That's how it is. But there's another tongue we've tied up out o' that same frindliness to you and yours, a tongue that was crazy to wag if we hadn't tied it tight. Niver was I glad before to have a grip on people until Nellie came to us with that story—"

"Nellie? The doctor's servant?"

"The same wan and a loose tongue she is. If it wasn't for this fear o' what I'd do to her whole family if she wagged it agin Fr. James and agin you, there wouldn't be a house in the village where they wouldn't be waggin' their finger o' derision, runnin' to tell wan another o' the goin's-on between the docthor's wife and her uncle's curate, a preesht o' God. But, faix, I fixed that. 'Let me hear even wan whishper of a breath an' it's out on the road yer father an' mother an' their eight childher'll be—' Aye, Father, that's what I said to her whin she cum runnin' to us with her shtories o' what she saw whin she opened the door of the parlour by mishtake without givin' any warnin' to the pair that was inside and the docthor away. The craythurs thimselves didn't see her whin she bursht in on thim, they wor so taken up with one another, or they'd ha' been ashamed o' their lives, so they would an', be the grace o' God, it was shtrait to Mary she cum in her fright at seein' thim like that."

He drained his glass.

"I wish you'd take yours, Father. There's no use worryin' over things that pass. We'll all pass, God help us, us an' all the things we be worryin' foolishly about. An' as for Maggie Mickle John, the craythur, I'm not the wan to have ill feelin'. 'Tis only human nachur to do what she done, fashen it on the highesht she could. If she'd known about Fr. James 'tis on him she ha' fashened it, God help her. An', talkin' of help, it's up to us that has to help thim that hasn't. 'Tis the Irish way, the besht in the world, and, for all that Mickle John and poor Maggie has been thryin' to fashen their throuble on Tony, I'm not goin' to shtint a bit o' help to thim because o' that. God help the craythurs; who is goin' to help them if we don't?"

Chapter XXIII

THE DOOR OPENED. FR. NED TURNED. IT WAS JAMES, HIS EYES ABLAZE.

"I suppose it's the Maggie Mickle John business," the P.P. groaned inwardly, "if it isn't some worse foolishness. Well, he'll get it in the neck, if it's Maggie. I can't spare the poor fool this time. I should have got him transferred even if it would have seemed a victory for Pat Culkin and got his Lordship suspicious."

"Pull down a chair, James. You can feel a real touch of winter today," he said.

"No, the armchair, James. You look too much like a Reverend Mother, sitting bolt upright on that high chair," but Fr. James's face did not relax.

"Yes, we're in for it again," the parish priest thought wearily. "Trouble on trouble. I was wrong in trying to spare him. He'll have to be changed and it will worsen my whole position. Pat Culkin will take it as a sure proof of victory and what reasons can I give his Lordship for the transfer?"

"Well, James, what is it now?" he asked.

Fr. James's eyes snapped with passionate rage.

"Maggie Mickle John has had the baby. She gave birth to it last night. We can't let the matter lie any longer."

Fr. Ned stirred uneasily.

"That's bad, very bad," he said.

"It has got to be stopped. This isn't the first time. There was another girl, before I was curate here. It was hushed up, Mickle John said."

He looked accusingly at Fr. Ned. Fr. Ned stared into the fire. There had been another girl, Babs Kelly, another strap. The affair had been hushed up. Pat Culkin had refused to accept that Tony was the father, and he was probably right, but to avoid a scandal he had as an act of charity given the family enough money privately to get the girl away to England [and] provide for the child. The father and mother, poor creatures, with ten mouths to feed, had been glad to get a little money [and] avoid the disgrace of an illegitimate child.

Babs had gone to the devil afterwards in England. It would have been difficult to prevent, in any case. [Fr. Ned] had been miserable over the affair, but, even if he was sure Tony Culkin was the father—a thing of which he had no proof—he did not see what good he could have done by making a public stink in the parish [and] disgracing both families.

He could feel James's eyes on him.

"The thing has got to be dealt with. We can't keep quiet any longer."

The curate's voice had a fierce ring.

"Lust and adultery have got to be stamped out of this country. The purity of Irish men and women has been one of God's greatest gifts to us, a shining light for all the world—"

"What course are you thinking of, James?"

"The course I've advised already: to denounce the ruffian from the altar [and] make it clear to Culkin and all his tribe that there is no room in Lochnamara, no, more anywhere in the diocese or in Ireland for a man of his kidney.* Mickle John tells me he has good reason to think that Maggie isn't the only one . . . that in a short time we may have a second or even a third fruit of his lust on our hands. Hushing up won't do this time—"

His voice had a vindictive ring.

"You'd almost think he envied Tony Culkin," Fr. Ned thought, then immediately repented.

"Oh God forgive me! God forgive me for my shameless lack of charity because James is going to raise trouble for himself and me."

"There will have to be something done certainly, James," he said reflectively.

Fr. James looked at him with indignation.

"Something! There's only one thing to be done, hound him out of this parish [and] out of the country. When I was a boy, one of the old R.I.C. got a girl into trouble in our parish.[36] If the thing had been let go, others would have tried the same game, but Fr. O'Brien wasn't the sort of man to stand for that. He gave the fellow his chance to marry the girl. When he refused, Fr. O'Brien told him he'd teach him a lesson he'd never forget. He hounded him out of town. When the fellow got a transfer to the other end of the country, he got after him there [and] got him out of that district. For years he ran that man from district to district, like a pack of hounds running a fox from covert to covert. In the end he had to leave the Force [and] hide his head in Dublin or some English city. All the country watched the hunt. I can tell you, Fr. Ned, no gentleman tried to tamper with the girls of our parish while Fr. O'Brien was there to protect them."

The parish priest sighed heavily.

"Those were great days, James, great days when a priest had such power, but I'm afraid they're gone . . . forever."

"You mean that—"

Fr. Ned put up his hand.

"Pat Culkin isn't a policeman. There's the law of libel. Pat Culkin wouldn't hesitate to take an action against you for defamation, and what defense would you have? What proof have you except Mickle John's word [and] the word of his daughter? All the countryside knows what she is."

Fr. James got up [and] stood looking down fiercely at the grey head bowed over the hearth. When he spoke, his voice was quivering with indignation.

"Do you mean to tell me, Fr. Ned, that I am to let this parish be fouled with lust for fear of an action of defamation, [or] let girl after girl be ruined by that drunken hound because his father is Pat Culkin, the shebeen man, the gombeen man who has made slaves of our congregation?"

Fr. Ned didn't look up at him. The personal ferocity in his voice was raising an instinctive fear in him.

"It's not only Maggie Mickle John that's getting him," he thought. "He wants to strike back at Culkin for all he's been doing to Nan. Poor fellow—poor James. Does he think he can make up for his own sin by this sort of cleaning up?"

He shook his head over his thoughts [and] thrust them back. He might well be wronging James, but his instinct had rarely failed him. It was that instinctive feeling that had so often guided him to motives underlying the actions of a penitent—motives of which the penitent was not often conscious.

"I agree something has to be done, James," he said softly. "All I meant is that it won't do to rush into Pat Culkin's net. He's raging about Tony's loss of the dispensary. Now, on account of Nan marrying Ederney, his rage is transferred to us. To be fair to the man, it's quite intelligible that he couldn't make head or tail of our letting Nan marry an atheist who doesn't conceal his opinions. What else could a man like Culkin think but that we did it from the lowest motives, the only sort he understands? And I'm afraid the sequel isn't any great proof that we were right. Have you seen any progress, even the slightest progress in Ederney's attitude toward religion? I haven't."

Fr. James frowned blackly.

"One can't expect immediate results. With Nan beside him day and night—"

He paused.

"Day and *night*," he repeated with a savage satisfaction.

Fr. Ned caught the emphasis on the word "night."

"What agonies the unfortunate fellow is suffering," he thought. "Yes, he's suffering agonies and using them as a scourge for his sin."

James's voice was beating on his ears like a savage drum. Let the Culkins do their worst, take and win their action for defamation. He would gladly face it for the love of God, the protection of God's poor against the ruffians of the world. Money he had none to pay, but he could pay by his sufferings, jail, disgrace—whatever God willed. What he would not do would be to deny God [and] his duty to the poor and the weak who could not protect themselves.

"I tell you frankly, Fr. Ned, if you refuse me permission to denounce that man from the altar, I will denounce him in every house in the parish [and at] every crossroads. You cannot prevent me from speaking the truth in the highways and by-ways. Then let Mr. Pat Culkin place me in the dock. It will not be the first time the servants of God were sent to the court and the prisons for proclaiming that God's laws are higher than any mere human suffering."

Fr. Ned got up, selected a pipe from the bundle on the mantelpiece, tapped it against the fender and began to fill it in a leisurely way.

"I don't think you need to trouble yourself about thoughts of prison, James," he said casually. "Unless the libel is a criminal one, prison doesn't come into the picture. There would only be a question of damages and you've no goods to claim on. Besides, I expect that the plea that you were acting in the course of your priestly duties would be sufficient defence. Put thoughts of martyrdom out of your head."

Fr. James's face darkened.

"I hope I haven't been thinking of myself as a martyr," he said in a hurt voice.

The parish priest shook his head emphatically.

"I have no doubt you haven't, James. It would be others, I imagine, who would have to bear the martyrdom. Culkin's lawyers would take the opportunity to wash all the dirty line of this parish in a public court, drag down Nan's marriage to Ederney—"

Fr. James flung up his head.

"What has that got to do with it?"

The parish priest nodded.

"Nothing, absolutely nothing, but the lawyers' game would be to foul us [and] show that you and I cared little for Christianity when it was a question of getting Nan married. They'd work it in in some way, you may be sure, foul Nan and Ederney, our cloth— everything—in their attempt to show that your action in attacking young Culkin was personal malice, revenge for the boycott of Ederney [and] the accusations his father has been making against us to the Bishop."

"I don't see how they could possibly drag Nan into it."

James's voice was fiercely rebellious.

"They mightn't, but you know what Culkin is. What better platform than a libel action could he have to vent his charges against us? Even if he lost, it would be well worth his while to foul us in the face of the world, and he mightn't lose."

The young priest began to pace up and down the room.

"What are you asking me, Fr. Ned?" he cried.

"I'm not asking anything."

The parish priest's voice was suddenly sharp and stern.

"It is my duty to put all the facts before you as I see them. Having done that, my position is clear. I will not forbid your denouncing Culkin from the altar, but I will not repeat your denunciations at the late Mass. I haven't sufficient evidence of Culkin's being the father to take such an extreme step against one of my parishioners. What's more, Pat Culkin has a story about you and Nan that he'd have no scruple in using."

James Clogher's face went white. His staring horrified eyes made the parish priest feel like a murderer.

Then James was on his knees before him, his shoulders shaking convulsively.

"The story is true, Fr. Ned, true, true. Yes, Fr. Ned, I have sinned," he cried. "Grievously I have sinned. Since that moment, I have prayed and worked—"

Fr. Ned waved the tragedy aside.

"Don't make too much of it, James. I didn't intend to bother you about it. You can judge from that how little I think it matters. I wish you or Nan had told me before Pat Culkin mentioned it. He wouldn't have caught me off my balance, but that's neither here nor there. I've questioned Nan about it since, and it's clear that if there's blame anywhere, which I doubt, it doesn't lie with you. She threw her arms around your neck as if you were her brother. You couldn't help consoling her. You were taken unawares, but you did no more than if she were your sister. I assure you that anyone might have done it, but it isn't everyone who would have done what you did immediately, not even every priest. You've never been near Nan since, she tells me—"

The curate made a gesture of despair.

"I've never been anywhere else but near her, Fr. Ned. God forgive me. In my sickcalls on the mountain, in the darkness, in the confession box, even at the Holy Sacrifice on the altar, she has been with me. Oh God, forgive me."

The parish priest put his hand on [James's] shoulder.

"A man can't help these storms, James. Every man gets them. There's only one way to meet them—prayer and the avoidance of the place of temptation. I know you have prayed. I have seen your face turned toward God in the agony of repentance, I knew you were lacerating yourself for some imaginary sin. Several times I was on the point of speaking to you, telling you there has been no sin. There was not the slightest premeditation. You were simply overwhelmed for a moment by Nan's misery. There was no intention, no dwelling on the satisfaction—"

The curate cut him off with a cry.

"Again and again those moments come to me [and] with them an ecstasy such as I should only feel for God."

Fr. Ned pressed the young man's shoulder.

"What mountains you make out of molehills, James. Your one weakness is passionate exaggeration. How can a man prevent thoughts from entering his mind? As long as he refuses to entertain them, as you've refused—however, there's no sense in talking about all that. There's only one thing to be done now—to leave the scene of temptation. I'll talk to his Lordship about it. He will arrange for a transfer. Meanwhile, I would suggest that you go into retreat. There's one being conducted for young priests in Roymore. It begins next week."

Fr. James stiffened.

"Then I am not to be allowed to do my duty about Maggie Mickle John."

"If I were your confessor, James, I'm afraid I should have to warn you that pride is your besetting sin, not a hunger for the sins or loves of the flesh."

The curate wilted.

"You are right, Fr. Ned. It was for that sin of pride that God hurled me down from the pedestal. It was the same sinful pride that made me question his Lordship's views when he wished me to become a professor in the Diocesan College. I wanted to be a martyr, a servant of the poor [and] the miserable. Now you find me being righteous again, denouncing the lusts of others—what right has a man like me to denounce the lusts of others?"

Fr. Ned smiled as a father might smile at a willful son.

"And your exaggeration of your sins, James—don't you think that might be part of the same pride, making a great sinner of yourself, you that hardly ever committed a sin in your life, barring the excess of your love for God and your terror that you might have offended Him by your [zealousness], and, if you like to put it that way your pride in virtue and piety and goodness? Now, there's a good man. I'll see about the transfer. You will go to the retreat in Roymore. When that has healed your mind, your work in your new place will fill it."

Fr. James did not turn back to wave at him as he always did when he shut the garden gate. The parish priest watched the crouched back [and] the drooping head till they were out of sight. The mask of courage and knowledge that had concealed his own fears was gone from his face. It had fallen in [and] become the face of an old man.

"How badly he has taken it," he muttered. "The unfortunate fellow can't bear the thought of being separated from her. That's what his 'making an Act' has come to."

In the sitting room he fumbled for his rosary beads [and] sank wearily into the chair fingering the beads.

He had accused James of foolish pride. It was he, not James, who was guilty of that contemptible sin, the vainglory of the worm exulting in its own goodness.

He had accepted Fr. Carmody's flattery—the belief that God has chosen him amongst all the priests of Ireland to save Philip Ederney. He had sold Nan for that hope [and] risked her happiness for his own vainglory. Now James had got caught in the net.

He crushed the rosary beads in his fingers.

"Oh Mary, Mother of God, Mother of suffering," he cried. "Mary, Mother of the Crucified, will you not come to our aid? Without you, we are lost."

He threw himself on his knees and began the Sorrowful Mysteries.

Chapter XXIV

THE TWENTY-THREE CABINS OF LOCHNAMARA HAD TURNED THEIR backs to the sea, barred and bagged the doors that looked out on its white-topped mass of water. Yesterday the village had faced the west. Today, with a protective about-turn, it had reversed its street to face the mountain. Back doors had become front doors, facing dirty back yards littered with dung-heaps. The older children, playing in the spaces between the cabins, were pleased with the change and with the opportunity the dung-heaps provided of playing "King of the Castle." . . . On this side they felt the snugness of the leeward of a boat running before the storm.

Between them and the outer tumult, the thatched roofs of the cabins, moored with lumps of stone and short straw ropes, rocked and shivered. Round [the cabins] the pigs put up long snouts and grunted in angry protest when a rush of children disturbed them in their rootings. As blast after blast swept between the gables, hens cackled wildly and ran on long legs to the shelter of the kitchens, to

be driven out again by the women whose hands were already full
enough with the squalling children.

From time to time the spray from a wave greater than the others
struck the more westerly doors with a thud that made the dogs
whine and creep closer to the turf fires, but the street was filled
with people moving in one direction—toward the most exposed
cabin of all, the gable house of the village. They were not hurrying.
Their sense of decorum did not permit that, but they were moving
as quickly as decency allowed. Even the men who had been "holding up the gables," were joining the throng, for word had flown that
Bid Faherty, the fighting woman of the village, and the new curate,
Fr. Roche, were in each others wool.`

"If it's what you're after tellin' me, Father, that I must die for
fear Patch'll commit mortial sins with others, thin I'm tellin' him
an' you he can go shtraight to hell."

The words came in a screech to meet the astonished ears of the
newcomers. Never before had they heard such words flung in the
face of a priest, but Bid's tongue was the limit if she was provoked.

"Aye, rowl in the dunghape of mortial sin with the divils in hell,
wan afther th'other, till his belly burshts, that's what Pat Flaherty
can do, if he wants it, down in the pit o' hell, but my life he won't
take for his shport; becripes he won't, your holy Riverince, not even
with your Rivirence's blessing, not if I've to brain the bloody divil
with the tongs to keep him off."

The curate, a square butt of a man with a rough weatherbeaten
face, came backing out of the door into the crowd, Bid's voice in
pursuit. She appeared in the doorway, her hands on her hips.

"To talk to a dacent married woman like that!" she cried, "a dacent married woman that niver let a foul word or an indacent hy-
perbole be shpoke in her presence!"

The priest backed still further into the crowd. Over the roof a
sweep of spray sent a shower of brine over him and the group
around him, drenching them, but they hardly noticed it.

Over the howling of the wind, Bid's voice trumpeted.

"If you lit him at you agin, sez the docthor, 'tisn't but the coffin.
An' now, the preesht of God comes along and sez I'm to prepare for
the coffin, thinkin' in his granjur he's the cock o' the walk an' me
wan o' the hill-billies he can give his ordhers to, tellin' me whether
I'm to live or die. Well, me answer is plain and shtraight. Three
years I shpent in London in the middle o' the black Proteshtans,
an' in all thim years, I didn't hear as much indacency as I've heard
in this house this blessed day, not in all thim years, an' today I'm
tellin' Patch Faherty and thim that's behind him and forgets I'm a

dacent married woman, that the day he thries his murther on me'll be the last day he'll iver thry to force any humum beam to do anythin' on this earth, whativer he may do in the pit o'hell afther I'm finished with him—"

Her fists went up so close to the priest's nose that he stepped back hurriedly. Her husband, a thin gaunt man, threw himself between them. The priest's face was flaming.

"So we have a London rip,˙ a Piccadilly girl to deal with, as well as an atheist doctor," he said grimly.

For the moment she stared at him as if she could hardly believe her ears. The next moment she had flung her husband aside and was on the priest, her nails tearing his face.

"A Piccadilly gerrel!" she screamed, "you blaggard! you lyin' defamin' scoundrel! I'll have the law on you if I had to folly you to hell to get it!"

The priest flung her off. Her husband sprang at her. The neighbours had her by the shoulders [and] arms [and] were dragging her back.

"A shtreet gerrel!" she screamed, struggling to be free. "A shtreet gerrel, that's what he's afther callin' me, the blashted liar! A shtreet gerrel! Me, a dacent married woman with her nine childher rared in lawful marriage."

The crowd were between her and the priest. Women were running for cloths to wipe the blood off his face where she had scored it. It was livid now and the pale glare of the skin was showing angry red furrows.

The woman went silent, staring at the blood dripping from the priest's cheeks. Except for the thunder of the breakers and the bellowing of the wind, there was silence in the street. The priest stood bewildered while the women wiped the blood off his face. He let them do it passively, sharply conscious of the reek of flannel clothes and the turf smoke that seemed to be part of them.

He had come from the eastern part of the diocese, civilised parishes where faces were not turbulent and barbaric like these. Never, in all the eleven years of his mission, had such an outrage been committed against him. That it could happen had been beyond his experience. Why it had happened now he could not understand. He must have made a bad mistake, but how? The faces of these people were condemning him, not the woman. He had a feeling of being surrounded by wild animals with instincts and values so different from his own that at any moment they might throw themselves on him. He knew that the feeling was absurd. They were not wild beasts, but good practising Catholic people. No Catholic crowd would attack a priest. Yet, though he had acted rightly, they certainly felt he had wronged the woman. The swift savagery of her action had showed that she also felt she had been wronged. Her outrageous attack on him was the instinctive reaction of a good woman.

He looked round at the ring of faces. They were waiting for him to speak, their eyes filled with expectation mixed with exultation, hostility [and] fear.

He wanted to speak, but no words would come. The wild faces, the acrid smells, the thunder of the sea, the reek of fish and seaweed were confusing him; yet, he must speak, [he] must say something.

"My friends, I have come to the conclusion that I have done wrong, grievous wrong in suggesting that Mrs. Faherty was other than a pure woman. I beg her forgiveness and yours for the bad example I have given."

The faces changed; heads nodded in agreement. Bid Faherty stared at him [and] looked round in triumph at the faces. In those faces she saw the triumph was his, not hers. He had done the right thing.

For a moment she was nonplussed, then she fell on her knees [and] began to beat her breasts wildly.

"God in Heaven, forgive me! God an' His Holy Mother look down in pity on me this day," she cried, "for what I done, layin' me vilent hands on the face of a holy preesht o'God—"

A thud of heavy waves struck the sea door, sending a stream of water through the sacks with which it was stuffed.

She sprang up from her knees, ran into the house [and] began to push the sacks back into their places. Other women ran after her, caught up bags [and] began to mop the floor. . . . Their hunger for a dramatic scene had been fulfilled. Bid's denunciation of Patch and the new priest, the priest's scandalous accusation, Bid's terrible action, the priest's acceptance of his own wrongdoing, Bid's grand repentance—it was as good as a Mass or a Benediction, barring the smell of the incense and the tinkling of the bells.

The men, disdaining household chores, gathered round the priest. He wasn't much to look at or even to pass the time of day with, like poor Fr. James, the craythur, but he wasn't as ignorant and thick as they [had] thought, not all out. If he was, he wouldn't have done the right thing in the end. Bid Faherty's nails had learnt him manners, though 'twas an awful thing to do to a priest. Now 'twas up to them to show him how mannerly and decent they could be and how respectful to a priest of God once he knew his place.

They began to talk soothingly in their soft western voices blaming
Bid and thanking God for her repentance, for the priest's saintliness, for everything.

The curate, watching the line of yellow teeth under the scraggy
beards, was sharply conscious of the insincerity behind their words.
Their thoughts were that he had acted like a boor. The wild turbu-
lence behind the bog-stained faces, the fear and hostility in their
eyes were accusing him. It was a new experience for him to feel
accused [and] uncertain in a crowd of Irish Catholic people. He
could not grasp it, yet there was no doubt that behind the soothing
words there was distrust [and] disapprobation.

Through the door he could see the knot of women gathered
round Bid Faherty. What were they thinking [and] saying to one
another?

Some of them had thrown their red petticoats over their heads
as if they were cutting him and the men off from the sight of their
faces. There was rebellion there, a primitive ferocity that he had
never experienced before in Irish women.

The priest sighed. He had envisaged a very different congregation when he heard he was being transferred to Lochnamara. Although the curacy was a bad one, he knew that the transfer had
been an honour. The situation in the parish had become so bad
that his Lordship had found it advisable to pick a strong man and
an experienced one.

His eyes came back to the ring of men's faces. The wild, watchful
eyes were measuring [and] judging him. He would have to deal
firmly, drastically, with the situation, yet he felt himself unable to
handle this people or their women-folk. The one person he felt he
could deal with was the doctor, a man, who, for all the gulf between
them, was at the same stage of humanity as himself.

Against him he could act and it was clear that he would have to
act drastically and quickly before more harm was done.

"It isn't Mrs. Faherty who's to blame for this, but those who are
behind her," he said authoritatively. "It is with them I must deal.
God be with you, my friends. God guard and protect you."

As he walked away in dignified slowness, Pat Mickle John looked
after him meditatively.

" 'Tis how he tuk it dacenter than any wan'ud expec an' him so
thick an' ignorant in other ways," he said softly.

Jimmy Gill scratched his head [and] launched a large spit into
the dung-pond in front of the door.

"Mebbe 'twas dacency," in a sort or an aside, "an' mebbe agin, it
wasn't."

Pat Mickle John eyed him.

"An' what wud it be, if it wasn't the dacency, me wise man?" he asked with a malignant look.

The pretenses of Jimmy Gill to be the knowing man of the townland were sickening.

"Mebbe 'twould be Bid's scratchin' nails and th' edge o' her foul tongue. How'd any wan know what that rip o' the divil'd be up to nexsht, if he kept on at her?"

The others watched them in silence. The old quarrel between these two was one of the standing entertainments of the village, always sure to draw out something worth hearing.

Pat Mickle John's nose wrinkled in disgust.

"So 'tis how you be difindin' her is it, sayin' mebbe she did the right thing?" he asked scornfully.

"Me difindin' her! Me! Rip o' the divil I said."

He turned indignantly to the group.

"Ye heard me—rip o' the divil—'twas that, I said, wasn't it?"

Pat Mickle John looked contemptuously at him.

"Yah, 'twas that you said, but 'twasn't that was behind yer words, not that at all, but satisfacshun that the preesht o' God got a durty blow. 'Tis a bad day for Lochnamara, a bad unlucky day whin the likes o' that cud happen in a house in it, an' a man to be found in this townland who'd be exultin' over it. There's no sort o' luck cud come o' conduc' like that, nothin' but misfortune an' bad luck an' disgrace, no matther hoe ignorant an' unmannerly the preesht shown himsel'."

An old man with a yellow weather-beaten face and mild blue eyes came between them.

"Let ye be quiet with wan another now, dacent and neighborly like the good God wants Christian min to be," he said softly.

Red and grey beards stained with tobacco juice wagged in agreement. The sage of the village had spoken.

The old man turned to Bid Faherty. His large blue eyes, like the eyes of an animal, contemplated her mildly.

"Childher is God's offspring. There isn't a chile but is made by God Himsell in His own image an' likeness," he said. "Whin you're refusin' Patch, 'tis God Himsell you're refusin. D'ye iver think o' that, Bid?"

She made no answer. The faces round her were so full of respect for the old man's words that she thought it wise to hold back the answer that was on her lips. Owney Foran was the saint of the village who could not be gainsaid.

"There wor things you said while the preesht wor here," he went

on, "things I didn't want to dhraw down in his prisince. Whin a
stranger is there, wan doesn't foul wan's own, but now that there's
nobody here but oursel' 'twill have to be said. 'Tis blashphemy you
wor committin' in your talk, Bid Faherty, blashphemy agin God an'
the Holy Ghosht. 'Tis a bad day for Lochnamara, a bad day an' an
eevil wan, whin a dacent woman cud get her tongue to say the
things you wor sayin' this day, God in His holy pity an' mercy, forgive you."

Round him the stained beards were wagging in agreement with
his words. Behind the men, the women were nodding their heads.
Now that the scene was over they were guiltily conscious of their
sinful enjoyment of it.

Owney went to the door [and] looked out into the storm.

"I'll be goin' now, Patch," he said, "but tonight I'll be sayin' the
Rosary for pace in this house, pace an' the grace an' the mercy iv
our Divine Lor' an' His Blessed Mother, our Glorious Virgin. There
isn't on the whole wide earth any power like the power o' prayer an'
what I'm askin' ye now is for ye all to sind up yer voices with me to
the Maker iv all things to reshtore to this house the pace and holi-
ness an' happiness God intinded to be in it an' in ivry Christian
house in the parish of Lochnamara and the seven villages o' the
Black Shore an' beyant."

For a minute or so he stood at the door without moving, as if he
was listening to the thudding of waves. Then he turned slowly [and]
came back to the cabin.

"There's another thing that wants to be said an' 'tis how for a
while back now I been thinkin' o' sayin' it, for 'tis a thing that wants
badly to be said. The docthor, forgive him, has been a cause o'
throuble in this parish. A quare, conthrairy man he is in many a
way, quare an' conthrairy, God help him an' a grate sinner, God in
his mercy, forgive him; but there's wan thing that has to be rimimbered for him, rimimbered and niver forgotten be thim he helped
an' saved an' dhrew out o' the jaws o' death an' that thing is the
way he give himsell up to save the min an' wimmin an' childher o'
this parish, whin they wor in their sorest need. Night an' day he
tiled in thim eevil days o' the faver to bring health an' halin' to the
people o' the Black Shore. Many a man an' woman an' chile he
dhrew back out o' the mouth of death an' the thing that has to be
said about him an' us now is this—'tis poorly we're rewardin' him
for the pasht few weeks, for all he's done for us, peltin' an' nick-
namin' an' boycottin' him at the behesh o' some that aren't fit, as
the Holy word says, to loosen the latch in his boots."

He stopped [and] looked around at the faces full of fear. He struck his stick on the floor.

"What I've said, I've said, an' I'm not takin' it back," he went on in a loud voice. " 'Tis God's charity is the wan guide that ought to be ladin' us, God's charity and the prayers that cums from it, not the words o' thim that has niver brought anythin' but the worsht o' bad luck to the people o' Lochnamara from the day they cum back to it, to its sorrow, up to this day o' days."[37]

Chapter XXV

FR. NED, LOOKING ACROSS AT THE NAIL-MARKS ON THE FACE OF THE NEW curate, thought, not for the first time, that the Bishop had not shown his usual knowledge of human nature—in this case, suiting the man to the temper of the parish. Even if his Lordship had felt that the parish priest was falling down on the job and needed a bit of stiffening, this insensitive man was not the sort he ought to have picked for a parish of the touchiest people in the diocese.

The P.P. groaned inwardly. That was the worst of choosing as bishops whose lives had been spent in teaching or diocesan secretarial work. It was quite likely that his Lordship thought that, because these people of the Black Shore were miserably poor, they were dull and insensitive, whereas there wasn't a district in the diocese where a priest had to be more careful of his step than in the Seven Parishes.

The P.P. watched the angry red scorings rise and fall as the curate worked through the bacon and cabbage and the roast mutton. If the man were even capable of learning the lesson of those nail-marks it might have been a good thing that the attack had been made on him; but he had no doubt now that Tim Roche wasn't the sort to whom experience taught anything.

At first, when the curate had come to him in confusion and obvious dismay, he had high hopes that the lesson had not been wasted. Now he had no longer any such hopes. Second thoughts in the curate's head had been foolish thoughts. Angry resentment had replaced the dismay. The man was determined to get back "face." It was the defiant swagger of his walk, the set of his shoulders, the exaggerated confidence of his voice [and] gestures.

From the day he came, he had been acting the strong man sent to clean up the mess left by the weak P.P. and his complacent curate, but the acting had not been too crudely intrusive. Since the disaster in Patch Faherty's cabin it had become aggressive. Today he was certainly going to raise the whole question of Ederney and Nan. The P.P. could see it in every move of his, and the worst of it was that there was no defense to offer. He himself and Fr. James had laid themselves open to attack [and] to censure if the Bishop had not been too considerate and gentle to express his open displeasure.

The curate raised his head from its concentration on the bacon and cabbage. The "old man" certainly knew everything there was to be known about the good things in life as far as a priest's life permitted. His whiskey was the best, his bacon and cabbage as good as his whiskey, and that was saying something. If he did let things slide, that only made him a grand parish priest for a curate who knew his own mind.

To be sure, he let the outside of the chapel run down a bit while he dolled up the inside with pictures and statues that cost more than would have put a grand face on the outside; but, after all, it was his own little bit of money that went on these folderols. He never asked a penny from the parish for them, not even saddled it with a debt, though it was the sign of a good energetic P.P. to leave debts behind him for the church and the schools when he moved on to heaven or a better parish.

Harmless, harmless, for all his negligence, except for that one black spot, his tolerance of an atheist doctor, a man who ought never to have been allowed to set foot in the parish. Well, that blot would soon be removed. With God's holy help he himself would soon have the parish cleaned up from that plague spot, even if he had to ride roughshod over Fr. Ned's love for his erring niece.

He pushed his plate away.

"That's as nice a bit o' bacon as I've ever tasted, Fr. Ned," he said, "an' as for your mountain mutton, it takes the biscuit."

He wiped his mouth with his napkin.

The parish priest got up and selected a pipe from the pile on the mantelpiece, put it back again, came to the table and sat down.

"There's an apple tart," he said.

The curate waved his hand.

"To tell you the truth, Fr. Ned," he said, "I wouldn't have the room, but go on yourself."

Fr. Ned shook his head.

"I'm off food a bit lately," he said.

The young man looked at the parish priest's plate.

"You are that," he said. " 'Tisn't much you gave yourself and it's still less you took."

He shook his head.

"If I was you, Fr. Ned, I'd take more exercise. If we could only get a golf course laid out for tourists, it would help the place no end [and] get us out of the house, too. Nothing like a golf course for getting a man out of doors. I must see if the Tourist Board mightn't be able to give a little help to start one."

"Aye, I'm afraid I'm neglecting my exercise," the other murmured.

"Will he ever come to it?" he thought.

"A glass of punch, Fr. Tim?" he said.

The curate nodded jovially.

"Always room for that, Fr. Ned," he chuckled.

Kate came in with the tart.

"I think we'll postpone it, Kate," the parish priest said. "Your bacon and roast mutton has tempted us too much, but we'd be glad for a glass of punch if you'd bring the kettle."

Kate took her tart away with a stony face [and] brought in the kettle.

"To think that poor Fr. James had to go to make place for this new fellow. Not much of a family he ever came from you could see by the way he sat and talked, puffing himself up with the noise of his own blather," she erupted to Babs who helped in the kitchen.

"Aye faith, Mrs. Conner. 'Tis a durty loud voice he have surely and him always blamin' an' attackin' the people," she agreed.

The curate, unconscious of their disapproval, was stirring the sugar round and round in his glass. It wasn't so easy for a curate to open up a thing like this with the parish priest. When the P.P. was such a decent, friendly sort of man, as kind and decent as they make them, if a bit feeble. Still, God's holy will was more sacred than the feelings of even the decentest parish priest.

"There's a thing on my mind, Fr. Ned, and when there's a thing on your mind, it's better get it off without carrying it round with you."

The parish priest nodded.

"Nothing like it, Fr. Tim," he said encouragingly. "Never let a thing lie festering in your mind. It isn't true that I agree with all this new psychiatry stuff, but there's something in it."

The curate watched him triumphantly. So, the thing had been

gnawing at the P.P.'s mind. All that sludge about his having welcomed Ederney in order to save the doctor's soul was running off by now [and] leaving a bad smell behind it.

The parish priest was making figures on the cloth with his fingers—very nervous, he was, poor man.

"Yes, Fr. Tim," he said without lifting his head.

The curate took a sip of the punch.

"It's about the doctor, Fr. Ned. I was telling you about Bid Faherty and indeed I'm ashamed of myself the way I let my temper get the better of me there for a minute or two—"

"Ah well, I'm afraid Bid's a bit of a rip, all right," Fr. Ned murmured.

"Still and all, Fr. Ned, I must acknowledge she made amends for it, went down on her knees before them all—"

Fr. Ned stared at the table. He could see Bid putting on her act, all the fine gestures of indignation and repentance. What born actors they were, those people of his, God bless them, and what a consolation it was to them, this power of dramatising their misery with all that repertory of splendid attitudes and situations.

"Ah, they're a grand people at heart," he murmured.

"They are that, Fr. Ned. It was most edifying, I must say, the good example she gave before the eyes of the people."

He paused. There was something in the parish priest's attitude that was giving him a feeling of uneasiness. He hadn't noticed it at first. It was coming very softly, sliding towards him in that queer way things came to him from this P.P.

It was very important that he should convince the P.P., make him see that he had been justified by the reactions of the people to what he had done; but, for all the old man's quietness, he felt he was making no headway.

A queer old fish the P.P. was, queer and disturbing with something, in fact, that reminded him of the attitudes of the people themselves.

"He's been here too long," he thought, "too long altogether. He's got to be one of them, not wild and savage, of course—he's the opposite of that—but queer in himself like a person who hasn't been meeting proper human beings for years. I'll have to watch my step with him."

His eyes went round the room [and] came back to the parish priest's face.

"Have you any hope left at all, Fr. Ned, that Ederney might come back to the Faith?"

The parish priest shook his head.

"None. Fr. Darmody, who recommended him, thought the same. I let Nan marry him in the hope that she'd work it. I know how she's praying and praying, the first at the chapel every morning, a daily communicant, storming the stronghold of Heaven with prayer, as she says herself, but I must confess that I can't see that she's making the slightest progress in bringing the doctor back to the Faith. I'm glad you've raised the matter, Fr. Tim. It's the sort of thing that ought to be discussed between the priests of a parish."

The curate's face brightened.

"Your delay does you credit, Fr. Ned. I can see what you were up against. You didn't want to risk her eternal salvation, an' no wonder. If we drive the doctor out, he'll take her with him. Back to England—that's where he'll bring her—into that cesspool of sin and unbelief—"

He got up and leaned his elbow on the mantelpiece.

"It's no wonder you waited and waited, hopin' God would intervene."

The parish priest looked up at him.

"I'm afraid I can't even claim the merit you're so kind as to allow me, Fr. Tim," he said coldly. "Dr. Ederney won't leave here, and there's no way you can get him out. There's no charge the Local Government Department could listen to. He's the best doctor in this country, perhaps, the province. He lives for his job. The Government couldn't touch him even if they wanted to cooperate with us."

The curate smiled grimly.

"I don't think we need trouble them," he said. "If we make up our minds that he must go for the sake of the parish, go he will. I think I can guarantee you that. A man of his station who refuses to go to Mass, to go to his duties, a man who is openly perverting the minds of the people isn't merely a bad Catholic. He's a bad doctor, a menace to the community, a far greater menace for instance than a boozer like that unfortunate young Culkin who sins through negligence [and] overindulgence, but whose faith is sound. I feel certain that with a little judicious pressure, we can get the Board of Health to see eye to eye with us on that. If they don't, I'll guarantee the priests of the country will make it clear to them that it will be a bad day for recalcitrants when the next local elections come round. Yes, I think we can make the County Board of Health sit up and take notice."

The parish priest's face was noncommittal. To the curate it seemed almost disapproving.

"Pat Culkin has been hounding Ederney down. Pat's name

doesn't smell too well here, or indeed in any part of the diocese. I'm not sure that his Lordship would like the idea of anything that looked like cooperation between us and him."

The curate looked his superior squarely in the eyes.

"So, he thinks he'll be able to block me," he thought, "draggin in the Bishop's dislike of Pat Culkin."

"I can't see what his Lordship would think except that, in a crisis of this sort, we couldn't afford to leave any weapon unused. Pat Culkin is certainly not the ally I'd choose if we had the choosing, but this time it happened he's on the right side of the angels, you might say. His Lordship could hardly expect us to fall down on the job merely to avoid being on the same side as Pat Culkin."

The parish priest toyed with the salt cellar, but made no answer.

The curate's face softened. The old man was being hard hit, but he'd have to agree in the end. In spite of his wishy-washiness, he was honest and pious, as good as they make them.

"If we could only avoid it, there's nobody it would make happier than myself," he said.

He took a sip of punch.

"Great stuff, that, Fr. Ned. Wherever you get that whiskey, I don't think there's anything equal to it in the diocese."

He waited for a little, but the parish priest still said nothing.

"It's those boys and girls going and coming to and fro from England who are troubling me," the curate began, "working amongst a pagan people, losing their faith there, then coming back to find the same thing started here at home, right in their midst by an educated man they look up to, and with our connivance as you might say, if we let the thing go on any longer. It's that is the real danger."

The parish priest sighed heavily. He had been given powers from God, the greatest and most sacred powers a man could receive— the power to turn the wafer into the flesh and blood of God, the power to bind and unloose. Had he misused them, been deflected from using them by his love for Nan? Was he making obstacles now in the path of a man who wanted only to do his duty, because of that love and because he disliked that man? He had prayed night and day, but prayers demanded acts and he had funked* the acts that alone could have given meaning to the prayers.

His mind brooded heavily on his own default. For weeks [and] months he had known that Ederney was immovable in his unbelief. He had let him run on, hoping against all reason that Nan could bring him back to the fold. Now his Lordship, under the inspiration of the Holy Ghost, had sent this priest to put an end to all that, and he was secretly resenting it, judging his Lordship for his wisdom.

"I fear, Fr. Tim," he said at last, "that I have connived at disbelief, impiety [and] defiance of God. I am glad you have spoken so fearlessly. It cannot have been easy for you to do it, but the time for shilly-shally is past."

He got up [and] stood with his elbow on the mantelpiece staring down into the fire. He had no doubt now that he had defaulted in his duty [and] allowed himself to be deflected by his love of Nan from the path he should have followed.

The curate put out his hand, but [Fr. Ned] did not see it.

The curate caught his hand and squeezed it. In his triumph he felt like being generous. He had won more easily than he had hoped. What a bad conscience the poor P.P. must have been nursing.

"Fr. Ned, Fr. Ned," he cried. "I know how much it will cost you to do it. There's nothing I wouldn't do to save you the misery of having to do it. If you think that even now I might be any use going to the doctor and Mrs. Ederney, I'll go gladly, no matter how they receive me."

The parish priest shook his head.

"I don't think it would be the slightest use, Fr. Tim. Again and again I've tried to come closer to the man. He has always brushed me aside as if my touch were pollution. In the early days I know that Nan had high hopes. What hopes she can entertain now must be slight indeed. She still spends herself in prayer, but she has ceased to talk to me about her trouble—a bad sign. She does not want to depress me. That, I know, is the meaning of her silence."

"Still, they ought to get a formal warning," the curate said.

The parish priest shook his head.

"Perhaps. I could tell Nan, of course. As for any attempt to talk the matter over with him, I fear it would be worse than useless."

The curate smiled.

"One can never tell," he said, "with a man like him, repentance sometimes comes suddenly in a flash of light when the truth is revealed to him."

The parish priest groaned inwardly.

"Revelation from Tim Roche!" he thought, "and I used to rebuke poor James Clogher for the sin of spiritual pride—James, who had more brains and more sanctity in his little finger than this rhinoceros has under his whole thick hide."

"As for going to the Bishop with our trouble," the curate went on, "his Lordship certainly didn't send me here to come trotting back to him with every trouble that's bothering me. Often I've heard him say it's the sign of a courageous priest to handle his own stuff and, if you don't mind my saying so, I think it's up to you and me, Fr. Ned, to deal with the doctor off our own bats without worrying about either his Lordship's opinions or Pat Culkin's cooperation.

Chapter XXVI

IT WAS RAINING, A STEADY PITILESS RAIN THAT DRUMMED ON THE SODden thatch of the roofs in the little valley, drew steam from the heaps of seaweed on the Black Shore.

To Nan, standing at the window of the doctor's house, it brought back the memory of that other day of driving rain and miserable thoughts when James Clogher had come as an angel of healing. Now he was gone from her, lost to himself, they said.

A blast of wind came roaring up from the sea [and] shook the house as if it was going to tear from its foundations. On the water, the white waves were toppling madly into black gulfs.

Through the wind she could hear the steady roar of the sea, the thunder of the waves tumbling on the shore [and] the groaning of the stones dragged down by the receding water.

James Clogher was being dragged down by another sea, the dark invisible sea of his incompatible loves—for God, for her—while she, who could heal him, had to remain here.

She sighed heavily.

If it were any other time, she could leave Philip for a while, but not now when this storm was about to break.

A favourite phrase of her husband's came back to her.

"The secret of the cure of the patient is the caring for the patient."

Strange words from the lips of Philip who never had seen a human being complete and entire in his life. But the words were true. What doctor could heal James as she could, if only they would let her come to him?

The latch of the gate clicked. The new curate was scudding before a fierce blast.

"What is this for?" Nan wondered. "It can't be his dues—they've

already been paid—and it's hardly a social visit. The storm Fr. Ned
has warned me of must be about to burst."

The door opened. Nellie stuck her head in.

"Fr. Roche, ma'am," she cried.

The priest's rugged face appeared behind her. Nan, shaking
hands, rested her eyes on the red [scratches]. Bid Faherty had certainly left her mark when she had got the chance.

The priest laughed.

"They all look at it, Mrs. Ederney. The story's all over the place,
so I expect you know how I got it."

She nodded.

"Bid has the name of being a very wild bird, even now when she
has the burden of nine children; but come down to the fire, Father.
You'll have a glass of something."

"Thanks, Mrs. Ederney. It's a day when surely one feels the need
of a bit of comfort in a place like this. What I can't understand is
how you're letting your doctor hang on here when he could have
the pick of some of the best jobs in England."

Nan handed him the glass, placed the decanter and the soda-
water on a low table beside him, took the other armchair and
watched him sip his whiskey.

"So it's that he's come to talk about," she thought. "The storm is
going to break."

The curate held up the glass.

"It's like me to have forgotten to say, 'Here's how,' Mrs. Ederney.
Already Fr. Ned has told me twenty times I was never born to be a
diplomat, but here's how, at last. Better late than never. All the
best, Mrs. Ederney, and a quick departure from this miserable hole
for you and the doctor."

Nan shook her head.

"Thanks for the wish, Father, but I'm afraid it has little chance
of being realised. My husband came here deliberately because it
was so badly stricken with disease and misery. His idea was that if
he could make it a model dispensary district, the example might set
others to do similar work. In his own way he's full of the missionary
spirit."

The curate's face set grimly.

"An excellent thing, Mrs. Ederney, a most excellent thing if he
had the wisdom to confine his missionary zeal to his own field. He'd
have us all behind him if only he would, even now, agree to do
that."

Nan got up.

"I'm afraid there's not much use talking about these matters to me, Fr. Tim. My husband is cooking up some germs in an oven in his own room. Hadn't I better call him?"

The priest put up his hand.

"You know what it will come to if he forces us to act, Mrs. Ederney?"

She nodded.

"Fr. Ned warned me already. You feel you'll have to preach against him, get the district to avoid contact with him, ostracise him, as far as they can afford to ostracise their dispensary doctor."

The priest looked relieved.

"I'm very glad, very glad indeed, Fr. Ned has explained it all to you. As a pious Catholic you will realise that we have no alternative if you cannot get the doctor to leave for some place where his great gifts will not be marred by the still greater harm he's doing here. Some English dispensary district, or, better still, some university post in England or Scotland, for instance, would be the ideal place for a man of his attainments."

Nan shook her head.

"There's no chance whatever of my being able to move him."

"But you must know he'll be beaten in the end, that the only result will be a public scandal followed by a dismissal."

Nan got up.

"That won't deter my husband. He is one of those people you can't frighten. He may indeed welcome a public show-down. There's no use in your talking to me about it, Father. He and I never discuss these things. It's part of the compact we made when I accepted him. He has kept his side of the bargain and I must keep mine."

The priest looked bewildered.

"But Fr. Ned has been hoping that you would be the means of converting him."

Nan gave a bitter laugh.

"I had that foolish notion too," she said. "It was a natural one, perhaps, but it was not through argument I hoped to convert him. I'm afraid my brain could not pit itself against his in discussion. What I did hope was that I might bring him gradually back to the fold through his love for me, get him to come to Mass, let the grace of God flow bit by bit into his soul. It was easy at first to hope that he could be weaned from his extraordinary idea of a world of emptiness [and meaninglessness], an accidental universe that came from nowhere [and] is going nowhere. All that is so incredible, so dreary and sad too, so miserable a faith that I could not believe he could not be saved from it. It was natural for us to hope that the beauty and promise of the Faith would take its place, by the grace of God, if only he could once be got to come to Mass."

The priest put his hand on her shoulder.

"Thank God, Mrs. Ederney, thanks be to God you're with us, heart and soul. You know, we hate having to take action against your husband. From everything I've heard, he's a grand nature—charitable [and] devoted to the poor and needy. Even now, if you could only get him to come back to us—"

Nan shook her head ruefully.

"Not the slightest hope, Father. Not the faintest chance either of his coming back to the faith or of his leaving here. Another thing I want you to understand also is that any boycott or attack on him will find me by his side, much as he and I differ about religion. However, I had better call him and let you hear his decision from himself."

She went to the door and called—

"Philip! Are you there, Philip?"

"Here, Nan, what is it?" came Ederney's voice.

"Fr. Roche is here and would be glad to have a chat with you."

"What the devil can *he* have to say to me?"

"He has important things to say and you better hear them."

"Oh all right—all right—I'm coming."

Nan came back to the fire [and] stood looking at the face of the priest.

"I need hardly warn you what his attitude will be, Father," she said. "He may even resent this call as an intrusion."

The priest's mouth set firmly.

"I'm prepared for that. What has to be done is long overdue. If he forces us to act, we will act. We must."

Nan hesitated.

"If I thought there was any use in my staying, I would stay, of course, but I'm afraid there's none."

"Thank you, Mrs. Ederney. On the whole I agree with you. If what you fear is true, things will have to be said that I would gladly spare you."

Philip Ederney came in [and] looked from one to the other. The priest got up. Nan nodded towards him.

"You haven't met Fr. Roche, I think, Philip."

The priest put out his hand. The doctor ignored it.

"No, I haven't had that honour," he said icily.

Nan made an unconscious grimace [and] left the room.

The two men stood facing each other. The priest, looking at the cold yet burning eyes of the doctor, found it difficult to say what he had come to say. The man's refusal of the ordinary courtesy of shaking hands gave him the feeling that he wasn't all there. He couldn't be anything else but mad to act like that, apart altogether from his insane craze to proselytise the parish of Lochnamara. If they could get him certified that would be the simplest way out, but unfortunately, insane eyes [and] insane beliefs were not grounds on which any mental specialist would certify insanity.

The doctor broke the silence.

"To what do I owe this honour, Mr. Roche?"

The priest drew a deep breath.

"To my foolish optimism, Dr. Ederney. I thought I might talk to a friend, a fellow Catholic who had strayed from the fold. I see now that I am in the presence of a madman, a pervert of such a lunatic type that friendly discussion, argument [or] persuasion would be out of place. I will therefore confine my message to a bare warning. Since you came to Lochnamara, the parish priest in his charity has given you the most extreme latitude in the hope that the grace of God might come to you in this intensely Catholic atmosphere. My predecessor was in complete agreement with his superior in that attitude. They both treated you with a kindness, a tolerance [and] a charity that would not have been extended to you, I believe, in any other parish in this diocese, not in any diocese. The only result has been that you have taken the fullest advantage of their tolerance to advertise your atheistic doctrines [and] give immoral instructions to the married women of this parish."

He paused, waiting for the doctor's reply, but the other merely nodded.

"Proceed, please," he said quietly.

"What I have to say is painful to me, still more painful to my superior for personal reasons. We do not deny your zeal and ability as a doctor. If deeper issues than the mere healing of bodies were not at stake, there is no one whom we would more gladly have in our midst. The spiritual issues have made that impossible. You have forced them into consideration. The souls of our people are of deeper importance even than their bodies. You have come here with the deliberate purpose of imperilling these. You have been given every chance. You have refused them all. Therefore, Dr. Ederney, I regret to have to tell you that we must lose your services."

The doctor smiled.

"Indeed," he said softly, "and how, may I ask, do you propose to dispense with them?"

"By warning the people from the altar that they are not to call in your aid."

"Then you will, I take it, have another doctor to take the sick calls."

"There will be no difficulty in arranging that. In the circumstances, all we have to do is send out the call, explaining the position, and we will have scores of volunteers."

"And if the people disobey you, if they call me in?"

"We can deal with that. They are good Catholics. Good Catholics do not persist in actions which their spiritual guides have banned. You do not understand the power of our Holy Faith, I fear, Dr. Ederney. It has no army or police behind it, yet its powers in a truly Catholic land like ours are greater and deeper than those that could be conferred by guns or armies. 'Thou art Peter and upon this rock I will build my church and the gates of Hell shall not prevail against it.' "[38]

"To descend from those heights to ordinary, mundane matters, Mr. Roche, since the powers of your omnipotent Church do not include the power to appoint or dismiss dispensary doctors, perhaps you could be so good as to explain how you can force me to go."

The priest moved a step towards him.

"I will tell you, Mr. Mocker. The Board of Health cannot afford to waste rates and taxes on payment of a doctor whose services people will not use. When the people refuse your services, the Board will have to dispense with them also, whether they like it or not, but I have little doubt they will be glad to do it when they have full evidence of the use you are making of your position here."

The doctor smiled bitterly.

"I have brought healing to your people," he said. "I have cleaned up the typhus [and] the filth that you and those like you have allowed to destroy this district for centuries. I am stamping out tuberculosis [and] a host of infantile and adult diseases. While I am engaged in this work of mercy, you stab me in the back because I will not accept your superstitions [or] inform women that it is their duty to die rather than deny their husbands' lusts. You threaten that if I do not cooperate in the evil you inculcate, I must go. Well, Mr. Roche, I will not cooperate, and I will not go until I am driven out. If and when that day comes, I will welcome it for the opportunity it will give me to expose the conditions here, to let the civilised world know how you have not only tolerated them, but battened on them. I do not think you will feel so triumphant, Mr. Priest, when the press of Great Britain and America carries the exposure of your lack of charity to the flock whose ignorance you exploit, the story of your hypocrisy and venom, the intolerance with which you have driven out a man who has come to try to make up for your own shameless negligence. Now, perhaps you will be so good as to spare me any more of this unpleasant interview."

He went to the door [and] opened it. The priest bowed his head [and] went out in silence.

In the hall he turned.

"The day after tomorrow is All Saints Day," he said. "On that day, if you have not repented, it will be my sorrowful duty to denounce you from the altar."

Nellie made a dash from the kitchen to open the front door for him. A gust of wind and rain swept the hall, but the priest remained standing in the gale as if he could not give up hope that at the last moment God might perform the miracle which alone could save the doctor's soul.

For a few moments the two men stood staring at each other, then, with a gesture of despair, the priest turned up his collar and went out into the storm.

Chapter XXVII

To NAN, WALKING ALONG THE SEA ROAD, THE LAND OF THE BLACK SHORE had taken on the look that made it so raw and ugly in autumn. In the little fields of oats and rye, the cornstalks had been pulled up by the roots, not leaving the decent skin of stubble that hides the nakedness of reaped cornfields in inland farms. The potato patches gave the same sense of being torn up, their hideousness bared. Over it all, the whine of autumn wind was keening.·

The sea was teeming with herring and mackerel shoals passing to the south in the outer seas where the shelf of Ireland ends and the waters go down into depths; but this year the people of Lochnamara had little share in the harvest of the sea. In the years when the shoals came inshore in pursuit of the sprat that moved in millions before them, the frail curraghs of the Black Shore were often loaded to the gunwale with their catch, but this year no sprat were lining the beach with their silver, and the canvas curraghs were too frail to go out into the ocean seas where others were gathering the harvest.

It was one of the evils Philip had hoped to remedy. Already he had been in communication with a government department about the possibility of supplying a loan for a fishing fleet of stout boats which could stand the Atlantic storms and would soon repay the expenditure. He had got a favourable reply, but the boycott would put an end to all that. There were many years when, owing to the caprice of the shoals, the fish did not come inshore, but this year the people had been told that their misfortune was due to the curse the atheist doctor had brought on the countryside.

Through the haze that lay over the water the flood tide was moving with a fermenting sound. That would be his doing, the devil's brew he had created which no shoal of sprat or herring or mackerel would dare to venture.

The village school came into sight round the bend in the road. Through the window a hymn was coming—'Immaculate, Immaculate.' The voices of the children were rising up in praise of the Mother of God, Virgin of virgins, Rose of all roses, 'Protector of the poor,' shield against evil.

Nan stood listening to that world of sweet hymns and sweet litanies, of flowers and incense and tender mysteries and sacraments. A wheezy harmonium was adding its contribution, but even it could not destroy the touch of radiance.

'Immaculate, Immaculate'—the soft western voices were rising up in joy and hope. Philip would say they were being turned into sleep-walkers, but she wanted to go in.

She didn't go. The sight of her on the threshold would be the signal for the singing to stop. That was certain. With the sight of her, the filth of their ordinary lives would be back.

She walked on and on, hating to turn, to come again to Lochnamara in the daylight which would show her sullen looks [and] the averted eyes of old friends.

When darkness fell, she turned.

It was Eehe Howna,˙ the night when men and ghosts mingle. Through the villages of the Black Shore and along the sea-road and up the mountainside a cold blustery wind was blowing, crowded with wandering spirits, but every door was open on the road and boreen˙ and mountainside to let the spirits of the blessed dead who had been waiting so eagerly in Heaven for the return home granted to them on this one night.

Below, there were other gates open, the souls of the damned hurrying through to taste their one night of freedom from fire and torment. They too, poor creatures, would come home, and so, tonight, every door in the seven villages and along the wild mountainside would be marked with a cross of limewash to keep the doomed ones away. The children would be drawn in from the street and boreen and midden to be kept safe under the picture of Christ and Mary Mother, protector of childhood, all things of the home made snug and tight against evil things.

There were others less easy to protect—the young and beautiful sought by the "good folk" who lived in the hills. Even they could not live forever. Their lives were counted in centuries, but even centuries come to an end and on this one night the people of the Sidhe had permission to leave their underground dwellings, ride the Four Winds in search of the most beautiful young boys and girls of the countryside to fill their dwindling ranks. From the hills of Maeve and Knocknarea they would be riding in their silken cavalcades, snatching the beauty and youth of mortals [and] bringing them to strongholds where no priest or monk could pursue.[39]

A wild night it was, a crowded night on the earth and in the air over the seven villages of the Black Shore, and Nan, as she walked along the sea road in the starlight, looked with envious eyes through the doors [and] at the groups celebrating its mysteries.

On the wide hearth girls and boys were shouting and laughing round the nuts set to roast in pairs to see whose love would hold and whose would spring apart. In the middle of the floor, the big wooden tubs were surrounded by children ducking for apples. Fr. Ned had seen to it that no poor child in Lochnamara would be without a handful of apples tonight, nor any girl without the bit of lead to melt and pour through the keys of the bedroom door into the cold water that would give it the shape of the husband who was to come—farmer with his spade, tailor squatting on his bench, weaver at the loom, blacksmith with his sledge or anvil.

Yes: tonight they were happy, the old welcoming [and] visiting souls, the young glimpsing the future or dreaming of being taken into the hills of the Sidhe to be princes and princesses clad in silk and eating off plates of gold.

Tomorrow, All Saints Day, they would have high holiday again in honour of the glorious ones who had reached Everlasting Bliss. Then they would go back to the treadmill of poverty and misery, but the memory of those mysteries and splendours would gild their wretchedness over many a weary day.

When Nan reached home, she found the house empty. Philip had not got back from a sick call that was so urgent the family could not avoid sending for him in spite of the boycott. The little maid had gone to a neighbor's for the festivities.

As she mounted the stairs, they rang with emptiness. Instead of going to her own room, she turned into her husband's bedroom

[and] looked round. The room seemed squarer, more geometrical than ever. It was as it had been when she came into the house as a bride—a Euclidean space shaped to Philip Ederney's image. Her attempts to shape it [and] give it colour had been a hopeless task. She could see no impress of hers on its bleak walls.

She went to the dressing table of red maple her uncle had given her husband for a wedding present [and] caressed it with her fingers. Its rose flush would have warmed up any other bedroom. Here it was merely incongruous.

"Displaced," she whispered, as if she were in a room where a friend was lying dead.

The front door opened [and] shut softly. She slipped across the passage to her own room. There was a step on the stairs. Her husband tapped at her door. She wondered why he came. It was a rare thing for him to come to her bedroom.

"Tired, Philip?" she asked, moving the armchair over to him.

He passed his hand across his forehead [and] began to talk in a low voice.

"When you were marrying me, Nan, I know you did not calculate on this. You couldn't have known that I would bring you into such trouble."

She put her hand on his shoulder.

"On the contrary, Philip," she said softly, "I knew there was bound to be trouble; it could not be avoided."

"But not this—a denunciation from the altar by the priests. You couldn't have expected that. What I want to say, Nan, is that I don't think you should stay on here and have to endure it. It was never in our contract."

His face held a rigidity she had never seen in it before [and] behind the rigidity a dumbness that saddened her.

She pressed his arm [and] smiled sadly at him.

"Is that how you think of me, Philip?" she asked, "as a fair-weather wife waiting to desert you at the first storm?"

He caught her hand [and] covered it with kisses.

"Nan, Nan," he cried, "you're not going to desert me even now when your uncle [and] the Church are going to throw themselves on me?"

His face was so radiant she was filled with an overflowing pity.

"Poor Philip," she murmured, "poor, lonely Philip."

"Poor!" he cried, "I am the richest, the happiest man in Ireland! Tonight I can dream as I once was able to dream. With you behind me I cannot be beaten. When this storm is weathered, when they're beaten, as beaten they will be, then the new world is coming to the Black Shore, the world I've dreamed."

"The lunatic in him is eternal," she thought. "Is there another man in the world who couldn't see the futility of his dreams?"

She put her hand on his shoulder.

"You're very tired, Philip," she said. "Tomorrow we can talk over these things. Now you must go to bed and get a good sleep."

The morning came grey and unwelcoming. She dressed, went downstairs softly so as not to waken her husband. In the sitting-room she sat staring through the window at the cocks of seaweed, the upturned curraghs, the carrageen moss the women had spread to dry, the sea fumbling against the rocks.

Today, the Day of All Saints, Philip would be denounced from the altar [and] he and she finally cut off from the community they both loved in their so different ways. It was a struggle that any sensible man would have avoided. In the end they would be beaten, driven out, but, with her husband in his present mood, there was nothing she could do to prevent the disaster—nothing.

The door opened behind her. Her husband came in [and] touched her cheek with his lips.

"You should have taken the morning for your sleep," she said. "If a call came we could have wakened you."

"I've slept enough, Nan. My mind is so full of plans that I couldn't sleep, seeing this place as it will be inside a generation. When once this storm blows over, I will start at once to carry out the plans. In Lancashire I have good friends, men with money, who will see the enormous possibilities of the place, the profits that can be made from the iodine from the kelp, out of the supply of fish to the English markets when we have the new fleet of boats, from the agar-agar* waiting to be tapped in this western seaweed. Can't you see it all, Nan, the generating station turning turf into electric cur-rent, the Black Shore dotted with factories that will make it a land of plenty, rescue the people from all this misery [and] get them out of the clutches of the Culkins and other blood-suckers? Just think of the sanatorium we can have with its clean bright wards, its surgi-cal departments, its X-ray room, its lectures on cleanliness, sanita-tion [and] prevention of disease."

His eyes, filled with the visions, were fixed on her face, but saw nothing of it, of the despairing look in her eyes. The echoing voice reminded her of an illness she had had when she was a child, when she [had lain] awake listening to people talking, talking. Outside, men and women were moving in groups to Mass, looking up at the house of the man who was to be denounced from the altar. Far away she could see a grey mist creeping over the sea toward Lochnamara. In front of it the sea was darkening [and] taking on a despairing note.

Her gaze came back to the visionary stare in her husband's eyes.

"How strangely like those dreamers of fairies and 'good people' of Hallowe'en he is," she thought, "only more fantastic, more remote from reality than they. Poor Philip! and yet, perhaps, not so poor, since nothing in this life will ever be strong enough to deprive him of his dreams."

Chapter XXVIII

THE BLACK-HOODED HEADS WERE COMING ALONG THE ROADS FROM THE east and the west, [and] pouring down the mountain lanes. The day, bright and sunny, was turning the scarlet petticoats into flame. Behind their women, the men in blue and white flannel marched in groups, their newest white "drawers" covering the yellowed workaday ones. They smelled of peat-smoke, and fish and seaweed and, as they trudged along the roads and the lanes to Mass, they talked of fish and seaweed and kelp and what might happen in the chapel today. Around them the boggy earth, the outcrops of rock, the smell of the dank waters, [and] the sheep on the mountainside gave them their setting.

Through the groups, the school teachers' cars piled up with their families. The owners of the pubs and the shebeens that dotted the mountain road were there also. No man, woman, or child who could come was missing. It was still early for the late Mass, but nobody was going to be left in the chapel yard outside of the range of the sermon.

By half-past eleven the church was packed to the doors. Pat Culkin led off with the Rosary. The [responses] of the congregation went up to the roof in a deep wail.

The Rosary ceased. The altar boys filed out in their white surplices. Behind them Fr. Roche marched with a belligerent face.

The smell of peat-smoke and sweat grew stronger as the congregation strained forward.

"A grand face for a priest of God going to create the body of our Lord."

Tony Culkin's loud whisper scandalised the pews around him. Tony must be a bit soused already. If he was, the drink in him made him comment on the sermon [and] they could look forward to scenes such as had never been witnessed before in Lochnamara. If he was properly soused, even Pat Culkin might not be able to restrain him.

The Mass moved rapidly.

"Faith, Roche is in a hurry today. I bet he'll get through it in fifteen minutes. Any takers?

Tony looked round with a grin at the faces that were trying hard to register disapproval. His father caught his shoulder [and] swung him to face the altar.

"By dog and by devil ye're a grand pious crowd. Y'are so y'are," Tony said in a loud voice that made the altar boys turn their heads.

Mass was over. Fr. Roche was mounting the little pulpit Fr. Ned had brought home from Italy the year he went to Rome. Nan's eyes fixed on the prominent rugged face [and] saw eyes that looked ferociously focussed [and] lips thrust out belligerently.

"Dearly beloved Brethren—"

The lips paused [and] drew a deep breath expressive of sorrow and reluctance.

"Brothers and Sisters in Christ, today I have a heavy task to perform, a burden I take on myself with feelings of the deepest grief and shame—"

Again he paused as if the words were reluctant to come.

"There has come amongst us an envoy of Satan. In the guise of a Catholic he has come to us, in the guise of a healer. The Evil One sends his emissaries forth on their foul errands in many a shape, but never has the Enemy of God been so cunning in his craftiness as in the disguise in which he has sent this agent among the pious, God-fearing people of Lochnamara. If he had come as a Protestant missionary offering the soup and the leaflets, you would have known how to deal with him as your fathers did of old, but this demoniac Monster has failed in that guise too often not to know the reception such an agent would get from the Catholic people of Lochnamara. Today he comes in a more deadly shape as a healer, a doctor who would cure our bodies, if only we sell him our immortal souls, turn against God's holy laws, deny Christ, refuse to obey God's command to Adam's breed that they are to increase and multiply in lawful marriage, allowing no obstacle to come between them and His commands. Never, my dearly beloved brethren, has Satan laid a more cunning snare to entangle souls."

The priest's breast was heaving with emotion. The congregation, staring at those heaving shoulders, answered with little cries, "God in His mercy protect us! God and Mary protect us!"

Tony Culkin slumped in his seat [and] closed his eyes. Even in his drunken condition he felt the weight of his father's hand.

The priest's voice rose in a passionate cry. This Catholic community must take every precaution, guard themselves to the utmost against the snares that had been laid for their feet. No man or woman who called himself or herself a Catholic could call in the agent of Satan except under pressure of the most urgent necessity.

From the back of the chapel an angry voice came in protest—

"If I hadn't called the docthor in whin Bartly was in the mouth o' death, 'tisn't here at Mass be me side he'd be today, but down rottin' in the earth."

A few voices joined it in murmurs of dissent, then tailed away as the priest, raising his voice, drowned the cries.

The shouting voice rang round the church, full of menace [and] power. The hooded women on their knees threw themselves forward on their faces. "The cross of Christ about us," they moaned in unison. "God have mercy on us! Holy Mother of Jesus intercede for us!"

At their backs under the gallery, the men made the sign of the cross on their foreheads. As the priest's voice broke over them in billows, they swayed, moving their bodies from side to side; but in the chapel yard after Mass there was a little group talking angrily. Whatever foolishness the doctor had committed, he didn't spare himself when Lochnamara was in sore need. They wouldn't forget that to him. From other groups cries came that the priest was right [and] only doing what needed doing long before.

The men began to shout at one another, to move towards one another. The older men came between them.

"Shame on ye," they cried, "shame an' disgrace on ye dishonourin' and insultin' God's house."

In the private lounge a crowd of mountain men were standing round Pat Culkin. It was a very great privilege for them to be admitted into that sanctuary, but Pat had special work for them to do and the flattery of this admission would help him get them into a cooperative mood.

"Drinks on the house, boys—how many of ye is there? Twintyseven. Twenty-seven large brandies for the boys, Mary—Mary, I say, Mary—'

"Where the hell is that bloody gerrel? Well, it can't be helped. I'll get the stuff mesel' for ye, boys, an' while ye're waitin', Dr. Tony'll give ye a song—"

Tony waited until his father disappeared into the bar.

Well then, I won't then, and God damn the lot o' ye."

"Come on, now, Dr. Tony, isn't it all for you th'ould man is workin.' 'Phil the Fluther's Ball,' Dr. Tony, that's the shtuff we want to hear tonight."

"I'd sooner have 'Yip, I addie, I ay'—come on now, Dr. Tony, 'Yip I addie, I ay."

Tony got up.

"Blast the lot o' you, you dirty pack of boozers and blackguards, yes, hired blackguards ready to sell your souls for liquor."

The men were all around him. He could feel the hot smell of the potheen his father had been stuffing them with.

"An' isn't it yoursel' has the right to talk iv us sellin' ourselves for likker, Dr. Tony, you that sold yoursel' for the same thing long ago."

"Whisht now.' Don't be gettin' the doctor's rag up. Shure 'tis how 'tis somethin' classy the doctor'd soon be givin' us—'Tis that that's worryin' him."

Tony's face went white at the insulting words—the horrible, true words.

Over there in that bloody white house up on the hill they'd be sitting, she reading, perhaps. She was never much for knitting or sewing or crocheting or—or—oh God damn that fellow. He could have saved her all this, saved her and Fr. Ned and the whole bloody lot if he'd even the sense of a louse—but he hadn't, never would have, and the dad'd get him. The dad'd get everyone—every bloody whore—"not the way he got me," he thought, "but the way he gets all the others. Yes, he'll get the damn fool and Nan with him."

" 'Tis somethin' classy the doctor is thinking about."

Pat Culkin came in carrying a tray with tumblers of brandy.

"Ye haven't got the docthor to sing yet boys. What are ye waitin' for?"

" 'Tis how the docthor is choosin' a song, Mr. Culkin."

In spite of the hard names he had called them, they'd never let Tony down [or] let Pat Culkin know what he was thinking of the whole business.

> Have ye heard of Phil the Fluther
> From the town of Ballymuck

> The times was goin' hard wid him
> In fact the man was bruck

Tony's voice was rising full and clear.

"After all, what choice have I?" he thought. "Nobody could save Ederney or anybody that has the misfortune to be tied to him. God help Nan. I can't."

The rich pungency of brandy was filling the room.

The docthor'll dhrink with ye too, boys. You'll have a glass, Tony, won't you?"

"Yes, father."

> So he sint out a notice to his nabors wan an all
> O' how he'd like their company that evening at a ball.
> There was little Mickey Mulligan that kep' The Running Dog. . . .

Chapter XXIX

IN THE PARLOUR OF THE DOCTOR'S HOUSE NAN AND MARY CULKIN AND the doctor sat with the windows shuttered and barred.

"It was like you to come to us on a night when every man's hand is against us," Nan was saying.

Mary looked at the doctor. He took no notice. The feeling of her damp sweaty hand was still in his, giving him that physical repulsion she always roused in him. She turned to Nan—

"If you saw the crowd that's drinking themselves blind in Dad's lounge, you'd understand the danger. They're mad drunk already and, when dark falls, they'll be here. God knows what'll happen then. If the shutters weren't closed they'd break in through the windows. Even with the shutters barred, heaven alone knows what they'll do. Poteen drives even the decentest men crazy and these men are a lot of mountainy savages that think the doctor is Satan himself in disguise. Fr. Roche's sermon this morning was one of the worst things I've ever heard. How a priest could get himself to preach such wickedness I can't imagine, but they believe every word they heard about Dr. Ederney being an emissary of the devil—"

Both women looked across at the doctor. When Mary Culkin

came in, he had been on the point of going out and had come back
to hear her news, but had forgotten to take off his hat. Like the rest
of his clothes it was old and frayed. Under the battered hat, his face
looked pathetic, but Nan didn't feel the pathos. Why couldn't he let
the people alone [and] not start all this hell's racket about their
souls? He didn't believe they had souls; if they hadn't, why couldn't
he let them alone about them? He wasn't even angry now. There
wasn't another man in Ireland or elsewhere who wouldn't have
been angry, and there he sat under that battered old hat, a pathetic
ass cluttered up with his own conceit and his belief in the goodness
of humanity. His eyes were so gentle they would have disarmed
anybody, but she didn't want to be disarmed. She had no illusions
about the root of that gentleness. It was sheer stark conceit.

She had been fooled too often before to be taken in again. Blather
of his about the love that comes in hospital wards came back to her
maddeningly. He could see that, but he couldn't see all the happiness they could have together if only he could get himself to be a
natural human man.

A shower of stones against the shutters and the shattering of
glass interrupted her thoughts. The mob had come. If Mary Culkin
hadn't warned them to close the shutters in the sittingroom, they
would have been injured, perhaps killed, by the stones that were
coming in showers.

Philip got up and was moving towards the door. She caught him
by the shoulders.

"Don't go out, Philip," she cried, "they'll murder you."

Yells mixed with the crashing of glass drowned her voice. They
were calling to him to come out, show himself a man.

"You hear them, Nan," he said softly. "They want me to come
out [and] show that I have the courage of my convictions."

"Convictions!" she cried. "Much they know about convictions.
Have you left your senses, Philip! You'll be knocked down, trampled
on, murdered."

He smiled quietly.

"They couldn't do that to me, Nan. There's hardly a man in this
parish whose family I haven't helped or cured."

The thudding of stones against the shutters answered him. She
felt like striking his stupid face with her fists.

"You hear that," she cried. "If you go out, they'll knock you
down, smash your chest [and] face in. You won't have a bone left in
your body by the time they've done with you. You don't know what
savages, cavemen, these fellows are when they've been set mad

with potheen. You won't go, Philip; you won't go. I won't let you go, Philip."

She held him tight in her arms, but she thought—

"God, how I hate you!"

Mary Culkin got up [and] gave them a long look. The love they felt for each other was the love she always longed for [and] never could reach. She slipped out of the room. It was her father who had worked the mob up to this. It was her duty to go out [and] try to undo what could be undone of the harm. They would not dare to touch her and she might persuade them to go home.

Nan did not see her go. She was holding her husband tight in her arms, thinking that it was the first time she had ever had her arms round him. What a pair they were. Never had she hated him as she did tonight—his incurable, imbecile egoism. She pressed him closer to her.

"Philip," she said softly. "Philip darling, for my sake you won't go out tonight."

They were banging at the door [and] the shutters.

"Come out an' fight, ye bloody basthard," they yelled, but he didn't seem to hear them any longer. He put his arms round her [and] brushed her hair with his lips.

"Nan! Nan!" he murmured. "Oh God, how I love you!"

She closed her eyes [and] pressed her face against his breast. The strange unaccustomed words were shaking her. What had been wrong with her that she had been so blind?

Michael's face came up before her [and] the ecstatic child's face of James Clogher. What were these men to her compared to this man, her husband? She had done with them. This man loved her [and] needed her as neither of them ever could.

The thudding of the stones against the shutters had ceased, the cries of the mob also. She pressed closer to him. She was almost glad now that this thing had happened for the way it had brought them together. She was listening eagerly, not for the sounds from outside, but for those words of love from him to which he could respond.

"Poor devils!" he said softly, "poor devils; but I'll lift the veils from their eyes yet [and] show them the road to freedom."

She flung him from her. It was not of her he was thinking.

"Hadn't we better see if there's any room in the house with a whole window?" she said coldly.

"I expect they've broken them all," he said calmly. "Tomorrow they'll be sorry when they see what they've done."

She looked away angrily. He was incorrigible in his conceit.

"Tomorrow," she muttered, "tomorrow!"

"Blinded by conceit," she cried to herself as she ran to the door and up the stairs. "How could I have ever thought we could come together?"

Her bedroom was a sorry sight, the carpet spattered with broken glass, the mirror smashed, the floor strewn with heavy stones. His was even a worse wreck.

She ran downstairs to the kitchen. Her china and crockery were lying in fragments all round the floor. The dresser and chairs had been hacked to pieces. They must have [hoisted] a boy through the small kitchen windows.

"And he's done it all," she muttered, "done it as surely as if he smashed them with his own hand."

She came back wearily to the sitting-room. Her husband wasn't there.

"Philip," she called out, "Philip!"

The waves were pounding against the shore, drowning her cries. She let her voice go in the screams that were forcing themselves from her.

"Philip! Philip! Oh my God! Philip, come back to me."

Two men came along the road. She ran toward them. Philip must have gone to the neighboring cabin for help. The men shone a torch on her. It was not Philip and another, only two Civil Guards who had been drawn by her cries.

"What is it, Mrs. Ederney?" one of them asked.

"My husband—the doctor—have you seen him?" she shouted at them.

"No, ma'am. We heard some kind of a disturbance in this direction and came out to investigate; but we didn't meet the doctor. Sure, nothing would happen to him. Even if the people don't like some of his ways, nobody in Lochnamara would touch a hair of his head."

"You don't know what's happened then. How innocent you are! You don't know that a mob has wrecked our house, you poor little innocents," she cried bitterly. "Of course, you don't. How could you, not even if a man has been murdered."

"Wrecked your house, ma'am! Why didn't you send for us at wance?"

"Send for you! Whom would we send? The old woman who did the housework for me has deserted us; but my husband—my husband!"

"You'll find him home waitin' for you and worryin'. Now go back like a good woman. He'll be at the door lookin' out for you, so he will."

She threw his hand off her shoulder angrily. This looked like a put-up job.

They couldn't not have heard the yells of the mob. They had lain low, afraid of the anger of Fr. Roche and Pat Culkin. Now they were saving their faces [by] coming on a belated investigation.

The man's voice was going on soothingly.

"You go home, Mrs. Ederney, and we'll soon find the doctor for you. He must ha' gone to the barracks to report the outrage [and] passed us in the dark. Now just run on home like a good woman and have a cup o' tay ready for him by the time we bring him back."

She stamped angrily.

"He did not go to the barracks to report them. It's the last thing he'd ever do—the last thing. He was an angel, an angel, I tell you, among devils."

Her voice had risen to a scream. What was coming over her? She pulled herself together [and] began to talk quietly.

"He loved them. He believed in them. He believes in them still, if he's alive. What are we standing here for? He may be dying, crying out for help."

The gardai started. A dead man would mean an inquest, charges of murder perhaps—either bad trouble or a chance for an officer to get [a] promotion if it was an ordinary case. But this wasn't an ordinary case. There wouldn't be any promotion from an arrest [or even] a conviction. Pat Culkin would see to it that they got no evidence. If they did get evidence, he'd see to it that the gardai who used it would suffer. There mustn't be any death.

The older of the two men sprang into action.

"Run back to the barracks, Peter," he said. "Get every man out on the search. Come on, Mrs. Ederney. You and I will find the doctor. He can't be far away. Where'd he go on a night like this if he didn't go to the barracks? Sure, there's no place else he could go. There wouldn't be a sick call, not after what Fr. Roche said today."

He had her by the arm.

"His boat! I'll bet he went down to the boat to see if they damaged her," he said. "That's it—that's it. Why didn't I think of that before?"

He was hurrying toward the beach. She let herself be dragged. Now she seemed incapable of volition. She shouldn't have left Philip alone for a moment. He was capable of any foolishness.

The mob had stopped their cries too suddenly. It was a trap, an ambush. They were waiting for him in the darkness, expecting him to come round the house to see what damage they had done. If he hadn't come, they would have got him some other way, sent a boy on a sick call knowing he would not refuse such a summons.

The boat was lying on the shingle above the tide. The torches showed that it had not been touched.

"I was sure we'd meet him goin' or comin'," the garda muttered. "Must have passed him in the dark."

"We couldn't [have]," she said hopelessly. "He'd have seen our torches."

She was sure he was dead now, thrown head foremost into a bog-hole. Her mind was wandering. The bog-hole would preserve him as he was. He would never grow old. Some day, years ahead, when she was an old woman, they would find him [and] bring him to her.

"The young man Danny Malone, the old woman Molly Magee." She had read that story somewhere, in Tennyson, or some other.[40]

He'll be back in the house, waitin' for you, worryin' about you," the garda's voice was saying; but it wasn't true. He wouldn't be at home worrying or believing any more.

At the house the men in uniform were waiting for them. One of them with stripes on his arm spoke in what he meant to be a reassuring voice—

"We found him, Mrs. Ederney. He's in the house. We've telephoned to Roymore for an ambulance."

"Is he dying?" she asked calmly.

"Dyin'? Sorra fear for him. He'll be all right in a week or two. We'll catch the blaggards who did it. They won't get away with it."

They had laid him on a sofa in the sitting-room. His hair was matted with blood where they had struck him with a heavy stick or stone. His eyes were closed as if he were asleep. On the floor beside the sofa, his battered hat was lying covered with mud. The worn sports jacket was black with mud mixed with blood.

Nan knelt beside him and felt his heart. It was beating feebly. There was a black swelling over his right eye. She felt it. It was hot and angry. She went to the cupboard for disinfectant, washed the wound and dressed it.

I'd give my davy* that wound was inflicted with a spanner,'" said the Sergeant. "In the dark they got him with a spanner. That's how they got him down. It was lucky that it wasn't an inch lower. They'd have smashed the eye, so they would; but we'll get them, Mrs. Ederney. Never fear, we'll get the blaggards that did it."

She finished the dressing [and] took up the hat from the floor, straightened it carefully [and] put it on the table.

"There was only one thing he cared for," she said slowly, "the good of the people, and this is what they do to him."

"We'll get them, Mrs. Ederney. Fr. Roche never meant them to do that sort of thing."

"No," she said. "He only turned his back while Pat Culkin egged them on to murder the man who spent his days saving their lives."

"Now, now, Mrs. Ederney. Mr. Culkin wouldn't do that. It's thim mountain blaggards back from English back streets forgettin' their Holy Faith and morals when the dhrink has thim maddened."

He drew a chair over to the sofa.

"You'd like to sit down beside him, Mrs. Ederney, so you would. The ambulance will be here inside an hour—less—and thin he'll be as right as rain. In a couple o' weeks you'll have him back fit as a fiddle, see if you don't."

Chapter XXX

When shall the swan, her death-note singing,
Sleep with wings in darkness furled?
When will Heaven, its sweet bell ringing
Call my spirit from this boozy world?[41]

Tony Culkin's voice was booming through the ward. The voice of a nurse cut him off—

"Dr. Culkin! Dr. Culkin! By right you shouldn't be here at all at this hour, you know. If you weren't a doctor, Dr. Ederney's physician—or you said you were—"

"Right, Nurse. Right as rain! Always right by dog and by devil. It'll be—"

Silent, oh Moyle, be the roar of thy waters.
Break not, ye breezes, your chain of repose.[42]

"Silent and sweet it'll be with me, by all the ten thousand devils of the Black Shore and beyond. There now, isn't that the right dope, Nursie?"

There was a scuffling sound, then Tony's chuckle.

"Now, now, that's a good girl—no harm meant."

His head appeared round the screen.

"Aye, faith, there you are, Darby and Joan, Jarby and Doan."[43]

The nurse passed him [and] began to apologise.

"He's chronic, Mrs. Ederney, impossible to handle. I'd have to get the police to keep him out."

"I'm glad he came, " Nan told her. "He'll cheer us up."

"And if there's a man in Roymore can carry his drink with wisdom, understanding, counsel, fortitude, knowledge, piety and the fear of the Lord, it's Anthony Patrick Joseph Culkin of Culkin's Fishing and Commercial Hotel, Lochnamara. You tell nursie that, Nan. She won't take it from me."

He stood by the bed, looked solemnly at Ederney and began to intone as if he was preaching a sermon—

"It was on a Sunday it happened, Dr. Philip, the blessed day of the week, a day you haven't been respecting doctor, as a Christian gentleman ought to, but, if you don't keep the anniversary of last Sunday as a day of days, well, I'll be jiggered—"

He felt the bottom of the bed.

"If I sat down on it, I wouldn't be hurting the hot water bottle [and] getting myself and your hubby into hot water again, would I?" he asked Nan.

She drew a chair over to the bed for him, but he waved it away.

"I want to feel Ederney's vibrations when he hears the great news, Nan. I've done the forty-five Irish miles from Lochnamara in three quarters of an hour on that old tin-can of mine, all to feel them, and I'm not going to be done out of the happiness."

Nan waved him on impatiently.

"For Heaven's sake, Tony, cut the cackle. You know how we're burning to hear the news."

Tony settled himself on the end of the bed.

"It was a sermon, Ederney. Any objection to hearing a bit of a sermon by a bishop?"

Nan put up her hands in a despairing gesture.

Tony wagged his finger at her.

"Now, now, Nan—a sermon should have a slow and dignified delivery. See *Instructions to Young Priests* by the Reverend Dr. John Dooley, and this sermon deserves it above all sermons, a homily by a bishop about Pat Culkin and Philip Ederney at the last Mass in the great Metropolitan Church of Lochnamara—a great Christian homily on the evil and the scandal and sin of the attack on Philip Ederney. I think the bed is beginning to vibrate, Nan."

"No, Tony," Ederney said in a low voice, "the bed is not beginning to vibrate."

Tony shook his head mournfully.

"A Doubting Thomas. You can't get yourself to believe that his Lordship came down himself all the way to Lochnamara to condemn the attack on you, Ederney."

"I have no reason to doubt your word for it, Culkin, but it isn't what his Lordship said or did or ever will say or do but what the people of Lochnamara have done that has got me down," Ederney said in the same low voice.

"All in its good time, Ederney—all in its own good time, but first let me quote a few of his Lordship's sentences from last Sunday's sermon."

" 'The attack on Dr. Ederney is a disgrace to this parish, to the whole diocese, a disgusting exhibition of blackguardism hiding itself under the name of Christianity. Drunken hooliganism is not the weapon by which good Catholics defend their faith.' "

"You should have seen the dad's face at that swipe, the delight of the congregation nearly breaking their necks, craning back and forward, to get a look at his phiz. Poor dad! Whoever enjoyed that scolding, it shouldn't have been me, but God forgive me, I believe there wasn't a sinner there got more fun out of the whaling the dad got than his son Anthony Patrick Joseph."

" 'Scoundrels who used Fr. Roche's sermon as an excuse for their private feuds—men who have no scruple in using even our Holy Faith for their private ends, without shame, without any sense of sacrilege. . . .' "

"Faith, his Lordship, when he opened his mouth, let it say what it liked and if you ask me, it must have been burning for many a long day to say things about Patrick Culkin, the stoutest upholder of the Faith in the parish of Lochnamara. It isn't that I ever thought, to be sure, that his Lordship was a Pat Culkin fan, but the sting of that sermon lay in the fact that his Lordship made it as clear as the day to everybody that, if he had to choose between Dr. Philip Ederney and Patrick Joseph Culkin, there wouldn't be a doubt in his mind as to which he'd keep on in the parish of Lochnamara."

He turned to Nan.

"And still the bed isn't beginning to vibrate, Nan."

"It's no wonder it's not shaking, Tony. It isn't the Church has been getting Philip down, but the ingratitude of the people who could allow him to be treated that way after all he's done for them. He expected nothing from the Bishop and, though his Lordship has been decent and generous and Christian, it isn't what *he* thinks that matters to my husband."

Tony nodded.

"Then the real good news is to come."

"What is the real good news?"

"The right-about turn the parish made when the news spread about the attack on the doctor. 'Tisn't often the dad puts his foot in it in his dealings with the people of the Black Shore, but, faith, he put that foot right up to the leg in it when he sent his hill-billies to wreck your house on the evening of All Saints Day. The jump-round of the parish in the doctor's favour was one of the greatest surprises the dad ever got in his life. He couldn't believe it at first, but today, when his Lordship himself came down to your side, Ederney, the dad threw in his hand. 'Tisn't as if his Lordship con-doned your sins—"

" 'His errors are grievous. They must be rejected. If possible this good man must be saved. There is one all-potent weapon against such mistakes and errors as his, the weapon of prayer. My dearly beloved brethren, I beg of you to pray day and night for the soul of our dearly beloved son who has strayed from the fold.' "

Tony joined his hands [and] pointed them upward in an attitude of prayer.

"If you [could] only [have] heard them, Ederney. The chapel was ringing with it, prayers for you, for me, for themselves and their children, even for the blackguards who put you out of action. Owney Foran had the time of his life leading them. Even Fr. Tim Roche wasn't able to take the lead out of his mouth, though the poor man has been doing his damnedest to get back in God's favour since he saw the use the dad made of him. Of all the venom I ever saw, the wickedest has been the venom of Tim Roche against the dad for making such a fool of him and such a tool of him before the eyes of the parish."

He paused [and] turned [his] large eyes on Nan, [and] from Nan to the doctor.

"There's a girl says I've got her into trouble."

"Another one, Tony?"

He nodded to Nan.

"Another one, Nan. As the grocers say, it makes the round half dozen, if I did it, but did I? If a girl is in trouble potheen is a great convenience when I'm the lad that fills the glass and gives a poor decent straying girl the chance of getting a little money from Pat Culkin—becoming a wage-earner, you might say, instead of being in disgrace for a bog-trotter with nothing to show for it. Even with-out the money, to be the young doctor's girl is a grand way out, an honour to the family instead of the disgrace of being the girl of a mountainy lad. So, they see their chance [and] come whispering to Fr. Tim, and Fr. Tim lends an ear to their sad tale—a Godsend it must have seemed to him, coming the time it did."

"But Fr. Roche must have known your reputation, Tony, before he agreed to back you against Philip," Nan said.

Tony grinned up at her.

"Damn well he knew, Nan, but they didn't come to him wanting him to break the bargain with the dad. Our people of the Black Shore are gentlemen. They knew as well as you or me that, when Roche made the alliance with the dad, the price was for him to swallow me hook, line, and sinker, booze and babies and all. What a grand song that'd make, Nan—"

> Booze, babies and all,
> Babies and boozin' and all,
> Fr. Tim was to swallow bould Tony
> Booze and babies and all.

Nan caught his arm [and] shook him—

"Get on with the story, Tony," she cried.

Tony grinned.

"Right, Nan, right. Where was I? Oh yes, Roche's part was to swallow me, good old Tony as the devil made him. The good people of Lochnamara knew that as well as he did and the devil a bit they wanted from Fr. Tim but for him to go to his dear old friend Pat Culkin, get a bit of money for the girl and have everybody happy. They never thought that, instead of getting the money, he'd take the chance of getting back on the dad for the trick the dad played on him on All Souls Eve. The idea that he'd start denouncing me from the altar and losing the chance of the bit of money for Sara Connor came as a terrible shock to them. The worst of bad taste, it seemed to them, for all they themselves condemned the dad's actions. A pair of thieves, you see, shouldn't round back on each other. Besides, it's the worst of bad business too—for now, the girl, they're afraid, won't get a penny because Roche sacrificed her to his own venom against the dad."

"I don't pity Fr. Roche in the least," Nan said bitterly. "Those that touch pitch. . . ."

Tony chuckled.

"Easy now, Nan. The dad isn't a shining angel, but—pitch!—ah now, Mrs. Philip Ederney! There's no denying that the dad's soul mayn't be as white as it would be if he hadn't spent ten years as a chucker-out in a speak-easy in Chicago. Souls get a bit blind and tough in that sort of job and, sure enough, the poor man is as bewildered by Fr. Roche objecting to his giving him the helping hand he gave him as he is by the way the people took it. All bewildered and resentful the dad is. He just doesn't understand Roche's rage [and] thinks he's reneging on him when he found out that beating up the doctor didn't pay. Well I can tell you the dirty dog who reneges on the dad will wish the devil had flown away with him before he's done with Pat Culkin. That's the way the dad sees it and, queerly enough, that's the way most of the parish sees it, too, for all their own vexation over the dad's setting the boys to beat up the doctor. A queer lot they are, for, strange and wonderful to relate, Tony is the man they look on as the gentleman of Lochnamara. They think he's the real thing, God help them. They always suspected Roche wasn't from the first day he set foot in Lochnamara and now they're certain he isn't. That gave a chance to the lads whose hands have long been itching to give Roche what's coming to him. Them lads that were in England during the war, or out on the front, aren't just as fond of priests as they might be, and the girls back from England aren't far behind them. If they didn't hit back when Roche started to use his blackthorn* on them, when he found them lying in the dark, it wasn't the fear of God that prevented them, but the fear of Pat Culkin's grip on their bits of holdings."

Nan frowned.

"So Pat Culkin is going to get his own back on the Church by turning the ruffians loose on Fr. Roche?"

Tony lifted his hands deprecatingly.

"Now did I ever say that, Nan? Did I ever suggest it? Could you expect the dad to spend his time protecting Roche from them blackguards after the dirty trick he's played on him?"

He shook his head solemnly.

"Roche has let the girl down [and] lost her the bit of money they expected he'd get for her. He has turned on his own dear confederate when he found that playing with him didn't pay. That's the way the countryside sees it—Roche reneging [and] losing the girl the bit of money that was coming to her. After the sermon on the doctor, they get a sermon against Tony. 'Whin he's goin' easht he'd be, 'tis goin' wesht he'd be'—that's the word that's gone round the parish about him. To the simple minds of this countryside it looks like a lot of backhanded tricks, the sort of high and mighty moralist like Roche shouldn't think of playing on the dad or Tony Culkin or, least of all, on a decent family that has just lost their cow and [needs] money to get another in her place. As for my own part in the game, I'm not saying I did it, and I'm not saying I didn't. If I knew, I'd tell you, Nan. Roche says I tampered with the girl and mebbe I did. That's the thing I don't know. What I do know is that there are a good dozen of girls in this parish that are screeching out to be tampered with; aye, faith, yelling for it, and no lack of mountainy boys willing and anxious to oblige, and, if and when they do oblige, the countryside ready to do a good turn by fathering it on Tony in one of his boozing fits and screwing a bit of their own back out of the pockets of Pat Culkin for the poor girl and her decent people. All one grand big family we are here in Lochnamara, with Pat Culkin the head of it always willing and ready with the money to make amends for the sake of his own soul and Tony's, if only his back isn't got up by blackguardly conduct like Fr. Tim's."

He gave her his broad happy grin.

"Even now he'll give it, Nan, in spite of Roche's antics. I'll take care he does, in case. Isn't it the dad and myself are the true Christian men in this world of thieves, Mrs. Ederney, seeing the point of view of our enemies and holding up the other cheek?"

Nan shook her head.

"Pat Culkin can't be white-washed, Tony. He's just a plain scoundrel, and, as for you, everybody knows you're irresponsible and irrepressible."

Tony caught her hand.

"Who cares, Nan? Who the devil cares and what the blazes does it matter? It's what happens to the doctor that matters, and I can guarantee you that when he goes back to the parish of Lochnamara, he'll find people waiting for him with a hundred welcomes to make up for the bad return that was made him for all his kindness."

He pointed his hand past her. Philip had lifted himself on his hands. His face was lit up.

"They know what I've done for them," he cried. "I knew the day would come when they'd know it. I knew it. I knew it."

Tony laughed heartily.

"So the vibrations are on at last. I thought 'twas that was getting you down, Ederney—man's ingratitude. Wait till you go back and get the welcome the whole parish is preparing for you. I don't say they'll have tar-barrels,[44] but, if you don't get as many sick calls as you can handle inside a week, I'm not Tony Culkin, and this time the pigs won't be taken out of your way. That's one thing the Bishop's sermon has washed out. If you only heard him hinting that, if there were devils inside the skin of people in the parish, it wouldn't be a doctor's skin that contains them."

He turned to Nan.

"I wouldn't be greatly surprised if even Fr. Tim Roche mayn't find himself amongst the doctor's patients, Nan."

"All the time you're just hoping your father will turn his hooligans on to him."

Tony spread his hands deprecatingly.

"Well now, I wouldn't say that, Nan. I'm thinking the dad is too cool a head to have anything to do with turning hooligans on to a priest. Whatever the dad is, he isn't a damn fool, and nobody but a damn fool would turn the mountainy men on to a limb of the Church, whomever else he'd let them loose on. As for myself, I'm not denying that if Roche got a welt or two, 'twouldn't keep me awake of nights. It might even be the best thing in the world for the man himself, teach him things he ought to learn in the early days of his mission if he's to escape worse later on. He's so thick and ignorant that he hasn't discovered yet that this isn't the middle of the nineteenth century when the priest could drive the people with a stick as if they were pigs and, if he doesn't learn it quick, there's just the danger that some day he'll learn it sudden and unprovided when it's too late. That'll be a pity too. He's an east-county bullock, beef to the heels and the brain, but he's a good enough priest in his own way and he'd get along all right if only he'd learn that the proper use of the blackthorn on a dark night is for walking quietly along the road feeling for bog-holes and the goats and asses that might be bedded down on it. Now Fr. James wasn't exactly a tower of horse sense, but there's one thing I will say for him—he was the most sympathetic poor devil that ever walked a parish, one of God's own gentlemen. Lochnamara is a poor, God-forgotten hole, its people a poor God-forgotten lot, but this I'll say for it and them, if there's one place in the world knows a gentleman when it sees him, it's the seven villages of the Black Shore."

"Is there any better news of Fr. James?" Nan asked him.

Tony shook his head.

"The news is bad, Nan. The man is falling into a condition of permanent melancholia. I wish they'd left him here with Fr. Ned. He was at home here and happy as far as a soul like his ever could be happy in this vale of tears and Tony Culkins. Over there in the fat flatlands he has neither home nor rest."

Nan went to the window [and] stood looking out.

When she turned back, her face was set.

"I've been thinking of late of a holiday in Dublin, Philip," she said. "Since you've [arrived] you've had no holiday."

He shook his head.

"Some other time, Nan. I couldn't take a holiday now, not with all those arrears of work. You go. You've been having a hard time of it of late. You've friends in Dublin and a holiday there will take your mind off Lochnamara and do you an amount of good."

She nodded.

"I think I will take one, Philip. With all Lochnamara behind you, you'll not need me so much any longer."

Ederney's eyes as he stared up at the ceiling held a denial of her words, but she did not see them.

When she came back from seeing Tony out, he tried to lift himself in the bed.

"I didn't dream, Nan, that the Bishop would—" he began, but she pressed him back gently on the pillow.

"There are many things about Bishops and their people you've never dreamt, Philip," she said.

"But—"

"But nothing. Now you'll sleep, my good patient and perhaps in your sleep you'll start to dream truer dreams."

Chapter XXXI

N AN LOOKED DOWN FROM THE UPPER DECK OF THE TERENURE TRAM AT the passers-by. They seemed artificial figures, mincing and posturing. When she got off at the top of Grafton Street and walked through Stephen's Green, it was an Abbey Theatre scene. Even the poor women, sitting on the seats in the sun, weren't the poor women of life. They went with the foreign ducks with painted eyes and the idle men reading newspapers on the seats by the brinks of the ponds.

Sin and the wrath of God had been as near in Lochnamara as the morning of the sea. Here they were remote, shut away behind a protecting wall of pictures and newspapers and streams of faces. "Just the place," she thought wryly, "for Michael's nest with its warm lining of bridge and golf, race-meetings and dances and discreet booze."

She smiled ruefully. What an absurd slant for a young woman to have on a city, instead of hurrying to the shop windows, the cafes, the pictures. Was it some trick of her vanity crying out sour grapes?

200 THE BLACK SHORE

Well, vanity or wisdom, it was the place to bring James Clogher for a rest cure.

She began to go over and over again the words of her letter to James. "If you could find even a few days to come to Dublin [and] let me show you the enchanted road round Boharnabreena and Firhouse and Tibradden, feel the smell of the heather and gorse on the Hill of Howth or Bray or Killiney* where the sea is far below and very gentle, I cannot believe, Fr. James, that your melancholy could last beyond the first day."

Sentimental rubbish, perhaps, but James was a sentimentalist. Stuff of that sort would have to be ladled out to him in the first stages of his cure. Impossible to believe that she could ever get him to feel religion as the family party with God the Lelands and their like had made of it, but he might be dragged out of the funeral pyre his mania was building round himself. She owed him that at least since it was she who had flung him into the fire [and] made a hell of his life.

Her pace slowed down. The thought of his dependence on her was soothing to her vanity smarting from the failure she had made of her own life. From the beginning she had been making a mess of her life, running away from reality, as he was doing now. As a young girl she had thought of entering a convent. She made a grimace over that memory.

It had been the fragrance of the incense, the pageantry of the convent that had caught her, not any love for God or the poor. James Clogher had once confided to her that the beginning of his vocation was the fragrance of incense from his mother's hair [and] clothes when she came back from Benediction.

"A pair of fools," she thought bitterly. "Only I haven't walked into it as he has, through his childish vanity and conceit of his intimacy with God. Until I crossed his path, he was vain as a peacock of his own righteousness [and] his union with Christ who suffered on the Cross [and] the God of mercy and love. Now he is back in the furnace of fear, shivering with the dread of the loss of his priestly chastity before those unforgiving, all-seeing eyes. I wish to God, Fr. Ned hadn't lent him those mad French sermons."

"The deep and shameful wound of Nature, the carnal urge that has chained the soul to the filth of the flesh."

The greatest of French preachers had given utterance to these insanely inhuman thoughts. No wonder James Clogher's mind had been lacerated, facing that incredible dilemma of the spirit and the flesh.[45]

His ravaged face came up before her again. There was a debt there that would have to be paid.

She began to think out ways and means. Peace and rest were his need. If she could get a cottage in a quiet place near Dublin [and] a quiet companion to live with them [to] act as companion, house-keeper and chaperon, they might, between them, be able to do something to settle his mind.

꙰

As Nan walked up the path to the cottage she had found at Bo-harnabreena, the glow of the walls in the evening sun seemed to welcome her. She had had to sell most of her little nest-egg of shares in order to buy the house, but to what better use could she put the money than in providing a place of rest and quiet for James?

She opened the door [and] looked round the hall. Yellow light lay over it.

She looked up the stairs. For days she had been making the nest, "bringing the sticks," she said to herself. "A rook building up in the safety of a tree-top."

She went to the sitting room she had made on the left of the hall. It was full of evening sun. Beyond the valley of Glenasmole, the Glen of the Thrushes, lines of hills melted into one another catching the light.

She walked slowly round the room, touching the chairs, the table, the sofa.

"For the first time since I left Fr. Ned's I have been able to make a home, a new life," she thought. "Can a new life be borne so easily?"

She left the sitting room [and] went to the room she had furnished for James. Everything was ready for him—the pyjamas on the bed, the set of new underclothes in the cupboard.

She had to guess the sizes, but he wouldn't mind if they were a bit on the big side. He wouldn't have any interest in things like that and he would not bring any clothes himself. She was sure of that. If the blue slippers did not fit him, the shopman had promised to change them. They were the only thing he couldn't wear if they didn't fit.

She looked round the room appreciatively. It was homely already. The black-backed hair-brushes, the comb, the bottles of "Flowers and Honey," gave it a lived-in air. The blue-grey dressing gown on the hook of the door seemed amusing. She wondered if James had ever allowed himself to have a dressing gown before, [or] if now she could get him to wear it or to use the pyjamas.

She looked round once again, then walked slowly to her own room. The clothes she had brought with her were still unpacked. She had been afraid to take them out, afraid of the associations they might bring. Now she had no fears. She began to unpack the underclothes, the knitted jumpers* [and] put them away in drawers.

She had not brought the coat and skirt of Connemara tweed. They would smell too close to the past. These frilly Dublin things were like wings, light airy chiffons, striped cotton frocks with full skirts and low boat-shaped necks, the gay sash of scarlet taffeta, the soft blue wool frock, the bedjacket of red silk. She opened the hat box [and] took out the Basque beret. It sat primly on her head.

"James will like its primness," she thought.

She gave it a sideways backwards slant that changed it, made it into a piquant hat. The face in the mirror was that of the gay girl who had first met Michael. The year that had been pressing her down was gone. She was almost back to where she had been before Michael came.

"Rubbish!" she muttered. I'm being a sentimental fool, the old sentimental fool," but she went on trying on the dresses [and] hats she could not have worn in Lochnamara. There was a turban of boldly striped silk. Pulled down well over one ear, it had a careless, apache* look about it.

She stood in front of the mirror.

There was something desperate behind the eyes, something that was ridiculing her childishness.

"But is it so childish?" she thought.

"I'm not an old crone yet. I'm young still, though I have left so much behind," she said firmly.

She began to arrange the clothes, folding them with exaggerated care, then hurriedly.

"I must catch the next bus," she whispered. "James will be worried if I'm not on the platform waiting for him."

※

He stepped out of the carriage [and] stood looking around. His face made her conscious of the cold smell of the station. She shivered a little. A chill like the chill of a tunnel was creeping through her. She did not move to meet him.

"What have I begun?" she thought. "He will drag me down with him. I can still escape."

She saw his face, despairing, frightened, crying out for her. She ran to him [and] caught him by the arm.

"It's all right, James. I'm here," she cried.

He drew back from her.

Her mind shrivelled [and] fell together. Suddenly an explosion of rage was shaking her.

"Damnation!" she thought, "ten thousand damnations take the man, bursting into my play like a bull in a china shop. All the while he has been thinking of me as a woman, while I have been playing the fool-child."

"Nan! Nan! forgive me. It wasn't—I mean I didn't—I have offended—forgive me—won't you forgive me?"

"Fiddle-sticks," she snapped angrily. "Look here, Fr. James, let's come off this high-falutin'—"

He put up his hands as if to ward off a blow.

"Oh Nan, don't—"

"Don't what? Well, let me put it this way. I'm here as your nurse. What you need is a good rest cure and I've been trying to arrange for you to get it without having to go to a nursing home. They're dreary places, those nursing homes. What you need is a rest in some quiet spot like Glenasmole. I've rigged up a cottage for you there. If you feel like living alone, I'll get a woman in the neighbourhood who will do for you; but I'm not so sure loneliness would be good for you, so I've got a cottage that will hold three of us—you, me and a companion, if you feel you'd prefer to have company as I'm sure you would. There's a charming old lady, Mrs. Green, who is in need of a country holiday. She'd love to come if you have no objection."

He caught her arm.

"Nan, I've hurt you deeply."

She shook his hand off.

"My dear James, don't alarm yourself. You haven't said the slightest thing to hurt me. I'm your nurse [and] you, a man who has got to be taken out of himself. If we find that you and I can't do the cure alone, we'll get a psychiatrist. It may be that confession is what you need, not the confession of evil thoughts such as you've been making in the confessional-box, but a cleaning out of some of the diseased stuff you mind is filled with. Anyway, we'll try first what a quiet rest in Boharnabreena will do for you. Tomorrow Mrs. Green can be moving in to the cottage and you will come out to us."

In the taxi he sat with his knees pressed together [and] stared in front of him. When it stopped in front of a quiet hotel in Harcourt Street, his eyes were those of a beaten dog.

"You don't believe in me any longer, Nan," he said despairingly.

Her pity went out to him.

"Indeed I do, Fr. James," she said softly. "Do you think I would do all this for you if I didn't? You and I are bound together by the deep affection we feel for each other. If you had a sister, or your mother had lived, it would be they who would be doing this for you. I am taking their place. Fr. Ned and my husband, both from different angles, would wish me to do all I can for you."

He pressed her hands [and] ran up the steps.

Back in the house, Nan looked round coldly [and] collectedly.

"Doll's House," she said, "doll's house! I have found you out. Since Michael threw me off the main road of a woman's life, I have been trying to get back by mothering dolls. The poor typhus patients were dolls—nothing but dolls. When I was cut off from them, I was lost until James came along. How I threw myself on that poor fool, glad that he needed mothering so sorely. Now he has made himself impossible as a doll or anything else [and] forced me to see him for what he is—a poor diseased creature. I don't want to mother him any longer, though he needs mothering now more than ever. I merely resent him as I resented my husband because no human being could mother Philip [or] make a doll out of his hard geometrical life. You, James, and he have upset the little girl's play and she resents it. The grown up woman has no right to these silly resentments. Goodbye to them. Yes, goodbye. Another stage in my life has been passed."

She nodded her head at the room.

"Doll's House," she said softly, "piles of linen, apple-green plates, and all the rest, your use has changed. Tomorrow you will be part of real life, furniture of a nursing home for a diseased mind. Goodbye, fairy-gold.'"

Chapter XXXII

THE RAIN WAS COMING DOWN FROM SEEFIN, REMINDING NAN OF THE days in Lochnamara. Up above a heavy turban of mist was hiding the mountaintop. The walls were wet, the hall full of a clinging damp.

She came down the stairs slowly, smelling the mist. It had prevented James from reading his breviary outside, up and down the path. Now he was sitting in the little front room they called the parlour.

She stood at the door looking down over the sweep of mountains that circled Dublin. On the plain the rain had stopped [and] the sun had scattered the mist, but [here] there was no sunlight. Beyond the city, the sea, cold and distant, held no menace like the sea of the Black Shore, nor any emotion.

She stretched her arms over her head and yawned. How sick she was of it all. Philip had been dreary at times, but Philip's dreariness had come from his caring for others, not from an obsession with himself. It had been nothing to the morass of boredom James had created with his fears, his doubts, his agonisings, until she had had the flash of inspiration to buy him the diary in which he had recorded, day after day, his feelings, his thoughts, his sins of omission and commission, the prayers that wiped them out [and] all his [other] transactions with God. It was a liberation of the spirit for her that lucky accounts book, particularly when the accounts balanced, as they had been doing more and more of late.

Cries of gratitude—"You have healed me, Nan. You have saved me," would have been a reward, if only the old chorus hadn't followed—"The miseries of the human state come from our frailty."

God, how sick she was of that tripe, of the man's picture of her as the source of thoughts that, even when he fought them, were eating him. Of late there had been less of that, more of the hymn of triumph. God was admitting him back into His Kingdom.

"Not wholly," Nan thought with a touch of malicious pleasure. Salvation had come back, but the ecstasy was gone. Ecstasy was silence. In those later days his piety had become garrulous—a good sign. He would not die now on any pyre or battlefield.

She walked slowly down the mountain road. She would be glad to be rid of him, though, when her task was done, there would be no doll left, no patient nor saint not sinner—nothing but to pack up and return to the lunatic land and sea of the Black Shore where no human being could keep sane, except, ironically, those who were already out of the bounds of sanity and free from its rules—a poet or saint caught up in his visions, a monomaniac like Philip, encased in his one idea, [or] a primitive brute like Pat Culkin, entrenched in the grossness of the earth.

She stood looking down at the fat suburban lands [and] the city that protected its dwellers' lives. She could see the safe drawing-rooms, the loaded tables, the golf links and race-courses—all the trash that came between them and the naked anarchy of God.

She turned away. These things were not for her.

When she got back James was standing at the door looking out at the mist.

"How are you feeling?" she asked him. It was the usual, expected question.

"I don't know what happened to me, Nan, but last night I had a collapse again—impossible to sleep, hateful to be awake. Inside me something seemed to be galloping at a demonic rate, tearing me apart."

She groaned inwardly. He was back in crisis again.

"If you would leave your thoughts to grow in peace instead of hunting them down as you're always doing, you would rest," she said. "As it is, how can you rest [when you let] nothing lie quietly in your head?"

She had said it so often before that it had become a cliché. God, how tired she was of it all—tired—tired and weary!

"You summon unhappiness deliberately, yes, quite deliberately. I've watched you do it," she added maliciously.

"That's a most shameful accusation to make. You know as well as I do that I've never had a chance. My parents, friends, relatives, the school teachers—not one of them understood me. You don't understand me either; you can't. You've always been surrounded by admiration [and] flattery. The point of the sword has never appeared before you unexpectedly. How can you know anything about a soul like mine? There is no sense handing me out refutations. I'm not going to listen to them—"

His voice had risen almost to a scream.

"I have been isolated—forced into isolation. It may be leading me to madness, but what do you know or care?"

"Why do you think I brought you here, James, if I did not care?"

"You flatter yourself with your pretense of caring. You are in love with yourself, with your own pretense of caring [and] being the great pity-giver, the maternal Goddess."

"He is furious because I do not love him. Yet, if I did, he would reject my love," she thought.

"All the time I've been with you, I've been imprisoned in a silence that has been strangling me," he cried.

"And yet, we've talked, James," she said.

"Yes, prattle—"

He broke off.

"Nan, Nan, I've hurt you. How ungrateful I must seem. You've done so much for me, but it's no use. Tomorrow I will go [and] relieve you of the burden."

"If only you would," she thought.

"It has been no burden, James."

"Your face belies your words, a face of refusal. You've said I deliberately call up unhappiness, play at being unhappy. Nobody who had the slightest sympathy or understanding of me could say a thing like that, but there I'm at it again. Don't think I'm ungrateful, Nan; you've done your best. It's your love for yourself that has got between us."

"Always somebody's fault—never his own," Nan thought wearily. "Strange how I never guessed the secret of the man [and] how incurable he is. He revels in misery, wallows in it. If I could make him happy today or tomorrow, I should destroy the springs that make life worth living for him—and always it must be others who are the cause of his misery."

"I try to keep on my feet [and] stand up against this attack humanity is directing at me, but there's nobody to help me. Nobody wants to help me. You—you mean well, or think you do. What is wrong with you is that you are in love with your own grandiose nobilities."

"True enough, I've been playing a part, too," Nan thought, "but it isn't my play-acting that's really getting the man, but the discovery that I don't love him [and] never could love him."

"When you sit at the table opposite me at meals I feel as if you were strangling me. I feel your fingers at my throat."

Nan moved past him into the hall. He pivoted around.

"You, you have nothing to say?"

"What can I say, James?" she said quietly. "I have failed badly [and] made you worse, perhaps. I have no doubt now that the sooner you part from me, the better for you—for both of us, perhaps."

He swung around angrily and rushed past her. That was not what he had wanted to hear.

She smiled sourly to herself.

"And to think I was mad at Philip when he shifted the rug in the bedroom, because it didn't catch the light properly the way he had it."

She went into the parlour. Outside on the gravel path, James was walking up and down furiously.

"The man isn't so far wrong about my make-up," she muttered. "He's sure I must have lounge-lizard tastes because I don't [share] his super-excellence, but is he so far wrong? There's nothing like an outraged vanity for sharpening the vision. What is Michael but a super lounge-lizard, a dough-chaser? Poor Philip! What trashy hands you've fallen into."

James came in.

"I'm sorry for all that, Nan. You've been doing the right thing for me all the time [by] trying to get me to take myself in hand."

Nan, watching the blinking eyes, began to feel pity gripping her, but that was unjustified. She mustn't be caught again. It was another trick of his, unconscious perhaps, this confession, [this] self-castigation. She'd have to get rid of this incubus [and] get back to freedom [and] Philip. A while ago she was sure she had got rid of him, but here he was, back again, determined to stay, or, perhaps, unable to go.

"If you feel you're quite normal—" she began.

He cut her short.

"You mean you don't think I am. Three nights ago you were sure I was cured."

She looked into his eyes. His flickered away. He wasn't cured, never would be cured, but she could do no more for him.

He looked back, baffled.

"Who is paying for all this? Is it your husband's money?"

The question was so unexpected that she stared back at him.

"You aren't going to tell me?"

"I haven't the slightest objection telling you. Philip has no money to spare. You can imagine the amount of fees he can collect on the Black Shore. It's my own money, the cash my parents left me."

"You've sold your shares to get this place?"

"Only some of them. For Heaven's sake, don't start bothering me about that, James."

"Start *bothering*! That's the sort of thing you're handing out to me night and day. I'm not starting bothering as you so charmingly put it, but you don't think I can go on living on your charity and you don't want me to. Only a while ago you said I summon up my unhappiness deliberately [and] that you've watched me do it, as if a man could want to be in misery."

Her head was beginning to throb.

"I think I'll have to go and lie down, James," she said. "I've got a headache coming on."

"Nan, I've given you the headache! What a brute I've been to you."

His face wore a look of mingled sadness and heroism.

"It's all right, James. A couple of aspirins and a bit of rest will have me right again inside an hour."

As she went up the stairs, her mind went back to Philip [and to] the evenings they sat by the drawing-room fire and had tea and toast with the curtains drawn and everything so happy and comforting. Why had she given all that up to come on this wild goose-chase for this impossible creature?

The memory of those evenings was maddening.

"His accusations are perfectly true," she thought. "I came because I imagined myself as the great healer, the maternal Goddess full of pity and love. I'm still at it, mothering the dolls. My medical lounge-lizard has a great deal to answer for. Or is this more of the bogus stuff, shoving the fault on to Michael? Had I much there, waiting to be stirred up before ever a man came into my life?"

The headache was getting worse. She pressed her hands to her eyes.

"They're flickering like his were a few minutes ago. Is the damn thing catching, or am I as bad as he is?"

She went to the window. Outside, the sun was piercing veils of mist with shafts of light. She drew the curtains viciously. The loveliness was irritating her.

"Playing at being long suffering—am I in the same game?" she thought. "Well, the headache isn't bogus, in any case."

She was wakened by the crowing of a cock. For a while she lay on her back staring up at the ceiling. The sounds from the neighbouring farmyard came to her—the grunting of the pigs, the lowing of a cow from the field under the window, the chucklings and cacklings of hens—the sounds of the Black Shore. Suddenly she felt she could not stand this man or this place any longer.

She must get back home.

She got up [and] came downstairs softly. She began to laugh.

Fr. James was sitting in the parlour reading his Office. He looked up, saw her face and returned firmly to his Office.

"He knows what's coming," she thought.

"When you've finished your Office, Fr. James," she said, "I want to have a talk with you."

He read on for a few pages, then looked up, glanced again at her face and shut the Breviary. There was no use trying to put off the fatal announcement.

"I'm ready, Nan," he said quietly.

He felt cold and chilled and half dead, but nothing could be done to prevent the disaster that was looming over him.

"You probably guess what I'm going to say, Fr. James."

"Yes, you are going to leave me."

The sadness in his voice touched her, but she must harden herself against that sort of slop. She had been no use to him, just a goose who had thought of herself as a healer.

"Yes, Fr. James. I have failed. I have been dreaming of myself as a great maternal. You were quite right about that—playing a part I haven't an ounce of qualification for is a fool's game. I've decided that the best thing for both of us is that I should leave tomorrow. After all, I've a husband and a home to look after. It seems to me that I've forgotten my real duties."

The dull ache in her head was beginning again. His face floated in front of her. She hadn't noticed that it was so yellow.

"I hope he's not getting jaundice," she thought.

"You can stay on here, of course, if you feel like it. Mrs. Green will look after you."

Chapter XXXIII

PHILIP EDERNEY WALKED ALONG THE STRAND OF THE BLACK SHORE. THE thunder of the breakers was filling the air. Out to sea there must have been a storm. Though the day was dead calm, a ground swell was heaving heavy masses of water on the strand. From the shebeens where they sold potheen, the yells of the mountain men were answering the breakers.

"There must have been a new brew of potheen last night," he thought.

When he first came to Lochnamara those orgies when the potheen was distilled had filled him with disgust. The lewd ferocity of their yells had been part of the filth he had come to clear, dregs churning up from the bottom of brutalized minds.

Today he felt the danger no longer. Primitives, ridden by fear, they were easing themselves by this defiance hurled at the universe. They were still half-buried by primordial slime, but they were being lifted by this exhilaration. When they drank, the vision of their community grew more vivid. It gave meaning [and] purpose, a center to their squalid lives.

"My development had been too simple," he said to himself.

"There must have been make-believe in what I thought was my spiritual progress. Somewhere I took the wrong turning?"

He walked up the strand on to the road. In a field beyond the sea road, a man was feeding a calf with milk from a bucket, talking to it as if it were a child.

The doctor leant on the wall.

"That's a splendid calf you have, Michael," he said.

"God bless her. Say 'God bless her,' doctor," the man answered heartily.

"God bless her," the doctor repeated mechanically.

The man's face relaxed.

" 'Tis always safer to say 'God bless,' docthor, whin you shtart to praise a man or a woman or a chile or a bashte. It do turn the bad luck away."

"Why this collapse of all my standards, this feeling that my mind is losing its identity? Am I being taken over by the humanity I have refused to accept, or is the assault imaginary?"

> A turf an' a sod
> Shpells Nebuchod
> A knife an' a razor
> Shpells Nebuchodonayser
> Three pair o' boots
> An' five pair o' shoes
> Shpells Nebuchodonayser
> The king o' the Jews.

The children were coming home from school mimicking their lessons in fantastic rhymes. As they passed him, the little girls curtsied [and] the boys pulled the locks that hung over their foreheads.

"Parents, offspring, all that glutinous mass, why do I need it now, my mind crying out for the flimsy stuff I have always despised? Can it be so flimsy, or is it I who have no understanding of the recesses of life?"

His thoughts went to Nan. He face rose before him, the eyes closed. The face was not saying "I do not love you," it was saying "You are not in love with me. You are in love with your own theories. Always it is your own you love, only your own thoughts [and] feelings."

He remembered her always now with her eyes closed, shutting out his face, his words, his gestures, his visions which gave nothing. It was as if he was coming out from under an anaesthetic in which he had known [or] seen nothing . [He] should have been pierced by love, but had he [ever] known love?

Two women came toward him riding donkeys with loads of sea-weed balanced in baskets on their backs. As they passed they ducked to him.

"God and Mary to you, docthor," they said in their soft western voices.

"The same to you," he answered.

They stood looking after him.

" 'Tis grand an' aisy an' nacheral the docthor is in himsel' since he kem out, not throwin' shtones at the wind the way he ushed to be," one of them said to the other.

" 'Tis so indeed, Julia," the other answered, "an' 'tis all the work of Our Lady. 'Tis all them novenas' an' rosaries we wor sendin' up to her. Shure, her Divine Son couldn't refuse her anythin'. A terrible pity 'tis them poor Prodeshtans keepin' on denyin' her and her only waitin' ready an' angshus to help thim an' every other poor soul that's in throuble and axes her aid."

Unconscious of their thoughts, Philip Ederney walked on, his head on his chest.

"At home I grew more and more away from my father and mother, but it was my refusal, not theirs. Why did I draw away the skirts of my coat when my mother asked me to join in a harmless game of cards? It was not boredom. I would have enjoyed it. Was it part of the play-acting of not taking part? Now this woman has shattered the pretense. I feel defenseless against her as she sits there with closed eyes strangling me; or is it my pretense she is strangling? If I had been in Siam, Tibet, any other land where I wanted to be at one with the people [and] shape their lives, would I have done what I've been doing here—deliberately running counter to all their feelings [and] traditions, the rhythm to which their lives move? The thing is absurd. No scientific mind would have done it. Even Planck, quantum-theory Planck, the greatest physicist of our century accepted religious symbolism as a sign of something higher.[46] Why have I gone out of my way to reject it totally? Is the explanation to be found in resentment against the loss of that little Gaelic enclave, the *boma** hedged round by the Gaelic language and the rites of the Church from the jungle of atheist England? Outside the wild beasts devoured the souls of the unwary. Inside we were safe, decked round with good-conduct ribbons, the grand old Gaelic language—on our side virtue and Erin, on theirs, guilt.

"Why was the pretense not killed on that Sunday evening when doubt first came, the night I spent immersed in Lanson's *History of French Literature*, the book that blew our *boma* to shreds for me? That Sunday devoured whole years. Did it transform the ambitions

bred of them? Was it then I filled the sudden emptiness of the
world with another image, the image of myself, the liberator, the
man above all tribal beliefs?"[47]

As he looked back on that night he found it impossible to disentangle the mixtherum-gatherum of thoughts, feelings, ambitions
[and] resolutions that had filled his mind as he walked the empty
streets in the small hours, taking the place of the tender pieties, the
sanctified intimacies, the plans of his family to make him a priest,
his dreams of becoming a Bishop [or] Cardinal. Had it been only
Lanson, or had he been waiting angrily for this revulsion, stirred by
resentment of the Monsignor? The old priest, Fr. Pat, had been the
friend of his childhood, the simple unassuming man you ran to,
whose knees you hugged. Nobody could hug the new man's knees.
His smug, modulated voice, the Adam's apple moving up and down
in his plump throat barred that approach. Fried eggs and bacon
were not for him.

It was uncanny, the impact of that presence on him, the loss of
the intimacy with his mother when she started making such a fool
of herself over him. There had been that sudden horror, the night-
mare of the death of love. Revulsion, indifference, faith, scientific
beliefs, the heavy smell of his father's coat—they were all coming
back with memories of that secret torment that had [destroyed] so
much. Could it be the memory of that loss that made him so bitter?
Was there resentment for his own loss [of] those dreams of Bishop-
rics [and] Cardinalates adding to the bitterness? The mind of man
was a strange pool.

Men passed driving a flock of black-faced sheep.

" 'Tis how he's rastlin' agin the divil, poor man," one of them
whispered, "fightin' hard, God and' Mary Virgin help him."

The doctor looked up.

"God to you, docthor," they cried.

"And to you, my friends," he answered.

This silence around him, a hum that was silence when he tried
to listen to the separate noises, what was it? It seemed to come
from his thoughts of Nan, but how? why?

When he reached the house, her eyes were looking at him from
the top of the stairs [and] from the fire in the sitting-room. He stood
gazing down at her face in the fire. It faded away.

He looked round the room, almost expecting to see her. In her
absence the space looked empty.

When she came back, she would bring the image of the man she
loved with her, the cheap fellow who left her for the cash of Dublin.
They would merely begin again the life that led nowhere. But what

was the beginning? Had he been waiting hungry all those years for that small pale face?

"Will ye have yer tay now, docthor?"

Nellie's head stuck in the door was a ridiculous irritating interlude.

"Yes, yes, bring it in."

"Is there anythin' you'd like with it? There's a bit o' cowd mutton. Wud I bring a coupla slices?"

"Yes, yes, anything. It doesn't matter."

He stood in front of the fire. Layers of truth seemed to be in the flames, one behind [and] beneath the other—life under life.

Why had it needed her absence to make it possible for him to understand things that seemed so clear now?

He locked his hands behind his back and walked round the room. He had prisoned her spirit in a cold solitude, she whose presence had brought all the warmth of life to his.

Today he was close to her for the first time. It was strange how close she was to him, the doors of her life open so that he could go on and on through her thoughts.

On a corner shelf there was a little pile of books, her housekeeping accounts. He went to the shelf [and] took them down, fingering them with greedy curiosity.

Nellie came in with the tea-tray.

"Your tay, docthor."

He did not hear her. He stood absorbed, motionless, turning the leaves.

"I don't keep accounts in the Missus' book, sir," she began in a frightened voice.

She was sure he would ask for her accounts [and] discover how she had been cheating him, but she could think of nothing to say to put him off until she could make up something plausible.

He stared at her. Her scared expression was clear to him, [but] natural. . . .

"I do not want you," he said.

"Patch Mullen's wife, Delia, is havin' a baby tonight, they think, docthor. He was here, wondherin' if you'd come—"

"Is the midwife not available?"

His words were mechanical [and] automatic.

"She'll be there, he said, docthor, but if it come out dead, God bless the mark, Patch sez she'd nivver have the heart to shkelp it an' freeze it an' bile it an' welt it an' murdher it into life the way you do with thim dead babies, they say, docthor, save in your presence."

"They know I've brought life," he muttered, "brought it out of death."

"What's that, docthor?" she asked him.

"Nothing. Did he say they were expecting the child tonight?"

"He said they wor expectin' it any minnit, but shure, thim's the words that's allus in their mouths an' thim runnin' for a docthor. 'Tis little I'd be mindin' thim. 'Tis how it's shtarted to pelt rain outside. In bucketfulls 'tis comin, lashin' out of the hivans. Let you take yer tay, docthor, now, quiet an' aisy. Whin you have it dhrunk, mebbe the rain'll be over—an' anyway, it'll be time enuff—"

"If anybody else comes, tell them I'll be found at Patch Mullen's—"

"Your tay, docthor—"

He was putting the instruments in his bag. He shut it [and] went into the hall. She followed him with the tray.

"I'll pour ye out a cup, docthor, before ye go out into that dilige. 'Tis dhrowned ye'll be altogether."

"Good, good," he said mechanically, but, as she was pouring it out, he slammed the front door.

The smell of baking bread came to him from the houses that lined the road. A consignment of flour had come from Roymore to Pat Culkin's and the whole village was baking.

"I have brought life. I have held death away, and they know it," he muttered. "Can a time ever come when she knows it too?"

He breathed in the damp night air in gulps. The smell of wet earth [and] the steaming fields mixed with the smell of baking bread was filling him with an unreasonable exultation. A vista of days with Nan opened out before him. Their routine would go on and on. In time it would turn into something deeper than mere routine—perhaps.

Chapter XXXIV

WHEN HE CAME HOME, NELLIE CAME HURRYING OUT OF THE KITCHEN, her face puckered with excitement.

"Fr. Ned is wantin' to see you, sir. I put him in the parlour."

His heart missed a beat. Something must have happened to Nan.

The parish priest had never come to his house, never would come, if something hadn't happened.

Fr. Ned's face reassured him. The priest's cheeks were haggard, but there was no bad news in his eyes.

"You haven't bad news, Fr. Ned?"

The name had slipped out unconsciously, an echo of Nan's talk, but he did not want to withdraw it. He was unreasonably delighted to see Nan's uncle in the room. It seemed to bring her back, and the old man's face was kindly.

The priest's face relaxed. He had been doubtful of the welcome he would get from the doctor, even with the message of peace he had to deliver. He held out his hand. The doctor took it.

"You have heard from Nan?" he cried.

"Indeed, I wish I had, but she never sent me a line. Have you had any news from her, doctor?"

Philip Ederney shook his head [and] dropped the priest's hand. "None," he said.

From the fields outside came the bleating of sheep.

"There's a dog worrying those sheep or else they wouldn't be bleating at this hour of the night," said the priest.

He was watching the doctor's face covertly. What a curious fish the man was, innocent as a babe unborn of all that interchange and tangle of human relations that others grasped instinctively.

How could he ever be made to see the world of shifting dreams in which Nan lived?

"All those girls who were at school with her—they'll have her running from morning to night, not a moment's breathing space," the priest went on. "She has dozens of girl friends in Dublin. She was always a great favourite, a great favourite altogether."

Ederney pointed to the armchair.

"I imagine that," he said, but there was no conviction in his voice.

The priest suppressed a sigh. The man was suffering, sure she was spending her days, perhaps her nights, with Leland.

"You smoke, don't you? Those are some of Nan's cigarettes on the mantelpiece."

The doctor moved to get them, but the priest caught his arm.

"It's the pipe for me, doctor," he said, "always the pipe."

He felt in his pocket, took out his pipe and tobacco pouch. The doctor's attitude was relief. As he filled the pipe, he thanked God that it was a message of peace he had for him, one that might help bridge the gulf between them.

The doctor stooped forward to poke the fire. It did not need poking, but he felt shy [and] constricted. He wanted the man to stay. There was something coming from him, some of the lifegiving warmth Nan had brought into the house.

The hunger he felt for some human warmth gave him an acute feeling of his own loneliness.

Nellie put her head in the door.

"Will ye be havin' your supper now, docthor?"

Ederney hesitated awkwardly. He couldn't eat without inviting the other.

"I haven't had my supper yet, Fr. Ned. I wonder if you'd care to share it with me. It's nothing but cocoa and bread and butter and cold meat and a bit of salad—you know—"

He faltered. The words were coming out stiffly. His mouth found it hard to say them, but the priest was accepting the intention.

"I'd be delighted, doctor. It's lonely at home since Nan deserted me for you."

"Thin I'll lay two plates."

Nellie's face as she ran into the kitchen was bursting with delight over the success of her ruse.

"Indeed I'd have come in to see you long before now only I was afraid of intruding. Tonight I felt so lonely I couldn't resist the temptation."

Nellie put her head in the door again.

"Will I make the cocoa now, docthor?"

Her face was beaming, crying out, " 'Thanks be to God I've seen this day.' "

"Do, Nellie, and bring in the cold mutton and the watercress."

He turned to his visitor.

"I was very glad to hear, Fr. Ned, that you and Fr. Roche repudiated the attack on me the day after it was made."

Fr. Ned shook his head.

"It was scandalous of me not to have foreseen and prevented it. Pat Culkin has his good points, but fair play and decency to an enemy, when he has him down, isn't one of them. Fr. Roche couldn't have known that. He was a complete stranger here, but I should have known it [and] anticipated what would happen. His Lordship was outraged when he heard of it, and no wonder. It was poor Fr. Roche who took most of the knock I should have got."

The doctor waved his hand deprecatingly.

"Don't blame yourself, Fr. Ned. I've been thinking things over and I see now that, only for you, the attack would have come months before. You were holding it off from the start."

He stared at the priest's face. "Bilious," he thought. "The man is eating too much fat. The eyes are a bit yellowish too—wining too much, probably."

The priest watching him did not expect the automatic diagnosis.

"What different natures we have," he thought. "He takes colour from nothing round him [and] finds it hard to fit into any change, while I take colour from everything."

Nellie came in with the tray.

" 'Tis a bit of our own mountain mutton we have for you, Fr. Ned," she said. "The sweetest thing mouth ivver tashted, as 'tis yersel' knows, an' the wathercress from Doolin Pool, the healthiest thing a man ivver put in his stummick. They say that wance on a time an oul goat that was thrown out to die and was wandherin' in the head as well as the feet, kem on that gran' pool o' wathercress be accident, an' lo an' behould you, who did they see walkin' in to thim, tossin' her horns tin days afther, but me bould nanny, an' her jumpin' an' prancin' like a kid that 'ud be afther wanin' from her mother's milk—but shure, 'tis yersel' knows the virtues do be in the Doolin wathercress, your Rivirince. 'Tis many a day I seen you goin' down that way and comin' back with bunches and bunches of it."

She was bubbling over with joy.

Philip Ederney watching her, thought, "A fool, a female fool just like my mother. Is Nan one whit different from the fool? Will a time come when that knowledge will pass from my mind to my feelings [and] free me from her?"

He poured out the cocoa [and] moved the milk and sugar over to the priest.

"I hope you don't mind taking cocoa," he said, "but it's the only thing in the house. If Nan were here there would be tea, but I'm afraid I never think of visitors."

The priest nodded.

"I like cocoa. It's a bit of a change for me from the eternal tea. You should have gone with Nan, doctor. You'd done so much here before that scandalous attack was made on you that a substitute wouldn't have had the slightest trouble carrying on while you'd be away."

"The words aren't mere counters," he thought. "The man means them. He is afraid of what might be happening in Dublin."

"It would have made a big difference to Nan if you had been able to go. You can imagine how her girl friends all want to see you."

For a moment Philip Ederney believed the soothing words. Then Nan's face rose before him. She had not wanted him to come. That was not the issue now, but what would be said or left unsaid in the future.

"Later on, Fr. Ned, later on. There were arrears piling up while I was in hospital. Tony couldn't reach on the lot."

Fr. Ned, watching the doctor's face, thought, "How he loved her. Can it be that she is playing about with Leland? It wouldn't be like her, not like her. She keeps faith. Yet why has she not written? She must know how lonely the man is. I must get Nan's address from Phyllis Glengariff. She'll be sure to have it. It isn't possible Nan would leave the poor man alone any longer if she knew how loneliness is pressing him down," the priest thought. "What a misfortune that it isn't this decent soul she loves instead of that Dublin Jackeen.'"

When Fr. Ned got up to leave, the doctor [accompanied] him into the hall. The rain had ceased and through the open door the light of the stars came through a soft mist mingled with the smell of the sea and the mountain.

"What a lovely night," the priest said, "but I expect you're too tired after your heavy day, doctor, to come for a bit of fresh air along the sea-road."

"Do you know, I think I will. The air is like wine tonight," Philip said. "If you don't mind my coming a bit of the way with you, I'd like to get a breath of it."

"His frozen mind is beginning to thaw," the priest thought. "God knows what the man has been suffering inside that sheeting of ice. What insanely bad luck he has had. A disconcerting thing in life, that intrusion of bad luck into human affairs, worst of all, the disintegrating moral effect of bad luck on such a life as his."

"I'll be very glad of your company, doctor," he said. "The soutane gets us respect, but it does create a human desert round it. Nan was my only real companion here. I've been very lonely indeed since she went to Dublin."

They walked on in silence for a while. Then Ederney said, "You're a man with a long experience. Have you ever come across a case where a spiritual disaster had grown out of childish make-believe? I mean, pretense that grew into reality?"

"There have been cases. Even here on the Black Shore it would surprise you to know how much of [life] is shaped by make-believe. I've known them call up unhappiness deliberately as if the imagination in some way cancels out their actual misery."

The doctor pondered that.

"Two days ago I had the feeling that everything was ended. It is not like me to feel that life cannot be endured any longer. For a whole day my direction was gone. Was it real, or was it the same sort of pretense—a shielding against reality?"

"Possibly, doctor. There are times when it is impossible to disentangle truth from pretense in one's dealings with one's self."

As they passed through the village, the dogs woke and started barking. In Pat Culkin's drunken men were singing.

"Curious, the peace tonight," Philip said.

※

When he got back Nan came along the path to meet him.

"I heard you coming up the path, Philip," she said. "Your step isn't like that of anybody else. Also the kettle is on the boil. Nellie said you've had your supper already, but I'm going to have mine. I'm famished for a cup of tea and I'm sure you'll not refuse a cup of my famous brew while you tell me the news."

She was talking breathlessly. Why did she feel that the smallest breach in routine would blow everything to pieces?

She caught his arm, drew him into the sitting room [and] scrutinized his face. On her way home she had been obsessed by fears of how he would receive her.

"You've been overworking, Philip. You look all in."

The lamp on the table was throwing grotesque shadows, but they could not hide the pathetic gladness in the man's eyes.

"A couple of weeks in Dublin is as much as I can stand at a time," she said.

"I'll have to tell him about James," she thought, "but tonight isn't the night for it. No, not tonight." Some evening when we are sitting by the fire, I'll say, 'Guess how I spent the time in Dublin, Philip, but you'd never guess it—not in a hundred years, the thing was so idiotic.' "

Nellie put her head in the door.

"The kittle is bilin', ma'am."

"I expect you haven't had a decent cup of anything since I left. You'll get one now," Nan cried back to him as she ran to the kitchen. She was still talking breathlessly.

He stood staring after her.

"Why is she so excited?" he [wondered]. "She has the hungry look of a young animal greedy for life. Is that why she gives such freshness to life? Why have I never noticed how wide her mouth is? There must be a lot more to her than I've ever seen when I conjure up that image of a waxworks saint."

In the kitchen, Nan, making the tea, was thinking, "I must make him understand, but how can mere words get into his head the wild jumble of desires, feelings [and] thoughts that sent me away from him?"

The paraffin lamp in the kitchen was smoking.

"Will you trim that, Nellie, when I've made the tea?" she said to the [maid] who was circling round her, fussing.

"Trying to get a look at my waistline," Nan thought. "Hoping against hope that a child is coming. Has he such hopes? If I told him everything, could I get him to understand, or would it suffer the dusty change that overtakes everything in his mind? No use. He wouldn't understand half of it, least of all that never in all my life have I planned a day ahead, at least not until I started those ludicrous plans about James. Yes, the same old silent quarrel will begin again."

With the thought came the remembrance that it was cocoa he drank instead of tea. She straightened herself—"Oh damn! I forgot that he takes cocoa. Well, tea it will have to be this time. I'm too tired to make cocoa tonight."

The tea was made but still she stood listening. Dogs were answering one another in the village and [out on] the mountain. Through the open window a smell of heath came mixed with the eternal seaweed. She was conscious of a crazy new obsession beginning somewhere at the back of her mind—this time, an obsession about Philip Ederney. James had been the cause of that. Would it, could it last?

"'For better, for worse, for life, and for death.' So it ran, that crazy rhyme. 'For sickness, for health.' It reminded her of the rhyme about the magpies—'One for sorrow, two for joy, three for marriage, four for death.' "

"What a queer thing it would be to get an obsession about Philip after all that time I've spent hating life with him, but I'm capable of anything—a woman of obsession."

Chapter XXXV

NAN WALKED SWIFTLY EASTWARD ALONG THE ROAD THAT COILED BE-tween the mountain and the sea. Over her head a lark was singing clear and joyous, telling of spring coming over the ridges that separated Lochnamara from the happier lands. In the little fields redeemed from the bog, men were opening the sodden earth [and] women carrying up the seaweed fresh and glistening from the life of the sea.

Here it was the sea that gave life to the land waking from its darkness. In the little fields, tiny yellow lambs were staggering round their mothers on wobbling legs [and older] kids, nibbling the sweet grass that was pushing up between the crevices of the limestone slabs on the higher slopes.

Nan, swinging along the sea-road in the keen wind, felt her body throbbing with life. The song of the sea came to her with new meaning. She had come back to it with dread, fearing the loneliness of life with Philip. There was no loneliness. There was absorption [and] obsession. "Another of my crazy fits," she said to herself, but without conviction. Her heart was soaring upward, blending with the song of the larks, the bleating of the lambs, the men shouting at the women and the donkeys toiling up from the shore with heavy baskets of weed. It was not peace, but it could be called peace. She felt now that she could not do without the man. He was her prop, her support. Beside him, others seemed broken reeds, rotting wood. What more could a woman desire than to be held firmly by so strong a support? Yet, there was something missing. Else why was that edge of fear still lurking in the corner of her mind? Today the fear didn't matter, however. Nothing mattered this morning except that the sun was shining.

A boreen climbed the mountain to the right. She followed it [and] crossed a stile to the mountain slope. Maidenhair fern peered over the clefts in the crags. Sweet fragrances came to her from the patches of warm grass crushed by her feet. It would be unnatural to be at peace in Lochnamara where there never had been peace since the day Michael had come into her life. When he was with her, there had been that stormy, uneasy joy; with Philip, the storm of misery, struggle, boycott. Now there was this meaningless surge of joy.

When she got back for lunch he was waiting for her. From the shore the smell of burning seaweed filled the room. The kelpmakers were busy. All night they would sit round the fires, stoking [and] drinking. The girls would come with their dried fish and the country loaves. There would be dancing. None of these people ever felt alone. Unlike her they needed no analyses of their feelings, no explanations.

The talks with Philip she had planned had never taken place, never would take place, but why need they? Life could be filled with meaningless ecstasy, if only it would last.

※

Spring went its way under the appearance of peace. From the fields and the coarse tufts of grass between the rocks larks soared up from nests that rocked with the movements of little bodies whose gaping beaks had to be filled. In the cabins, hens and geese were sitting on clutches.

When Lent was over and the spring sowing done, horses came galloping madly along the Black Shore carrying brides riding pillion to their new homes. Wild carousings blazed up along the mountainside when the parish turned from its toil to celebrate some "dragging home" of a popular bride.

On the hillside, looking down at the sea, Nan felt like one who sits in some vast cathedral. When she came back to Philip's house, the sense of space and mystery did not vanish. It would be possible now to think of building a home—not the doll's house of her earlier dreams, but a home where a man and a woman could live together.

She sent to Roymore for a good house painter [and] had the walls of the dining room and Philip's consulting room done in a pale primrose, her own bedroom, in a delicate green. She had bought fresh linen [and] arranged it in the cupboards. She planted flowers along the walk in the garden, had seaweedy mulch applied to the earth round the fruit trees [and] cleared the old house at the bottom of the garden of the rubbish of years and made it into a summer house where she could sit and read in the sunlight, away from the sight of the sea.

Most of the day Philip was away on sick calls. When he came home she encouraged him to talk about his patients, their symptoms [and] the treatments.

At first he talked of these things timorously, tentatively, looking for reassurance; then the eager talk came in a torrent.

Sometimes he spoke about her own health, but lightly, almost timidly. He was afraid that since she came back she was smoking too much. He thought she should try to eat more nourishing food, not live almost entirely on coffee, tea and biscuits. Regular exercise would help give her an appetite.

She nodded [and] agreed that he was right. She had much to thank James for in this new vision of Philip. In the first days after her return from Dublin she had been in constant dread that their life together would shatter it. It had not shattered it. The man had changed, become more real, driving out other images.

When she thought of Michael Leland there was no throbbing in her mind any longer. She did not think she loved him still.

"It's hardly credible that I could love two men at the same time," she thought, "but unfortunately, I'm capable even of that. Yes, I'm capable of any absurdity."

"Michael will probably be falling to fat," she said to herself. "He will probably be doing himself well. Life means little else to him. He will be getting heavy, developing a waistline."

The memory of his body was no longer a torment, nor the loose, swinging grace, the curved sensuous mouth, the rounded chin, the lazy beauty of movement.

His mockery seemed to her now the best part of him. She hoped he would never hear of her attempt to cure James Clogher. How he would laugh, making the episode comic, ridiculous. When he dealt with feelings [and] suffering they lost all content [and] became meaningless and absurd.

It was a sign of returning sanity that she could think so calmly of him, of James, of all she had done so wrongly or left undone [and] not have her mind bothering with the mental tidying up that somehow or other had not succeeded in tidying up anything.

Philip, watching her with a professional eye, was making the same hopeful deductions. She was still a bit haggard, but she was coming back to normal. There could be no doubt about that. When she had married him he had expected the disturbance that followed. The love a marriageable woman felt for the man she selected was a thing no scientific mind could ignore as a biological factor. Her natural [attraction] toward Leland had been abruptly broken. The mental sickness and confusion that had followed was as inevitable as the results of any other mental shock—inhibitions, complexes, the whole Freudian brood.

If [these inhibitions and complexes] had been nursed, they would have been dangerous, [but Philip] had not given her any chance to nurse them. Everything he had done, down to urging her to go to Dublin, had been part of a cure. He was sure now the cure had been successful.

She had met Leland, spent her days in his company as far as he could spare it, had an affair with him, perhaps. The emotional boil had been let, perhaps permanently.

Since she had come back, her action, her moods, everything about her encouraged more and more hope.

He did not attempt to pretend to himself that he was not suffering from his knowledge of what had happened [and] might, perhaps, have to happen again and again. That sick longing to know, to touch something he couldn't define—that was as much a reality as any other pain; that, and the hatred of having to share her with another.

His feelings were part of his biological make-up, pain that would have to be borne like any other pain that came from the weakness of the human body [and] the neurotic obsessions with private pleasure. He did not struggle against it. His sudden crazy desires to kiss her neck [and] her bare arms, or to turn back from a sick call to see her eyes—all this neurosis he accepted for what it was—the adolescence of *Homo sapiens* as yet only in his growing stage.

When she was over with her uncle he allowed himself quite shamelessly to slip into her room for the mere delight of touching her things on the dressing table and fingering her dresses. Folly, but follies, if accepted, did not grow into complexes. There was no sense in breeding inhibitions by suppression.

In the kitchen he could hear Nellie's brother talking in his thick Connacht˙ brogue. The sound of his voice was comforting, though God alone knew what rubbish the man was talking, the gossip of the mountain and the shore they revelled in. That intense interest of theirs in one another's affairs was the cement of the community. For generations back they counted everybody's ancestors—John Malia Pat, Mairtheen Mullen Bob, Maggie Mickle John. It was one of the ways by which they kept themselves from being sucked down into the depths.

His thoughts, as always, came back to Nan. If he could get himself to question her, what would come of it—days of intimacy or still greater estrangement? She was walking with him now in the clearly marked ruts, but what was behind that seeming calm? The smile on her lips that made everyone say, 'What a charming woman,' was it real? She was smoking more than she had done before. What did that mean? If only he could get behind her mask.

The thought of questioning her came to him, but he was scared of questioning. Questioning might be fatal. If the wrong words came, the wrong answers, they might blow everything sky high. Better let sleeping dogs sleep on.

Chapter XXXVI

FR. NED WALKED BACK AND FORWARD ALONG THE ROAD BETWEEN HIS office and his house reading his breviary. At times he stopped his

Office to rejoice over the peace his devotions to Our Lady had brought back to Lochnamara. The waves rolling in sleepily [and] luxuriously, were full of rest. From the mountainside fragrance came in sweet wafts from little fields that were as full of sweet herbs as of grass.

Never in the fat lands of the eastern part of the diocese from which he had come, had he found that delicious fragrance of the earth's own sowing that he found in these barren lands.

When he had come to them, first as a young curate, he had been ravished by it—that and the vision of some deep, ancient peace beyond good and evil—a sinful, pagan thought. He had thrust the vision away, yet it had persisted, calling to him from the depths as if it were the very voice of God.

During [later] years in the comfortable curacies of fatter lands, he had not forgotten the call. When his time to get a parish came, he prayed that it would be along this barren mysterious shore. His Lordship knew of his desires. There had, indeed, been little competition for the parish along the Black Shore, but he had found happiness here—a happiness that had become almost too great when Nan came to share the life with him and found it as sweet as he had.

His thoughts went to James. When James had first come, his happiness had been complete. Then bit by bit, the hysteria in James had emerged, the crazy visions that led to the pit of melancholia when they foundered. Why had such fine fellows as James and Philip Ederney had their gifts destroyed so often by lunatic swellheadedness? The ways of God were surely strange. The Lord hath given, the Lord hath taken away.

Fr. Ned sighed [and] went on with his Office. By the time he reached the church he had finished it. He went in and looked with delight at the altar. Never, even in the days before all the trouble had come, had Nan been so zealous in keeping the altar fresh and beautiful with flowers—not only the flowers from her own garden and his, but wild flowers from the mountain that had a fragrance mixed with brine. At the feet of the statues of the Blessed Virgin and Saints Patrick and Bridget and Columcille, there were little bunches of tender flowers from the interstices of the rocks, flowers as delicate as a butterfly's wing.[48] In the niches for which he had not yet been able to get the statues he wanted, she had placed tall vases from which bog plants with great green pods sent out a scent of seaweed and bog—the very spirit of Lochnamara.

He knelt down [and] poured out his heart in gratitude to God and Our Lady who had done so much for him. He rose from his knees

[and] looked round the church with the joy of a creator. Irish Catholic churches had always been centres of deep devotion, but there were few amongst them in which devotion was shaped by the artistic feeling one found in the Catholic countries of the Continent. Gaudy, tawdry pictures and statues everywhere. They did express the feelings of the people, but he had never been able to get himself to let anything unworthy enter the house of God. Better leave the niches empty than fill them with the tawdry stuff one found everywhere in Irish parishes.

When he gave them a parting look, Bridget and Columcille seemed to be smiling at him.

He left the chapel [and] strolled along the road smiling to himself. In his early days as a priest, his conscience had often accused him of turning religion into sensuous enjoyment. In later days that fear had fallen away. His sense of an immanent spiritual world had become almost a solid thing, sufficiently deep to absorb the beauty and fragrance and music of the natural world as the great Catholic churches over the sea had accepted [and] absorbed it.

With the transmuting power of God's grace, the fear that, in his love of the beauty of this world, he was trying to serve two masters had died away.

His thoughts came back to James. If only James's sensuous feeling for beauty had been able to pour itself into God's service instead of tearing at itself—if he had been a priest in some Latin country where beauty and religion walked hand in hand—James might have completed himself, blended the artist with the saint. He should have been educated at Rome, Paris, Salamanca, instead of Maynooth where religion was muscular rather than emotional. That harsh virility, the hard, bony Catholicism of the Dunboyne post-graduate course could not satisfy a mind like his [or] transmute the emotion with which it was overflowing.

Fr. Ned sighed. He had seen too often how easy it was for this devotional ardour, if it was not transmuted, to pass from the spiritual to the physical, leaving in its wake the melancholia that the combination of sensuality and dream must produce in the end.

He lifted his head. Nan was calling to him from the road. She came along the path swinging her summer hat gaily, but, as she came nearer, he noted again how pale her face had grown.

"If I did not know that she had settled down, if not happily, at least contentedly, I would imagine that she was being eaten up by desires," he thought.

A warm breeze was coming from the sea laden with the smell of seaweed and brine. She stood drawing it in—

"You have no idea, Uncle," she said, "how sweet this air is. It would be worth your while leaving your beloved [Connacht]* for a while to realise how good a country it is, how fat the air of the inland places seems after it, how stale and used up, the air of the big towns."

He gave her a shrewd look. Which place did she want him to speak about—the flatlands where James was working out his melancholy, or the streets where Michael Leland was breathing the stale air of Dublin?

"When I cross the Shannon [and smell] the turf smoke of [Connacht], it is like a welcome home," she said.

"The doctor must have been glad to have you back. He must have felt the place lonely without you, Nan," the priest said.

She nodded.

"You know, I think he did, Uncle. He was a strange fixed creature, but since I got back, there's been something moving in his mind. I can't quite get what it means yet. By the way, have you had any news of Fr. James of late?"

"Yes, I had a letter from Fr. Glynn yesterday. The news is bad. James is back in his melancholia."

She swung away [and] resumed her walk.

"If he had been put through a course in boy-scouting when he was a lad, do you think it might have saved him from all this, Uncle?"

Fr. Ned smiled. The thought of James in shorts with kettles and pans on his back was so absurd that it eased his mind.

"You may have got something there, Nan. If James had been brought up by a tough man, instead of in the sugared atmosphere his mother created around him, he might have been different, but I'm afraid the trouble is deeper than that. Epilepsy has emerged in him, unfortunately. It must have been there dormant all the time."

She swung away from him [and] stood facing the sea for a few minutes.

"I've been thinking of having the garden dug up and planted with potatoes and cabbages next spring," she said.

The sudden change of subject astonished him so that all he could say was "Good, good."

It was good, he felt. It was strange that she took the news of epilepsy so lightly, but her return to interest in such ordinary things as the garden was a splendid sign of returning health.

She began to tell him of a letter she had got from a former schoolfellow, Phyllis Glengariff, that morning.

"Every happening of the day seems so vital to her," she said, "the fact that she got the 10:30 train to Dublin, spent the morning shopping on Grafton Street, lunched at Mitchell's on roast mutton and apple tart with a cup of coffee afterwards—not the sort of coffee one could get before the war, but good enough—went to the pictures [and] after that to Confession at Gardiner Street. . . . For a while it made me long to go round Dublin listening to her bubbling."

"Better not go for a while. The doctor will be very lonely if you leave him soon again. He was very depressed while you were away. Now he seems very happy."

She gave him a whimsical smile.

"I haven't any intention of going. I'm the bit of sweetness—the marzipan—in Philip's life," she said. "He does want me. Wasn't it you who told me, Uncle, that when St. Francis of Assisi was dying he asked Lady Giacomo to bring him some of her homemade marzipan?"

"Yes, Nan, but I confess I don't see the point," he said, "Philip isn't dying."

"No?" she said questioningly. Also you think he's not a saint, of course, and St. Francis being a saint was the point of the story, wasn't it?"

"Well, one might say your husband is a perverted sort of saint," the priest said.

Nan nodded.

"It's the perverted saint in him is dying. That's why he wants the marzipan."

"What a queer lass you are, Nan, a queer, whimsical lass, just like your father, God rest him."

Fr. Ned sighed.

"I loved him as I never loved any other, but to the end I never got to the bottom of that queer far-away mind of his."

Chapter XXXVII

NELLIE PUT HER HEAD IN THE SITTING ROOM.

"Dr. Leland, ma'am."

Nan sprang up. Michael's face appeared behind the old woman's.

"Nan."

His eyes held an eagerness she had never seen in them in the old days.

"What a surprise, Michael. Are you staying in Lochnamara, or only passing through?"

The wild beating of her heart was easing. This was not the Michael of her dreams. She stared at him, trying to get back the image his appearance had shattered. He had hardly changed, a little heavier, perhaps, but only a shade, a little less light in the eyes, the smile less assured.

He was uneasy under her scrutiny, ill at ease in a way that was strange for Michael Leland.

"I'm having a fishing holiday in Carrha, Nan. I thought I'd run over and see how you and Ederney are."

"My husband is out on a sick call. He'll be delighted to see you. You'll stay for dinner?"

Counters, more counters, but what could one pass with this Michael Leland but counters? What was missing? Was the change in herself? Had she been such a mere goose only one short year ago as to be wrecked by this man?

Her attitude was disconcerting him. It must be some profound change in her that was throwing him [off] his stride, producing this hesitating fellow in the place of the triumphant hero who had swept her off her feet [and] flung her away so casually.

"I'm burning to hear all about your marriage, your career, Michael. Has it been in Merrion Square or Fitzwilliam Square?"[49]

She did not mean the words to be mocking, but the moment she had spoken them, she was conscious of some inherent mockery.

"We've only Jameson, Michael. I remember you preferred scotch.[50] If I'd only known, I'd have had some in for you, but I never once thought of your coming to the west."

Why did everything she said sound like mockery? His face was registering blow after blow, but she had no intention of striking or mocking.

She went to the sideboard [and] brought the glass, the decanter and the soda water. What an extraordinary meeting with Michael, the sort she could not have imagined in a thousand years.

"How is the doctor getting on? I heard you've got over the bit of trouble he's had."

She began to tell him about the boycott. He made the suitable comments, but he wasn't listening. He was all tangled up in the extraordinary change in their relations. What had he expected?

She wished Philip would come. This was getting impossible.

"You wouldn't care for a run in the car, Nan? It's a most lovely evening."

"The very thing, Michael. Philip won't get a car, says it would be little use in the mountain boreens. A run along the sea will be a lovely treat."

"And a relief for him," she thought. "Sitting face to face like this, with my eyes no longer adoring, must be a bad upset for him, but what has happened to him or me?"

It was better in the car. With his eyes on the road in front it was easier to be natural.

"Do you remember those French songs, Nan? I've often wondered if you ever sing them now."

> Tu
> As perdu
> La raison

she hummed.

"Yes, I sometimes sing them for Philip. Do you remember that idiotic American one, Michael—

> I noo the summer night
> Could never hold the same delight,
> But never noo
> I'd be, oh, so blue.

He continued the song

> Sleeping or waking
> My whole heart is breaking
> My whole mind is aching
> For you.

It was not the light airy tone in which he sang it of old. His voice was full of passion.

"My God, he loves me now," she thought. "Loves me now, a year too late, and I've lost the old zest in the hunt. The whole affair smells stale. Am I getting sense, or is it old age that's claiming me already?"

"What idiots we must have been to wallow in that sort of muck," she said.

"Muck! Idiotic!" he muttered. "Only a year ago, just one short year, you didn't think it muck."

"Ah well," she said softly, "as the people say round here, 'Twelve months is a long time and God is good.' Perhaps the old song wasn't as idiotic as any of the others. They were all muck, though the French songs seemed to carry off the stuff. I can always make Philip laugh when I do the American one—

> I noo the summer night
> Could never hold the same delight,
> But never noo
> I'd be oh, so blue.

But, you haven't told me anything about yourself, Michael. I'm burning to hear it. The beginnings of a career must be fascinating!"

The car was accelerating. It must have been doing a good sixty.

"I'm getting on quite well—excellently, in fact, but—"

For a few minutes he drove in silence.

"Yes, Michael?" she encouraged.

"It's only that I want to forget shop, Nan. I've come down here to forget it, and there's really nothing to tell, nothing except shop—the day-to-day stuff—"

"Well then, forget it. Tell me about the fishing. Carrha Lake is a grand water for trout. Did you have any luck?"[51]

He began to talk about the fishing. The baffled note in his voice reminded her of Marie Angelouse. In the old days in the Convent of Le Sacre Coeur, Marie and she had been inseparable. She had adored Marie. Every girl in the school had adored Marie. Not for her beauty. Marie had a body like a bolster [and] a broad face split by an eternal grin. It was Marie's spirit that filled the school [and seemed to] fill the world.

"How empty the place is with Marie gone," many a girl had confided to her when Marie had left to get married.

Marie's absence had made the school a desert, a place where no one lived.

That had lasted until vacation had come [and] liberated her to fly and see Marie. She had found the bolster body, but Marie was gone. Their separation had been even shorter than her separation from Michael—only a few months. Yet Marie was gone, vanished into thin air.

When they got back, Philip was waiting for them on the road outside the house. She was glad he had got home before them. Nellie would have told him about Michael's visit. He would be prepared.

He *was* prepared, his face full of cordiality.

"So, he has learned to play the game," she thought. "The saint is dead at last, stone dead."

Dinner went off splendidly, triumphantly almost, with Michael and Philip discussing the Wasserman reaction [and] the percentages of portal thrombosis on the Black Shore compared to the city.[52]

"Sarcoma," "carcinoma," "portal thrombosis"—the words were buzzing in Nan's ears. A drowsiness from the run in the fresh air was enveloping her. Through it Michael's head kept nodding eager assent as if he was thinking of nothing but shop.

"What a comedy," Nan thought. "Is even Philip thinking only of those sarcomas and carcinomas?"

When Michael got into his car, they were still comparing notes.

"You must come over and lunch with me at Carrha," Michael said as they were parting.

"We'll both be delighted," Philip assured him. "The Roymore bus picks us up here and leaves us at the hotel door."

"O damn the bus. What's this car for? She does sixty an hour easily and Carrha isn't the full forty miles. A little over three-quarters of an hour will get us there on these level roads."

"Splendid," said Philip, "splendid, Leland."

Chapter XXXVIII

THE AFTERNOON WAS HOT, ONE OF THOSE BREATHLESS AFTERNOONS one often gets in summer by the western sea. In Mary Culkin's parlour she and the District Nurse had finished their afternoon tea and were having a little music.

Mary, at the piano, was warbling one of her favourite songs—

> A little bird was singing there
> A little bird so sweet and fair.

As the words floated through the open windows, Tony's voice came booming from below.

> A little bird so full of pep
> I'd like to wring his bloody neck.

"What a dear boy Tony is," [the Nurse] said softly.

Mary Culkin sat staring at the keys. "Heavens! Can it be that she's thinking of Tony now?" she thought. "Tony who wouldn't look the side of the road she was except to burst out laughing at the look of her. What a strength of hope she has. First Dr. Leland, then Dr. Ederney, then daddy and now Tony."

"Yes, Eily, Tony has his faults. The whole countryside knows them, poor boy, but a decenter freer soul never was in a man's body."

Nurse Bruton nodded vigorously.

"And he doesn't make a song and a sermon out of it, like some we know," she said. "I've seen him with the poor creatures. Like a mother he was. No mother could have been tenderer. Tender is always the word that comes to my mind when I think of him, Mary."

"She has taken it bad," Mary thought. "She's all a jelly over him, and a good thing it would be for Tony too if he could be got to see the grand woman that's in her alongside of the fool. She'd look after him in a way that neither dad nor I have been able to do."

She shut the piano [and] swung around. For a while she sat in silence looking at the thick torso, the body teeming with life.

"What a waste," she thought, "to have a great juicy body wither slowly away without any of the fruit it's longing to bear."

She began to search her mind for some parallel. The love stories she'd read had no use for such bodies as Eily Bruton's, but there was one other book, a treasure house of wisdom that she took down again and again when she needed deeper company than the heroines of The Young Ladies Journal.

It was the old elocution book which had been used to train them in clear enunciation at the Convent School and contained lovely things like

> The Isles of Greece, the Isles of Greece
> Where burning Sappho loved and sung[53]

and sweet mournful poems such as

> He who hath bent him o'er the dead
> Ere the first day of death is fled
> The first dark day of nothingness.[54]

The prose pieces were mostly too tough, but there was one bit o' splendour amongst them that she loved even more than any of the pieces of poetry. Now, as she looked at poor Eily Bruton's fruity richness, the beginning of it came to her—"It is now sixteen or seventeen years since I first saw the Queen of France, then the Dauphiness of Versailles, and surely, never lighted on this orb, which she scarcely seemed to touch, a more delightful vision. I saw her just above the horizon decorating and cheering the elevated sphere she had begun to move in, glittering like the morning star, full of life and splendour and joy—Oh what a revolution and what a heart one must have to contemplate without emotion that elevation and that fall."[55]

"Do you know, Eily, I often think of you when I say that speech of Mr. Burke's about Marie Antoinette to myself," she said softly.

Eily Bruton ran over to her, threw her arms around her [and] kissed her fervently.

"What a darling you are, Mary," she cried.

Mary Culkin sighed. Eily Bruton had taken it as a compliment to her charms. What a woman, throwing up surges of hope while she herself had given up the struggle long ago.

"What a happy woman you are, Eily," she said. "I wish and wish Tony would get married to somebody like you, somebody who would hold him straight [and] steady him. It would be the saving of Tony."

Eily Bruton nodded.

"He's a darling, a real darling."

Her eyes were glistening again, dewy with emotion. At the sight of those eyes, Mary Culkin felt a twinge of remorse. "What's the use of raising hopes that haven't the slightest chance of getting fulfilled?" she thought. "It's mere cruelty."

"Have you met Dr. Leland at all since he began to revisit us?" she asked.

Eily Bruton's face darkened.

"Leland? No. I've seen him pass in his car with her beside him. It's a pity that scandal is being started just when poor Ederney was beginning to hope she'd settle down. There are some who say it was a fixed-up affair, settled that time she went to Dublin, but I don't believe she'd do a thing like that, giddy as she is. All the same, it's a pity, a shocking pity, and the scandal it's giving the parish is even worse. I'm glad I haven't met Leland. I'd find it hard not to tell him what I think of their goings-on. First, it was every third day, then, every second day. Now it's every day, if you please, and that poor ape, Ederney, going round with his mouth open saying what a good thing it is that his wife is getting all that air and variety."

She wiped the blobs of sweat from her forehead [and] snapped the corners of her mouth down.

"Air and variety, indeed!" she said.

"You don't think there's anything wrong between them?" Mary asked expectantly. She loved Nan, but it was so rare that a tit-bit of romantic scandal brightened life in Lochnamara that she could not keep from hoping that there was something here worth tasting.

The nurse tossed her head.

"That's not the sort of thing would enter into my mind, Mary," she said virtuously.

Mary winced. That was a dig that got home. It was time to change the subject. "I hear that Fr. James is staying with his cousin, Fr. William over in Glownthawn."

The nurse smiled maliciously.

"So I hear," she said. "He's been seen in the vicinity of Lochnamara too, wandering around his old haunts, but I hear he hasn't gone near the Ederney's, not even near Fr. Ned, [but] kept to the hills looking down at us, as well he might, poor man.

They say he's fully cured, but if you ask me, I'd say why's he wandering round the Black Shore if he's as cured as all that. Some that have seen him say he doesn't look cured at all, but there are people like that, people who wallow, my dear, positively wallow in the misfortunes of their neighbours."

Chapter XXXIX

FR. NED SELECTED A PIPE WITH CARE FROM AMONGST THE HALF DOZEN briars on the mantelpiece [and] sat down weightily in the armchair. He began to fill the pipe in a leisurely way, glancing at Nan's face from time to time.

He was glad she had come to him. He hoped it was not going to be a troublesome talk, but this new Leland business was frightening him.

If he went to Leland, talked things over with him [and] persuaded him to stay away from Lochnamara, that might be the way out, but then again it mightn't. Cutting Leland off abruptly might make Nan desperate. Leland mightn't listen to him, of course, but he was prepared to meet that. It was Nan was the trouble.

"I told you one day, Uncle, that I thought that the saint in Philip was dying. I'm not so sure now."

The priest's heart sprang up. That was a splendid beginning, a most encouraging beginning.

"Why do you think that, Nan?" he asked.

"The way he's acting about Michael. You'd hardly believe it, Uncle, but he's practically forcing me to go for these runs in the car with him. Again and again I've refused, but twice as often as I have wanted to go he's made me give in to Michael's importunities."

"Michael's importunities!" The priest stared at her.

"You mean you haven't been wanting much to go with Michael?"

"To tell you the truth, Uncle, I can't disentangle my feelings. I like being with him well enough. He's amusing company, but all that cracked feeling is gone, how I ever felt it I can't make out, but there it is. If he left tomorrow it would matter nothing to me."

"Philip must think it would, surely, or he wouldn't press you to go. He's very shrewd in his way. You're sure you're not deceiving yourself?"

She laughed.

"From the first day of his return I've been asking myself what sort of lunatic germ got into me last year to make me make such a fool of myself. No, Uncle, I'm not deceiving myself. Either the Michael I knew was never there, or he's vanished, or I'm growing old and sensible. All the old tricks were there and a couple of new ones, but they were as dead and stale as old cabbage. It happened to me once before with a French girl. The thing sounds absurd, but I suppose one keeps on changing [and] developing. Whether the change is in Michael [or me] or both, it's certainly real and it's lasting. I've been with Michael enough for the past week to know that the change in me isn't a passing thing. As far as I'm concerned, Michael is washed out, but I can't get Philip to see it. I've told him time and time again that I don't give a curse whether Michael comes over or not. I've spoken to him about the gossip and whispers my racing around with Michael must be giving rise to, but I can't get him to believe it. The very next time Michael comes along, he insists on my going with him, making it almost impossible to refuse. If he were a good Catholic, I'd say he wants to make an Act of it. The thing is preposterous and I don't know what to do about it. Refusing Michael flat, when Philip is pressing me to go, seems damnably rude, if you'll excuse the adverb. Besides, as I said, I'm glad enough of a break in the monotony, but I simply can't get it into Philip's noodle that I'm not longing for the man, [or] hungering and thirsting and famishing for him. Was there ever so absurd a situation?"

The priest nodded.

"You've no idea how you've relieved me, Nan. If you think your husband would listen to me—"

Nan shook her head.

"I don't like the idea of his thinking you and I have been discussing my relations with him and Michael. There's nothing for it, I'm afraid, but to wait. Michael has only another week."

The priest nodded.

"That may be the best."

"What an idiot you must think me, Uncle, with all the special lunatic situations I seem to breed automatically."

She took out a packet of cigarettes, selected one carefully, lit it and blew the smoke thoughtfully up to the ceiling.

"By the way, I hear Fr. James is staying with Fr. William over in Glownthawn—completely recovered too, they say."

Fr. Ned shook his head.

"I wish I could believe in the reality of the recovery. Fr. William isn't so sure of it. He thinks if James could be got to make a long retreat with the Cisterians in Roscrea, it would do him a power of good.[56]

⁂

Philip Ederney crouched over the fire in the sitting-room. He wasn't cold, but he felt the need of warmth [and] comfort. There were times when he was tempted to take out the whiskey [or] brandy kept for visitors [to] drown his misery. The puritan in him shrank from that way out. The scientist confirmed the puritan's restraint. That road of escape was a blind alley, leading back again only to increased misery.

His must be the hard way—the strength to drink the draught no matter how bitter it tasted.

It was not all suffering. There was triumph in his power to face the situation as a scientific man should face it.

That the universe should be circumscribed to the contours of a woman's body, the lights on her cheek, [the lights] in her eyes, was a neurosis.

The depths of her eyes, like the greens of the sea, the purple of the mountain slopes, were illusory effects of light, to be taken seriously only by morbid minds—artists [and] poets—that sickly brood akin to the diseased minds that had escaped by the easy road of religion [and] filled the world with taboos and persecutions.

Being an animal, he could not escape the illusions. The scientist in him had accepted it as part of his outfit [and] his limitations. He was longing for a child. He made no attempt to conceal it from himself. If there had been one, it might have held a healing power for her as well as an irrational joy for him. But that was one more in-stance of the survival of the ape-man inside his skin.

In scientific reason, why should he need a child? His work was his child—this mission to save these people [and] create a commu-nity that would be a model for the new Ireland, the new world it was his task to help to create.

Later on, when the period of Nan's biological urge was past, she would return to him, eased of those emotional stresses and strains that were part of her biological make-up. Meantime the scientific course was to make it easier for her to bear them, as he was doing by helping her and Leland to come together.

In her irrational sense of shame, she was trying to conceal from him [and] from herself, her passionate need for Leland's company. She must not be allowed to do that—indulge in the follies of sex-shames that led to repression, complexes [and] evil. Neither must she be allowed to see the jealousy he was suffering.

Not that his feelings must be repressed. On the contrary, they must be treated with the same sympathy he was extending to hers. This constant nagging of his for her love must be accepted as freely as her love for Leland. No modern scientific man would be such a fool as to run the risk of breeding complexes by the suppression of feelings, however primitive. The thing to do was to accept them, label them for what they were—throw-backs to the ape, hungers shared with the cat and the dog.

The true line was the one he was taking—hiding his own suffer-ings from her, but not from himself [and] giving her the fullest scope to use up that primitive emotional urge as soon as possible [and] become the rational being who could share his purposes.

Already he thought this new life was beginning for her. When he came home late at night there was always a dainty supper waiting for him, different every evening. Every morning his clothes were carefully brushed and pressed—a thing he had begun to think de-sirable from some idea that the sight of his neatness and trimness would be a form of training for the people. For the same reason he had begun to have an almost unreasoning desire to have his boots polished so brightly that they shone. They had never shone so brightly as now.

Everything pointed to the attainment of the hopes the rational part of him was cherishing, and yet, for some reason he could not understand his own mind. Instead of becoming firmer [and] more rational, instead of grasping more firmly the fact that she was only a female, he was tending more and more to place on an absurd pinnacle above all the fleshly attributes that he knew she shared with the most primitive women of the mountainside.

However, there was nothing he could do about it except note his feelings and accept them as symptoms of the emotional fevers to which *Homo sapiens* was liable during the years when his sexual functions were at the most powerful.

There were odd times when he had a feeling of being abandoned—another remnant, this time, no doubt, of the gregariousness that made monkeys move in flocks. There was no meaning in that any longer.

Modern scientific man moved individually. When he grouped in battalions it was part of a scientific plan, not anything to do with primitive feelings of huddling together for company and love as he had huddled against his mother before he understood the meaninglessness of love—the illusion that a mother could protect [or] that any other human being could fill the loneliness that was the portion of a rational man.

To be able to dwell calmly on all this should have been a profound consolation, and yet, at the back of his mind there was no comfort—nothing but a nagging derision of all those grand scientific thoughts as merely monkey tricks, jargon by which he was trying to hide from himself the petty jealousies and miseries that were gnawing his mind.

Chapter XL

NAN LAY IN BED STARING AT THE CEILING. FROM THE VILLAGE THE sound of crowing cocks was coming to her.

"Am I capable only of obsession, not of real love?" she thought. "Is that why nothing real can happen to me?"

She sat up. "I have come to depend on Philip. What am I giving him in return?"

Bits of the conversation with him that she had imagined came back to her. Why had she not made that conversation? "He is himself, only himself, never can be part of another," she thought. "That was why I could not talk to him. But am I any better? If I could merge even one little bit of myself in him, all might be well."

She went to the window. A morning mist was draping the shore, hiding the sea beyond it. From the village the crowing of the cocks was coming lustily. She lit a cigarette. Not much use in moping. Why should she take the blame for their not being able to come together?

Sounds were coming up from below.

"He can't be up so early," she thought, but when she opened the door, the smell of tobacco came up the stairs. While she was away he had taken to smoking. "At least it's a breach in his lack of humanity," she muttered.

She pictured herself baring her heart to him, holding him beneath the spell of complete confession. They would come together in unison of understanding. Happiness might begin.

Her lips twisted in a sour smile. If she began a confession, he would interrupt her to say, "There's no need for confession, Nan, and it worries you," or "We'll have to get the lower floor cemented; it's beginning to show dry-rot" and she'd answer, "Whatever you like. Are you quite sure you're comfortable in that chair, Philip? Why don't you take the armchair," not caring a straw whether he took the armchair or not.

"If we had children it would help," she thought. "It would certainly help me [by giving] my maternal craze the food it's craving for. It might even help him. That sort of man is sometimes crazy on children."

She came out on the landing.

"Why are you up so early, Philip?" she called downstairs.

"Couldn't sleep. I hope I didn't waken you. I went as quietly as I knew how."

"No, you didn't waken me. I was lying awake most of the night."

"You need a holiday. What about a run to Dublin?"

"He wants to get rid of me," Nan thought. "The strain of trying to live with me is getting him down. What a genius he has for making me feel in the wrong."

She came down the stairs, took his arm [and] drew him into the sitting-room.

"Couldn't you come with me? You haven't had a holiday since you came here," she said. But when he explained that things weren't cleared up enough yet in Lochnamara for him to be able to take a holiday, it gave her a sense of liberation, but also a feeling of unison with him.

"Curious how the thought of leaving gets the barriers down between us. If I were completely free of him, we could perhaps come together. If I were a bachelor girl in a flat, able to go to the theatre, the pictures, concerts, art shows and I met him, I'd surely be interested in him. He *is* interesting. That's the way we should have met."

She began to explain it to him.

"Our acquaintance shouldn't have begun here in Lochnamara."

She began to accuse herself [and] to excuse herself.

"God knows what I wanted. I didn't know myself."

Her words came tumbling out. At last she had got free to tell him things, but she must hurry with it. At any moment the man might once again become a stranger.

"You're exciting yourself too much about it, Nan. That sort of worry has been getting you down."

The words were deadly. Could she never penetrate to him? All the while she was talking, he was thinking of her nerves, her health. She turned on her charm, a thing that now seemed hateful, but, if it could be got to work, to bring the man nearer to her—well, all was fair in love and war.

"Philip dear, it eases me to talk."

If only she could get him to listen.

"A month in Dublin will be just the thing for you. This house is getting you down."

" 'And you're getting me down also,' he means," she thought. "I may as well put up my charm."

"You won't be lonely here all by yourself?"

Why had she said that? The man revelled in loneliness. Well, what did it matter anyway? She'd have to give up trying.

She stood up. In her dark blue dress, holding her head high, she seemed to him so remote that she could never be reached. A car hooted as it passed through the village.

"I'll take dancing lessons," she thought. "It will help to while away the time. Perhaps even I'll take a course in ballet [and] meet dancers and actors. It would be funny if I drifted into debauchery. Serve him and me right!"

The thought of her breath smelling of gin made her smile.

"Of course I won't be lonely," he was saying. "No doctor could suffer from loneliness in Lochnamara."

Her mind kept on the ludicrous image of her debauchery.

" 'Drinks like a fish,' they'd say, 'and gets gayer and gayer the more she take.' "

"What a playactor I am," she thought, "always at it."

"Already you see you're smiling to yourself, gettin' a kick out of the thought of Dublin," Philip said.

"Getting a kick" wasn't like his vocabulary. He was desperately trying to come down to her level. It was the only way of familiarity he could think of.

"Michael didn't even cure me of love," she thought, "if it was love I felt for him. James didn't cure me of the maternity complex. I'm as chockfull of it as ever. The doll's house stuff is gone. Philip might cure me of myself in the end, if I'm curable, but am I? He'd have to uproot me, tear me to pieces and put me together again. Nobody could do that, least of all Philip, a mere pair of watching eyes, no ears to hear; and yet I can't afford to despair. I must try to get to him."

"When I think of all the pain Michael caused me I can't help laughing at myself—the man was such a superficial thing," she said. "You understand that now, Philip, don't you?"

"Of course I do, but why worry about it? It's all dead and gone."

"All the time I was trying to conceal it from you as if it was a sore on my body. I felt a sense of shame. I was sure you would feel nothing but disgust. It was foolish trying to show indifference, for you were watching all my twists and turnings. You were generous to me. You watched me with pity."

"But Nan, all that is dead and gone. Why trouble yourself about it now?"

"Because I must talk of it or burst—"

She stopped.

"Might as well be talking to the leg of the table. It's no use, no use at all."

She looked round the room. The morning was brightening, showing up all the familiar objects. Was he even capable of feeling compassion for her? Was everything the same to him—love, renunciation, despair? Had he only one cure for all of them—get your nervous system right, get your digestion right [and] everything else will follow?

"You can imagine my astonishment when I found that Michael had fallen in love with me while we were separated. That time I spent in Dublin, you were sure I was spending it with him. You'd never guess how I spent it—trying to cure James. That's what I was at—Fr. James, you know, the curate who was here before Fr. Roche. He went to pieces through falling in love with me, or I thought he did. I'm not so sure now, but I tried to cure him. It was laughable. When I was sure I had got him cured, he broke out again and then I realised that I had been merely using the man to get rid of my own complexes. It was a doll's house I was playing, always the doll's house, the maternal stuff. When the spring was over I felt like a thief, a particularly low form of thief. I hadn't even left him where I found him. He was worse, definitely worse. I can still see his poor haunted face the day I parted from him, but I felt no pity that day. I had played a squalid trick on the man, just used him for my own needs. But I'm only pestering you. Why are all the kelp-burners busy at this time of year? It isn't kelp season."

"Iodine has gone up and up. The Americans are crying out for it."

It was evident he was relieved by the change in conversation. Her confession had only embarrassed him.

"A thousand miles away from me," she thought, "and yet he has got me. If I leave him, he shall have no peace. There's something frightening about his sense of power over me and he knows nothing about it—nothing about anything. He's as innocent as the unborn babe. If only I could get a job, it might take my mind off him, but there's nothing for a married woman except going around selling things on a commission perhaps. Why has he got me now? Is it more of my pretense? He's what he always was, only a school-boy, an overgrown medical school-boy. How in the name of Heaven has he got to be the only living creature in my world?"

"If you pack up now you can get the afternoon bus to Roymore [and] catch the 4:30 mail train for Dublin. It has a dining car attached."

"Yes, and I think I'll bring my chinchilla coat. It's cold enough in Dublin some nights."

"That's the thing to do, and put all those old troubles behind you. They're past and gone."

"Oh, I'll have no difficulty about that. It has taken a couple of years to sort them out, but they're over and done with. I felt I had to tell you about them to get rid of the last of them."

Chapter XLI

NAN SAT IN THE HOTEL LOUNGE IN DUBLIN WITH A NOVEL IN HER HAND. She was not reading the novel. It was merely protective, a shield between her and other lounge users.

"I came to Dublin to get away from Philip, to bury myself in company, concerts, theatres, picture halls. I haven't gone to a picture, a play, a concert. I want only one thing—to get back to the house of that man. Here I am rootless."

> Crashaw Bailey had an engine.
> It was snorting—it was puffing
> It had gumption. It had power
> It could go three miles an hour.[57]

A party of northern English working-men on holidays had been imbibing. She listened mechanically.

"No 'sicklying o'er with the pale cast of thought' for those fellows," she said to herself.[58] "Why can't I be like them? If Philip were drowned tomorrow should I be free of him? What would be my future? A pitiful figure, playing a character, a woman who has suffered a fundamental loss? If I heard that Michael or James had committed suicide—but what's the use going on with this nonsense? I should hear the news with complete indifference. That family sitting over there by the fire—father and mother and children—mean more to me than those two men. The family, at least, is natural [and] human and they remind me of Philip who is neither natural nor human. Yes, Philip has got to be my family. That young man over by the window who wants to get to know me, I could snatch at him, but I don't want to snatch any longer. I might try to use that poor fellow as a buffer between me and this hunger, but I can't do it. Why is the idea of starting again on the same old round so repulsive now? It would be hateful to practise on that poor fellow in the cheap flannel trousers, the heavy woolen socks, the coarse country shoes, but it isn't that that's holding me back, but some inner revulsion. The coarse English brute with the blowsy wife has been making eyes at me and only gives me the same sense of revulsion, although he'd give any woman the horrors. No, it isn't mere revulsion. It's the possession of my mind by Philip. I'm really a monogamous woman, really and truly monogamous. What a thought!"

Waiters came into the room [and] began setting the tables for afternoon tea. She got up and wandered about the lounge aimlessly. She didn't want tea.

"Philip is so gentle with me now. Does that mean I am dead for him? Why should I think that? It is I who am imagining a corpse, staring too fixedly at the corpse of my youth. That lunacy of youth—the idea that I could pick and choose happiness [and] put off the choosing as long as I liked. But I did choose. With Philip beside me, I kept on loving the tawdry lounge lizard, Michael Leland."

Crawshaw Bailey had an engine,
It was snorting, it was puffing,
It was gumption, it was power,
It could go three miles an hour.
Did you ever know, did you ever, ever
Ever, ever know, such a happy hour?

They were passing again, full to the eyes with drink and devilment—a crazy lot, but oozing comfort [and] vitality, the breed of Philip Ederney, though he'd be astounded to hear it—the breed of men who went to the Arctic, the Antarctic, looking for the Poles, the men who climbed Katchenjunga, who first circumnavigated the world in ships that were cockle-shells, the men who drove thousands of miles across America in face of every damned obstacle.

Did you ever know, did you ever, ever
Ever, ever know such a happy hour?

The jingle was running through her head, a message from Philip. "Nothing is impossible to a live man," he had said to her once when he was trying to share his lunatic dreams with her. Had she robbed him of those dreams? Could she give them back to him? Was he having empty evenings, lonely nights waiting for the front door slamming? She always slammed doors. It was not in keeping with her character, Philip had often remarked. He had never understood the impatience that was part of her make-up.

There was a mirror over the mantelpiece. She stood in front of it looking at the lines that were beginning to show each side of her nose.

"I think I'll go to the pictures," she said.

At the door of the lounge, she halted.

"Why in heaven should I sit there in the dark engulfed in waves of boredom?" she thought. "Better go up to the room and reshape my hat."

But when she got to the room it seemed absurd to take down the hat.

"What's wrong with me is that I've reached a limit and won't acknowledge it."

She stood in the middle of the room listening to the noises from the street—the clanging of trams, the hooting of cars, the sound of a woman laughing.

"Yes, I've reached a limit. I've got to choose—and the choice is already made for me. What I need is to go back [and] take up life with that man even if he becomes a prison warder."

There was a knock at the door.

"A gentleman below asking for you, ma'am."

"A gentleman? Did he give a name?"

Yes ma'am. Dr. Culkin—Dr. Tony Culkin."

Tony was sitting in the lounge looking round at the faces.

"Damn queer lot, Nan," he said. "Was this the best you could do in Dublin?"

"Have to go on the cheap, Tony. Philip can't afford anything else. You know how much he gets from fees in Lochnamara. . . . But what in Heaven have you been doing with yourself? Boozing the head off yourself, I suppose. Your face looks all blowsy."

He sniffed.

"The damn place is like an old clo' shop. It smells like old clo', stale cabbage [and] cheap tobacco. What a hell of a hole for your hideout, Nan."

"It isn't a hideout, Tony. You're just trying to get away from my remarks on your face. You've gone to bits since I saw you last."

"I know, Nan. I know all about it. Dad has informed me firmly and courteously—very firmly and very courteously—about the—what do you call it?—the progressive deterioration of my appearance. I was thinking of trying some make-up, but you know how it is. They won't let a man do that. I suppose you're allowed to smoke in this dingy hole?"

"Yes, smoke away, Tony. Don't you mind looking so coarse? It's a damn shame for you to treat yourself the way you're doing."

But God, how glad she was to see him. Her scolding was her way of giving tongue to her delight.

Tony was laughing.

"The same old gag, Nan. I thought you might be different. But you're not looking so grand yourself. Those cheek bones of yours are showing a bit too much. What have *you* been doing with yourself, Nan? Will you come out and have a square meal this evening? After that we could go on to some show. Donald Wolfit's at the Gaiety. Ronald Ibbs is at the Gate. Synge is on at the Abbey—all the high-brow stuff, but that's your brand, isn't it?[59] I'd sooner have a bit of variety at the Capitol or the Royal, but name the trash, Nan."

"We can think of that afterward, Tony, when we've had a feed. Lord, how I long for a decent feed, but tell me about Philip. Does he feel me an unnatural wife?"

"He's lonely, Nan. That's one reason why I hunted you up. The fellow is lonely, and God, he knows you don't give the feeling yourself of having a hell of a time here in Dublin. The smell of slops in this bloody hole would get anybody down, but to come back to your darling hubby. First and foremost, however, you haven't been seeing that Merrion Square mug, the dough-man, have you?"

Nan laughed.

"That brackish water. No, Tony, not the dough-boy—never again—but go ahead about Philip."

"There's nothing much to tell except that the man's screeching lonely. The other day he said to me—'When she's not here, the whole thing isn't real.' The joke of the thing was that while he was saying it, he looked for all the world like a school-girl unbosoming herself."

Nan got up [and] started to do her hair in front of the glass.

"I'll go up for my hat. Be down in a few minutes."

✳

When they were sitting at dinner in the Hibernian, Nan asked, "Have you ever been in love, Tony?"[60] "The devil have I? I've been in love with you, Nan, since the first day you came to Lochnamara."

"With me!"

"Well, what's strange about that?"

"I never suspected it. You never gave the slightest sign."

"What was the use? They were round you like wasps round a piece of honey. Where could I have edged in? Anyway, the thing is neither here nor there. If you knew I was in love with you, you would have dodged me. I was able to see more of you because you never suspected it. But why did you ask me?"

"Didn't you expect anything? hope for anything? Did you just go on loving without hoping for anything in return, not even some little recognition?"

"Recognition my eye. What was the bloody use of hoping? There were times when I nearly fixed that rat Leland, when I saw that he was only laying with you, but that's old stuff—mouldy. What's the point of it now?"

"So there is such a thing as disinterested love, love that asks for nothing."

"Disinterested love my grandmother! If you're thinking of me as a Christian martyr, cut it out. Until you got married, I'd have asked quick enough if I thought there was hope."

"And now you've come to get me to hurry back to Philip. You can't grasp that he's better without me, that nobody outside himself is really necessary to him, that I've only been a nuisance. Now, don't try to pull wool over my eyes, Tony. It's no use."

There was a sharp edge in her voice.

"What a bloody fool you are, Nan. What particular brand of booze do you prefer? They've very good Burgundy here, or do you prefer Bordeaux? I'm sure champagne isn't your booze—too vulgar."

"Whichever you'd prefer, Tony. I know nothing about wines. Do you know I can feel the smell of the seaweed when I look at you?"

"Yes, the rotting seaweed—great stuff. I'll get Burgundy, if you've no preference, more body to it. Yes, I feel like a piece of bluish meat the flies have settled on. It's a great life—frees you from all—what is the grand word?—responsibility. Yes, that's it. Do you know what Dad's up to now? He wants me to make a good match. A doctor can always make a good match, he says, and marriage would steady me. A couple of children would turn the bluish lump back into the wholesome red—the litmus-paper touch. I'd be sitting in my consulting room like a sensible man, feeling pulses, testing lungs [and] hearts [and] the devil knows what—aye, and taking blood pressures. Out in the waiting room the crowds of patients would be turning over *The Sphere* or *The Tatler*; just the pair of shoes that would fit me, don't you think, Nan? 'Better than die in some home for incurable boozers,' sez you, and so sez I. I've fallen in with the notion. I'm on the look-out already. The kids and the wife for me, provided she's got the dough, as Leland used to say. That chap was great on 'the dough.' "

"It isn't a bad idea your getting married, Tony, if the woman is sensible."

"And tolerant. Truly, truly, Nan, you're right. Dieu et mon droit, provided she's tolerant—aye, faith, why shouldn't I do my bit in helping humanity reproduce itself?"[61]

His eyes were on Nan's face.

"Your face is getting a bit sketchy, Nan. Why that thusness?"

"Oh, the devil knows why, Tony. There are days when my eyes won't focus. This is one of them."

"Something you've taken that doesn't agree with you."

"It may be. I was putting it down to something more fundamental."

She was aware of a breathlessness in her voice.

"I'm thinking of going back to Philip for good. I hate the Black Shore. I love it too. It's Philip. I hate him and I love him, can't do without him. Can you understand that, Tony?"

He nodded.

"Yes, I hate the dad, but if he died tomorrow, I'd be in hell."

"I want to precipitate things, have everything settled once and for all. I can't stick the way I am. It isn't that I'm painting the future in a rosy light, Tony."

She caught the wine glass. Her hand was trembling. Tony had filled the glass to the brim and the wine spilled over. She began to dab at it with her napkin.

"Leave the damn thing alone, Nan. The waiters will mop it up. You aren't eating a thing, neither eating nor drinking, and you said you wanted a feed."

"I can't eat. Are you sure Philip really wants me, Tony? I've tried to take an interest in his theories, his patients, his medical stuff. I might as well be trying to work up an interest in the midnight orgies of Paludis Catastrophis.[62] The whole caboodle bores me to the back teeth—the only stuff the man cares a damn about. It isn't that I don't mean well, Tony. I'm chockfull of the most elegant meanings; my efforts have been monstrous, but unfortunately, the man has got to know the whole thing is bogus. Gone are the days when my heart was young and gay,[63] when I was cocksure I could fool idealists. Why are you grinning? You think I wanted to make the man my property? I never did. I don't want manly property. If I could have got the damn thing to work, I wouldn't have asked a bit more, but what's the use of all this blather? I don't know why I do it. I tried it with Philip and all the result was that he watched me just as you're watching me now, thinking I needed a rest, a tonic, some bloody external thing. But I tell you I don't want to own him. I know as well as you do that, if I did, he'd be a dead bird in my hand—"

She stopped. Outside cars were hooting, buses clanking. Tony was waiting patiently, watching her with a quiet stare.

"What a good doctor you'd be, Tony, if only you could keep off the booze," she said.

"It's the stuff about Philip I want to hear, Nan."

"I haven't any more to say about him, Tony. I want to go back to him, but I don't want him to see me as I really am, to be known by him. It would distress him too much. My life will be a lie, of course, or would you call it an effacement? It won't be so easy, but I could do it."

Tony gulped down his Burgundy.

"Great stuff, that."

"You've no advice to give me, Tony?"

"None, except to cut out that stuff about lies, effacements and the self-sacrifice gag. It's more of the play-acting, Nan. Go back to Philip just as you are. The man wants you, not some grand doll dressed up to fill his life, but just Nan as she is. Going doggo˙ like a spider when it sees a man isn't any use. A woman gone doggo is gone dead and damned, no good to any man. And, Nan, don't go explaining, for the Lord's sake. He doesn't want explanations. He

wants you. You think he sees only the life of the tree-tops. Perhaps
it's all he does see, but he wants to come down from that lofty elevation. That's your job. Get his feet into the lower branches."

"What does one talk about to a man like him, Tony?"

"Hell, Nan, stop blathering. You're in love with the man at last.
He's in love with you—always was. What the blazes more do you
want? Watching a man's Adam's apple isn't the way to live with
him."

"You're so sure there's room for a woman in his world, Tony, that
you almost convince me. When he asks me, 'What are you thinking
about, Nan?' and I say, 'about nothing, darling,' you're sure it will
be all right?"

Tony looked at her with a grin.

"What an ass you are, Nan, what a bloody, blighted ass."

"And that's all you've got to say, Tony?"

"The lot, Nan. When that's said, everything's said."

"Then I'm going back to Philip tomorrow."

"Good girl, but hark you, Nan, if the man starts scratching his
nose or rubbing his forehead when he sees you at the door, don't
get analysing it. If the damn thing means any more than that his
nose is itchy, it'll only be tongue tiedness. As an expounder of love,
your boy's not exactly in the first class. The doughboy could give
him miles and miles of odds at that."

"Right, Tony. I mean, thank you, doctor. As a psychiatrist, you'd
make a name in Harley Street.[64] The eyes that look out of your
childlike face alone would make your fortune."

"You know, Nan, that's an idea. There was a fellow in college
with me and he's one of the top psychiatrists in London today. He
was a complete dud. Couldn't even pronounce the word psychiatrist. He called it 'piskiatrist,' and, do you know that he made his
fortune? They thought it was some new advanced form of the damn
thing and they flocked to him. I might pick up a wife with a pot of
money that way. But you aren't listening to my blarney,˙ Nan. The
chirping of the birds in the ivy of the garden of the Residence, the
screaming of the gulls from the Black Shore—all those dear sweet
bloody sentimental things—it's that you're listening for, Nan, isn't
it?"

"I suppose it is. Anyway I'm going home tomorrow and I won't
start explaining [or] analysing. I shan't be able to help probing [and]
scratching the earth for the poor little worms of love. It's my nature,
but I won't show it. It will all come right, I've no doubt. By and by
I'll reach an animal quietude, go in for violet note-paper [and] fill
my mind with kitchen matters."

The waiter was hovering over them, holding out the menu.

"The sweet—what are you having?"

"You pick, Tony, it's all the same to me."

"Two vanilla ices," Tony said to the man.

"Well, I think that's all, Tony. You've done me a power of good, showing me that 'twas really all about nothing. And I won't bother Philip about his craze for old rags of coats and trousers, nor his way of putting the carpet so it won't catch the light. He hasn't bad taste in ties, but he puts them on shockingly. I won't bother him about that any more, nor about the way he has of twisting his finger in his ear when he's bothered, nor about the middle of his bedroom. The maid too will be a bit of a problem. You can't get maids now in Lochnamara. The moment you've trained them, they scoot off to Dublin or England. All that will keep me going. We'll be at odds most of the time, Philip and I, but he won't know it. In my own petty way I'm clever enough, and you say he can't do without me. Splendid, Tony. Could there be a better ending to the story of true love frustrated for so long? The tramp come home, the tinker* back in the little street for the winter—all so grand and cosy. Happy ever after. When he's cooking up his germs late at night, I'll go in with my sewing or knitting and sit beside him [and] listen to his talk about the bugs and the patients and the devil knows what, until I drop off, or make some coffee to keep me awake. Perhaps in the end he'll turn into a coarse, ordinary male, the sort every woman wants, Tony, my duck."

"He'll never do that, Nan, never. No waistcoat will ever show a bulge at the waistline. That's what's wrong with the man. You'll have to swallow it."

She ate the ice greedily.

"He'll talk about the price of kelp," she said, "and I'll be thinking about the waste stuff in his soul. Isn't that grand, Tony, me thinking about the waste stuff in a man's soul?"

"Oh go to hell, Nan, you're just gagging. Will you have a liqueur before we go to a show?"

"Surely, Tony, good doctor Tony, and after that we won't do any high-brow stuff, just the variety show at the Capitol or the Royal, anywhere in this town. Tonight, Tony, you and I have done the high-brow stuff already [and] arranged my destiny.

> Crashaw Bailey had an engine,
> It was puffing. It was snorting,
> It was gumption. It was power
> It could go three miles an hour.

Did you ever know, did you ever, ever
Ever, ever know such a happy hour?

Tony stared.

"What the blazes trash is that, Nan?"

"A song of triumph, Tony, my wedding-march, prothalamium, epithalamium, some sort of thalamium. I never can remember the difference between the 'pro' and the 'epi' stuff. Can't you see Philip and me walking in the moonlight with our arms around each other's waists, can't you, Tony, on the shore road, 'and the road grand and white beneath the moon,' as they say at the Abbey."

❋

Philip was startled by the banging of the front door. He came hurrying out of his den.

"It can't be Nan," he cried, "but who else would bang the front door?"

"Yes, it's me, Philip, me, the gate-crasher, the door-banger. I couldn't stick Dublin. I was longing for home and I won't bother you with explanations. I promise you that."

"Explanations, Nan?"

She made no answer. She was looking at the woolen undervest [and] the white skin of his bare arms.

"Have you any oranges in the house? I'm dying with thirst."

As she squeezed oranges, the sound of the Angelus coming on the east wind drew her eyes to him. That bell had always brought a frown to his face. Today that high denial forehead showed no sign of resentment. In an odd sort of way he seemed to have grown up. It meant no change in his opinions, of course.

"Have you anything in for dinner? I'm damnably hungry."

"There's some mince, I think, Nan. If I'd only known you were coming—"

"Yes. There's a bowl full, just what I was longing for, something light and tasty. Do you know, Philip, I think the love of seaweed has got into my blood—

"So it will go on and on," she thought, "on and on and on—forever and ever—amen. Down at last the plain bread of ordinary life," she thought. "Will he ever get there or am I the ground crew whose job it is to wait each time for his return to earth? It will be maddening at times, just plain infuriating, but I expect I can stick it, even if it goes on and on, on and on and on—forever and ever—

amen. What a long way round I've had to take to get where every other girl starts on her marriage night."

Epilogue

IN A TRAPPIST MONASTERY ON THE SLOPES OF WHAT HAD ONCE BEEN A barren hill, Brother Jerome toiled and prayed. At two o'clock every morning, he rose, filed into the church [and] joined in chanting the Office of Our Lady [by praying] as he had not been accustomed to pray, without a prayerbook, rosary beads, or a formula of words. By four o'clock, Matins and Lauds done [and] Mass heard, he joined in the milking of the cows.[65] At five he had his cup of coffee and a piece of dry bread. At five-thirty he went to the farm to do a labourer's work.

He had been told how to walk, to stand, to sit, to hold his head, his hands, his feet. He ate, drank, and slept according to rule. Nothing in life was his own. At eleven o'clock he sat down to a silent meal with sixty others. On Monday it was beans; on Tuesday, potatoes; on Wednesday, carrots; on Thursday, turnips; on Friday, spinach; on Saturday, cabbage; on Sunday, peas and parsnips; and on Monday, the beans again. The meals were as the life, a stream of days in which nothing happened, except the few signs which took the place of speech.

In the early days there was one oasis in this human desert, the brief instruction from the Master of Novices. It assuaged a little James Clogher's hunger for the sound of a human voice. When his novitiate was finished, even that ceased and with it all contact with humanity. To move in a herd of sixty silent men, to live without the books he loved, to give up the life of the intellect, the beauty and art and passionate joy of religion was death for James Clogher.

He had come here to give away his life, but the slow agony of this death had not been seen in his imagination. In time the hungry humanity in him would die, but that escape was distant.

In the depth of the night, the call of the world crying out the futility and folly of the Trappist life still twisted his soul so that night after night he decided that the moment dawn came he would go back to a world in which he would hear the music of speech [and]

take part in the kindly life of men. Our Lord himself had spoken
against the man who buried the talent. Was he not that man, bury-
ing his talent in a Trappist grave?

Our Lord had called to the apostles, "Come, and I will make you
fishers of men." To his disciples He had said, "The harvest is great,
the labourers few." In his flight from the world was he not denying
Christ whose short life was one of unceasing activity [and] passionate externality in behalf of men?

When morning came he did not go. Between him and flight there
was a vision barred his way—the image of himself as the scapegoat
called on to suffer for the sins of men.

In the outer world the tension between God's justice and God's
mercy had torn him apart. Here, with that image embodied in his
life, the tension had been resolved.

In the moments when the image held possession, his bed of
boards, the mattress of straw, the manual labour he hated, the refusal of the outward drama of which he had dreamed, the hair
shirt, the girdle of steel points, the lacerations that might make life
vivid were engulfed in that vision. The dull drabness of a Trappist's
day became illuminated, clad in the glory of the Lord who had
taken flesh to become the scapegoat for men.

Was this soul of his, wrapped up in its image, at last on the true
path? There were moments when that question troubled the mind
of James Clogher. That priest who had lived for the lepers and died
for them was a true servant of God. Even in this life he had his
reward in their companionship, their devotion, their love. He,
James Clogher, had no companionship, no devotion to make clear
to him that he was not living and dying for himself. But was there
any real proof of that? There had been the urge, the inexorable cla-
mour that gave him no choice, no power of refusal of the call; but
might that not be hysteria, illusion?

The question remained unanswered, but as the years rolled on
and the cries of the world grew distant, it became less urgent. Bit
by bit, the image faded, leaving him naked without the feeling of
nakedness. The eighteen hour day of the Trappist with its manual
labour is a deep anodyne, the daily round of silence and prayer, a
sedative for the soul. In the end Brother Jerome was at peace, nodding with the older men after supper while the refectory Brother
read chapters from the life of St. Bernard, St. Chrysostom, or St.
Francis de Sales.

Notes

1. Loch Orribsen is a fictional lake, as is the village of Lochnamara. O'Neill has set his novel on the northwest coast of Ireland in an area of seven villages he calls the Black Shore. Although somewhat speculative, the place he may have had in mind is the promontory jutting into Blacksod Bay, a fishing and kelp-gathering area slightly north of Achill Island. When he traveled as a secondary school inspector, he would certainly have become familiar with the area and its inhabitants. Further, the few Irish phrases O'Neill transcribes phonetically seem to be in northwest country dialect. For example, the schoolmaster says, *"Go mbeanai a dhai dhuit"* (God's blessing to you). In other parts of the country, this same greeting would be rendered *"Beannacht de leat."* If this speculation is correct, Loch Orribsen would be Carrowmore Lake.

2. "come to do locum": from "locum tenens," literally, holding a place down. In this case, a temporary substitute.

3. Maynooth: The most famous Jesuit Seminary in Ireland which O'Neill himself attended for a term.

4. "Sound the loud timbrel o'er Egypt's dark Sea / Jehovah has triumph'd— his people are free" are the last two lines from "Sound the Loud Timbrel" by Irish poet and lyricist Thomas More (1780–1865).

5. Seaweed/kelp is a major source of iodine.

6. A British term for quarantine.

7. The infamous Irish wake, synonymous with a drunken brawl, celebrated in literature and ballad, has been acknowledged as less a final send-off than an anesthetic to dull the fear of death. In modern Ireland, the wake is a much calmer, more dignified affair.

8. "decades" are groups of ten beads on a Roman Catholic rosary. There are ten decades, each separated by a single bead. Each bead of the decades is held while saying an "Ave Maria" and the single bead, a "Pater Noster."

9. O'Neill is satirizing himself here. In his early days as Permanent Secretary of the Department of Education, he was responsible for introducing compulsory Irish into the curriculum (see Introduction). In this passage and others in which Liam O'Roarty appears, O'Neill is having a great deal of fun and possibly some sweet revenge.

10. The Sacred Heart Badge is the visible sign of having pledged temperance.

11. "Where wealth accumulates . . ." is from Irish writer Oliver Goldsmith's "The Deserted Village." Here, it is purposefully misquoted, out of context on O'Roarty's part and ironic, on O'Neill's.

Ill fares the land, to hastening ills a prey,
Where wealth accumulates, and men decay;
Princes and lords may flourish or may fade;
A breath can make them as a breath has made;
But a bold peasantry, their country's pride
When once destroyed can never be supplied.

12. Once again, O'Neill seems to satirize the point of view that informed his *Day of Wrath* (see Introduction).

13. St. Teresa of Avila (1515–82), a Spanish mystic, was the founder of the Carmelite Order of nuns. Of course, St. Teresa, an ascetic, had no "grand sweet tooth."

14. John L. Sullivan (1858–1918) was an Irish-American heavyweight boxing champion, born in Roxbury, Massachusetts, a Boston Irish neighborhood in the nineteenth century. He won the bare-knuckles championship in 1882.

15. During the failure of the potato crop and subsequent famine of 1847, Church of Ireland Protestants from the cities brought soup to the villages of the starving Irish peasantry. They used this opportunity to proselytize. Although they and their soup and their Bibles were regarded with hostility, there is every indication that the Protestant soup was eaten rather than being dumped into the sea, as legend has it.

16. John Milton's *Samson Agonistes*, l. 80.

17. John Butler Yeats, Jr. (Jack), a well-known artist from the late nineteenth century until 1957 (the year of his death), was the younger brother of William Butler Yeats, possibly Ireland's most famous and finest poet. Both Yeatses were friends of the O'Neills, who owned at least one Jack Yeats painting. It is, however, doubtful that one of his works would have found its way to the Black Shore.

18. The Sacred Heart in Roman Catholic iconography is a frontal view of Jesus with an elaborate, bejeweled heart exposed.

19. Here, Pat Culkin is showing his ignorance of Roman Catholic practice. The Sorrowful Decades, the Joyous Decades, and the Glorious Decades are events from the life of Jesus to be meditated on while saying the rosary at various times of the year. They are never said at the same time. For example, the Joyous Mysteries—the Annunciation, the Visitation of the Holy Ghost, the Nativity, the Presentation of Jesus in the Temple, and the Finding of Jesus in the Temple are meditated upon on Mondays and Thursdays and all the Sundays of Advent, and so on.

20. "Like little wanton boys. . . ." William Shakespeare, *Henry VIII*, III.ii.360–62. In this passage, Henry VIII is soliloquizing, bidding farewell to his greatness. The last line is misquoted and should read, "But far beyond *my* depth. . . ." This misquotation is probably intentional.

21. Liscarna House, formerly an Anglo-Irish estate.

22. Another misquotation, this time from the Roman Catholic *Confiteor*, a part of the Mass. The correct phrase is *"Mea culpa, mea culpa, mea maxima culpa* ("Through my fault, through my fault, through my most grievous fault"). Not only does Culkin substitute *magnisima* ("most glorious") for *maxima* ("most grievous"), he gets the pronunciation wrong.

23. "Finn McCool Branch of the League:" The Gaelic League, established by first President of Ireland, Douglas Hyde, in 1893 had as its purpose the de-Anglicizing of Irish culture. It is impossible to trace down the "Finn McCool Branch" if it ever existed. The League had hundreds of branches. O'Roarty's knowledge here is suspect. How, in fact, does he know that Ederney ever belonged to the Gaelic League in London?

24. This line and the following are badly misquoted from John Milton's *Lycidas*, ll. 123ff.

The hungry sheep look up, and are not fed,
But, swol'n with wind and the rank mist they draw,
Rot inwardly and foul contagion spread;

> Besides what the grim wolf with privy paw
> Daily devours apace, and nothing said.

Presumably, O'Neill is substituting "Rot inwardly with privy paw" with "Rot inwardly with privy maw" because he wishes to express his feelings about what really is coming out of O'Roarty's mouth.

25. This is possibly a distortion of Anne and Jane Taylor's "Hymns for Infant Minds" (1810)

> I thank the goodness and the grace
>   Which on my birth hath sailed
> And made me in these Christian days
>   A happy Christian child.

This distortion is why Culkin cannot recall the verse.

26. John Milton, *Lycidas,* l. 130.

27. "The Pickwick, the Owl, and the Waverley pen:" The Pickwick and The Owl are gentlemen's clubs. The "Waverley pen" was a famous writing instrument manufactured by the company Waverley Cameron, founded during the reign of George III, known for one of the most famous advertising slogans for its pens:

> They come as a boon and a blessing to men,
> The Pickwick, the Owl, and the Waverley Pen.

28. The Roman Catholic belief that by reciting certain prayers and making certain Acts, a venial sinner can "bank" days off for good behavior if he or she is condemned to Purgatory (a finite state of punishment to be abolished at the Apocalypse).

29. The traditional pig story in many peasant cultures is that pigs, being transported by boat, all rush to one side of the craft, overturn it and drown because, although they can swim (like all animals), their legs are so short that their back hooves cut their jugular vein.

30. The credit system of Alberta: In the 1930s and 40s the Canadian province of Alberta was under the rule of the Social Credit Government which paid every Albertan a dividend.

31. A rent, the annual amount of which equals or almost equals the value of the property (cf. Irish writer Maria Edgeworth's *Castle Rackrent,* a satire on Anglo-Irish landlords of the eighteenth century, published in 1800).

32. One of O'Neill's favorite novels was Dostoievsky's *The Idiot,* whose epileptic, Christ-like hero, Prince Myshkin, experiences moments of spiritual ecstasy just before a seizure.

33. "long withdrawing roar" is a phrase from Matthew Arnold's poem *Dover Beach:* "And now I only hear its long withdrawing roar. . . ."

34. Dunboyne Post-Graduate Course. Named after a building on the Maynooth College campus, the Dunboyne course, or Fourth Divinity Program, takes place in the seventh year of study for matriculants. This is the course in pastoral studies which matriculants must take if they wish to join the priesthood. Ordination usually takes place during this year of studies at Easter.

35. "Order priests," such as Franciscans and Dominicans in Ireland, often travel, rather than being attached to one particular parish. A confession to an "Order priest" thus takes on a certain anonymity.

36. R.I.C. is the Royal Irish Constabulary. O'Neill's father was a member of

the R.I.C. in Tuam, County Galway, but was mysteriously transferred to the Aran Islands for three years.

37. This speech is an excellent example of O'Neill's ability to record the tendency and habit in Irish speech of saying the same thing at least three times.

38. Matthew XVI.18.

39. The People of the *Sidhe* (pronounced "shee") are the pre-Christian fairy-folk of Ireland. The *fersidhe* (males) and the *bensidhe* (females) are traditionally responsible for missing children. However distressing this is for parents, children have nothing to fear. In fact, they long to be abducted and brought to the fairy mounds where they enjoy a magic life. These fairy mounds were marked by stone circles, still evident throughout Ireland.

40. "The young man Danny Malone and the old woman Molly Magee" is an Irish ballad that tells the sad story of a young man drowned in the bogs and perfectly preserved. It is not by Tennyson, rather a staple of the Music Halls of the 1920s and 30s.

41. Song by Thomas More, with an improvised last line.

42. Song by Thomas More.

43. "Darby and Joan. . . ." A loving old-fashioned couple. The names belong to a ballad written by Henry Woodfall, and the characters are those of John Darby, of Bartholomew Close, who died in 1730, and his wife, "As chaste as a picture cut in alabaster. . . ."

44. tar-barrels: The image seems to conflict with the meaning of this sentence. Tarring and feathering is traditionally a form of punishment and humiliation.

45. "The greatest of French preachers . . ." is possibly Jacques Bossuet (1627–1704). The *Larousse Dictionary* writes: "Arrive en Paris en 1659, il devint rapidement l'orateur religieux le plus." Bossuet was known as a "fire and brimstone" preacher whose text dwelled on the dichotomy of body and spirit.

46. The physicist Max Planck (1858–1947) received the Nobel Prize in 1918. He died during the year O'Neill was writing *The Black Shore* and O'Neill presumably would have read about him at the time.

47. O'Neill often said that his own reading of Gustave Lanson's violently anti-clerical *History of French Literature* convinced him to leave Jesuitical studies at Maynooth (see Introduction).

48. St. Columcille (also Colmcille), ninth-century abbot of the Monastery of Iona and a great lover of poets and poetry.

49. Merrion Square and Fitzwilliam Square, now mostly offices, were once two of the most fashionable addresses in Dublin.

50. Jameson's is a popular brand of Irish whiskey.

51. If my speculation about the setting of the novel is correct, the best candidate for Lake Carrha is Lough Termocarragh.

52. Auguste von Wasserman (1866–1925). The "Wasserman reaction" is a diagnostic test for syphilis.

53. Lord Byron, *Don Juan*, Canto II, Stanza 86. Clearly, O'Neill means this to be absurd.

54. Lord Byron, *The Giaour*, ll. 68–72. These lines are also ironic since the District Nurse has no beauty to lose.

He who hath bent him o'er the dead
Ere the first day of death is fled—
The first dark day of nothingness,
The last of danger and distress,

Before decay's effacing fingers
Have swept the lines where beauty lingers.

55. Sir Edmund Burke (1729–97): *Reflections on the Revolution in France*.
56. Cisterians are a stricter and more austere branch of the order of Benedictine Monks.
57. "Crawshaw Bailey . . . ," a Welsh drinking song.
58. William Shakespeare, *Hamlet*, III.i. 90–91.

And thus the native hue of resolution
Is sicklied o'er with the pale cast of thought. . . .

59. Donald Wolfit, Ronald Ibbs, and [John Millington] Synge. Wolfit and Ibbs were actors, and John Synge (1871–1909), famous for his plays about the harsh life on the Aran Islands, is probably best known for *Riders to the Sea* and *Playboy of the Western World*. Established by W. B. Yeats, Lady Gregory, George Moore, and Edward Martyn, the Abbey Theatre in Dublin has produced plays by Irish writers from the time of its opening in December 1904 to the present.
60. The Hibernian was an upscale Dublin hotel.
61. "Dieu et mon droit." Tony Culkin is punning here, pretending that he is saying "My God, you're right!"
62. "the midnight orgies of Paludis Catastrophis . . ." refers to the *Carmina Catulli* (Songs of Catullus), a collection of bawdy Latin poetry.
63. This is a line from "Old Black Joe," by American nineteenth-century songwriter, Stephen Foster.
64. Harley Street, London, is a fashionable address for physicians.
65. "Matins and Lauds" are the first two of the seven canonical hours of the day. Prayers are recited at each of these hours.

Glossary of Irish Words and Slang

Acushla: An Irish term of endearment.

Allanah: An Irish term of endearment.

Apache: A Parisian thug, petty thief, "hood."

Bashte: O'Neill's regional phonetic spelling of "beast."

Batten: To feed gluttonously or greedily.

Bawneen: Heavy cable-knit fishermen's sweaters worn on the Aran Islands of the West Coast of Ireland; also known as the "Aran-knit." The elaborate cables varied from region to region and were used as marks of identification, in order to return a drowned fisherman to his native village.

Blackthorn: An Irish walking stick made out of hawthorn.

Blarney: Cajoling speech; legend has it that those who kiss the Blarney Stone are gifted with the art of persuasion.

Blood in 'ouns: An exclamation; "Blood in the wounds [of Christ]."

Boharnabreena, . . . Killiney: Areas just outside Dublin, either on the coast (Killiney, Howth) or in the Wicklow Mountains to the south of the city. O'Neill was particularly fond of walking in Wicklow. In fact, toward the end of his life he and his wife rented a cottage near Mount Tibradden.

Boma: Possibly regional pronunciation of *boim,* meaning "small piece" or "fragment." If Philip Ederney's family was Irish Catholic in the midst of an English Anglican Church culture, the meaning fits into the context.

Boreen: A little country road.

Chucker-out: A bouncer at a club or bar.

Cockshy: A game of throwing missiles at the target, or the target itself.

Cod/codded: A fool, to be fooled or made a dupe of.

Commercial: A traveling salesman.

Connacht (or) *Connaught*: Refers to the west and northwest of Ireland. Pre-Christian Ireland was divided into four vast tribal areas: Leinster, Munster, Ulster, and Connacht.

Cownshuch: A regional phonetic spelling of *oinseach,* a female fool.

Curragh: An open Irish fishing boat used in the Aran Islands and the west coast of Ireland. Curraghs, seventeen to twenty feet long, are made of a tarred canvas stretched over wood woven like a basket. They are rowed

261

by crosshand pulls on bladeless oars. Every curragh used to carry a bottle of holy water. O'Neill is mistaken about the seaworthiness of the curragh. Plying some of the roughest waters in the North Atlantic, between Galway and the Aran Islands, curraghs are designed to carry huge payloads, including horses and cattle.

Davy: Slang for "affidavit."

Disedification: A turning away from moral improvement or guidance.

Ducks: White cotton or linen trousers.

Eehe Howna: All Hallows Eve.

Faix: An exclamation; variant on "Faith. . . ."

Foundered: In the sense of having collapsed or failed.

Freethinkers: A synonym for skeptics, agnostics, or atheists.

Funked: To shrink from or shirk.

Gaeltacht: Areas where Irish is the spoken and written word.

Gaffin: Actually, "gaffing" (as in hooking a fish); slang for ticking or playing a hoax.

Garda: A policeman.

Gardai: Police, plural or collective.

Gerell: A regional pronunciation of "girl."

Going doggo: Slang; to wait for something without moving, like a trained working dog.

Gombeen: The "Gombeen men" of the Anglo-Irish Ascendancy were native Irish who were employed as caretakers of the "big houses," agents who managed these huge Anglo estates for the profit of the masters. They were universally despised by their fellow Irish and were occasionally murdered. Thus, a "gombeen" in modern parlance means an Irishman who exploits his own countrymen and women.

Gomeral: A simpleton, a fool.

Greeshach: The embers of a turf fire.

Gu manny a jay ghuit: A phonetic transcription of "Go mbeanai a dhia dhuit," an Irish greeting and blessing, roughly translated "The blessings of God to you." O'Neill ran into the same problems as Irish writers who use Irish words in their otherwise English-language texts: Does the writer spell them in Irish (which very few can read) or in a phonetic English?

Haporth: A half-penny, or ha'penny.

Haw-haw: Boisterous.

Jackeen: A pejorative term for a Dubliner; also, the Jack or Knave in a deck of cards. The "een" is an Anglo-Irish diminutive.

Jumpers: Sweaters.

Keening: Wailing uncontrollably; the traditional practice of women at Irish wakes.

Lashins: Slang for "plenty."

Lavins: A regional pronunciation for "leavings," meaning leftovers; often used in the phrase "Lashins and lavins."

Lordship: Always refers to the Bishop of the diocese.

Man of his kidney: Man of his kind, sort, class.

Midden: A dung heap.

Mug: Slang; an ugly face, probably originating from the eighteenth-century custom of fashioning ale mugs in the shape of grotesque faces.

Nacheral: Slang; a phonetic transcription of "natural," in the sense of someone who is unenlightened, crude, primitive.

Novena: Nine days of prayer for a special purpose.

Pattern: A form of dance in which dancers imitate the dance steps of the leader.

Potheen: Also spelled *poteen*; it is an illegally distilled alcoholic beverage of very high proof, made from potatoes.

P.P.: A parish priest.

Quid: Slang for Irish or British pound.

Rasher: Back bacon.

Ruck: A large number of undistinguished persons.

Sassenach: From the Irish, *Sasanach,* a term used by Scots and Irish to denote a Saxon, or Englishman or woman.

Shebeen, shebeen-man: A place to purchase and drink *potheen*. The person who runs such an establishment. Shebeens once dotted the country roads of Ireland. They are not pubs; they are not legal.

Shoneen: A flunky or toady.

Shtrap: (That is, "strap"), slang; a pejorative term for a large woman. It is interesting to note the variant of this word: "strapping" is a compliment when applied to males.

Snug: A small private room in a pub.

Soutane: A priest's cassock.

Spanner: A wrench.

Tail: An orderly line of children walking two by two.

Taped: Measured. In this case, "determined."

Thusness: A noun meaning "being." "Why are you looking that way?"

Trickie/Thrickie: A young woman employing craft or cunning devices in order to deceive.

Troteen: Slang; a deprecatory term and diminutive of "bog-trotter." The "trotter" refers to pigs' feet.

Viaticum: The Eucharist, administered to one who is dying or thought to be dying.

Votheen: Irish diminutive for "votive" candle.

Whisht now: A cautionary phrase, synonymous with "Be careful" or Be quiet."

Wool [*In each other's wool*]: Hair . . . as in "in each other's hair."